GRAPHIS DESIGN 90

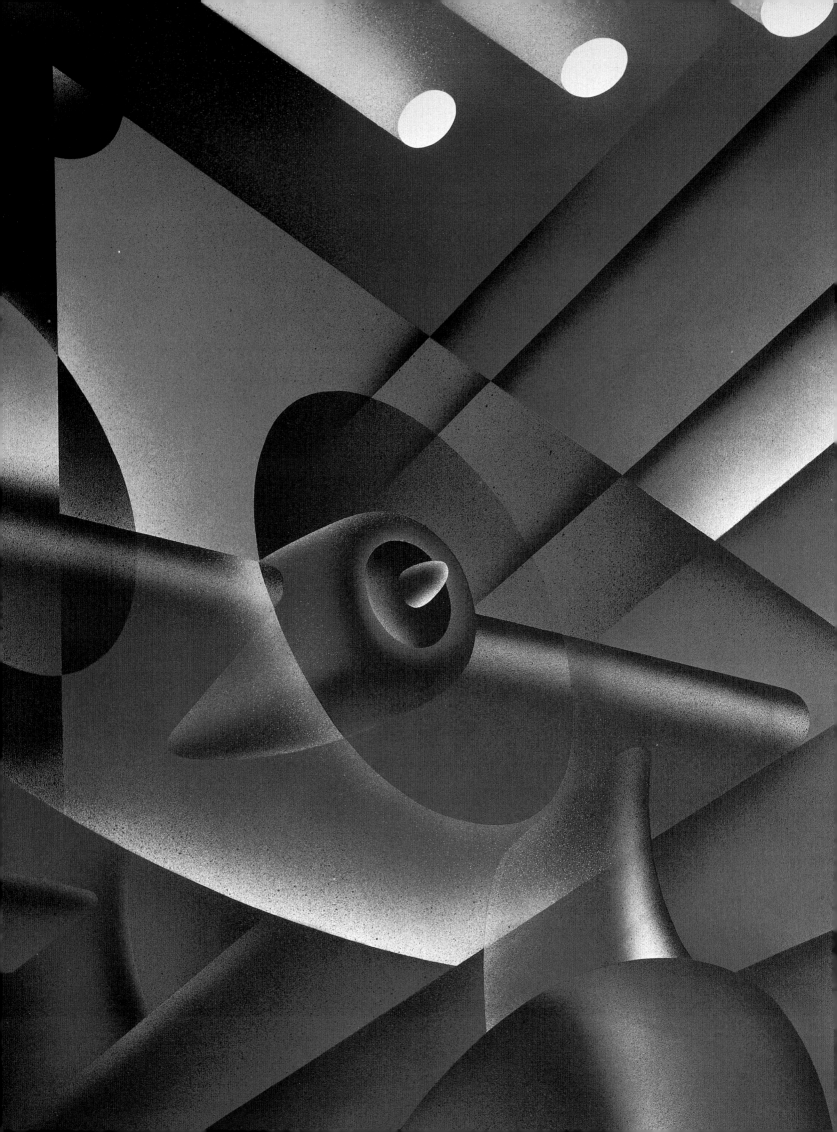

GRAPHIS DESIGN 90

THE INTERNATIONAL ANNUAL ON DESIGN AND ILLUSTRATION

DAS INTERNATIONALE JAHRBUCH ÜBER DESIGN UND ILLUSTRATION

LE RÉPERTOIRE INTERNATIONAL DE DESIGN ET ILLUSTRATION

EDITED BY/HERAUSGEGEBEN VON/RÉALISÉ PAR

B. MARTIN PEDERSEN

PUBLISHER AND CREATIVE DIRECTOR: B. MARTIN PEDERSEN

ASSISTANT EDITORS: ANNETTE CRANDALL, HEINKE JENSSEN

DESIGNERS: MARTIN BYLAND, UDI NADIV

PHOTOGRAPHER: WALTER ZUBER

GRAPHIS PRESS CORP., ZURICH (SWITZERLAND)

GRAPHIS PUBLICATIONS

GRAPHIS, International bi-monthly journal of graphic art and photography

GRAPHIS DESIGN, The international annual on design and illustration

GRAPHIS PHOTO, The international annual of photography

GRAPHIS POSTER, The international annual of poster art

GRAPHIS PACKAGING, An international survey of packaging design

GRAPHIS DIAGRAM, The graphic visualization of abstract, technical and statistical facts and functions

GRAPHIS COVERS, An anthology of all GRAPHIS covers from 1944–86 with artists' short biographies
 and indexes of all GRAPHIS issues

GRAPHIS ANNUAL REPORTS, An international compilation of the best designed annual reports

GRAPHIS CORPORATE IDENTITY 1, An international compilation of the best in Corporate Identity design

POSTERS MADE POSSIBLE BY A GRANT FROM MOBIL, A collection of 250 international posters commissioned by Mobil
 and selected by the Poster Society

GRAPHIS-PUBLIKATIONEN

GRAPHIS, Die internationale Zweimonatszeitschrift für Graphik und Photographie

GRAPHIS DESIGN, Das internationale Jahrbuch über Design und Illustration

GRAPHIS PHOTO, Das internationale Jahrbuch der Photographie

GRAPHIS POSTER, Das internationale Jahrbuch der Plakatkunst

GRAPHIS PACKUNGEN, Ein internationaler Überblick der Packungsgestaltung

GRAPHIS DIAGRAM, Die graphische Darstellung abstrakter, technischer und statistischer Daten und Fakten

GRAPHIS COVERS, Eine Sammlung aller GRAPHIS-Umschläge von 1944–86 mit Informationen über die Künstler
 und Inhaltsübersichten aller Ausgaben der Zeitschrift GRAPHIS

GRAPHIS ANNUAL REPORTS, Ein internationaler Überblick über die Gestaltung von Jahresberichten

GRAPHIS CORPORATE IDENTITY 1, Eine internationale Auswahl des besten Corporate Identity Design

POSTERS MADE POSSIBLE BY A GRANT FROM MOBIL, Eine Sammlung von 250 internationalen Plakaten, von Mobil
 in Auftrag gegeben und von der Poster Society ausgewählt

PUBLICATIONS GRAPHIS

GRAPHIS, La revue bimestrielle internationale d'arts graphiques et de la photographie

GRAPHIS DESIGN, Le répertoire international de la communication visuelle

GRAPHIS PHOTO, Le répertoire international de la photographie

GRAPHIS POSTER, Le répertoire international de l'art de l'affiche

GRAPHIS EMBALLAGES, Le répertoire international des formes de l'emballage

GRAPHIS DIAGRAM, La représentation graphique de faits et données abstraits, techniques et statistiques

GRAPHIS COVERS, Recueil de toutes les couvertures de GRAPHIS de 1944–86 avec des notices biographiques
 des artistes et le sommaire de tous les numéros du magazine GRAPHIS.

GRAPHIS ANNUAL REPORTS, Panorama international du design de rapports annuels d'entreprises

GRAPHIS CORPORATE IDENTITY 1, Panorama international du meilleur design de l'identité corporate

POSTERS MADE POSSIBLE BY A GRANT FROM MOBIL, Une collection de 250 affiches internationales commandées par Mobil
 et choisies par la Poster Society

PUBLICATION No. 197 (ISBN 3-85709-189-3)

© Copyright under Universal Copyright Convention

Copyright 1989 by Graphis Press Corp., 107 Dufourstrasse, 8008 Zurich, Switzerland

No part of this book may be reproduced in any form without written permission of the publisher

Printed in Japan by Toppan

Typeset in Switzerland by Setzerei Heller, Zurich

Typefaces: Garamond ITC Light Condensed, Futura Extra Bold

I have taken part a number of times on national and international juries and whenever I look at the thousands of contributions by devotees and willing contributors, one fact always strikes me. That over 90 percent of all the works presented will remain unconsidered. Which is another way of saying that only a maximum of ten percent of the contributions are truly "outstanding" and, as one says in German, mature enough for the "cabinet" – or showcase. The German term "cabinet" is pertinent, since in its original and historic sense it meant a "special room for studies and treasures". Well, many of the selected works do have the quality of studies – and many are real treasures. □ But in spite of that a sneaky doubt creeps up on any experienced and practiced adjudicator as to whether these selected "cabinet pieces" still have all that much to do with everyday life. Do they? Honestly? □ Just think it over. For, as is all too obvious, a great many of the pieces originate from within the realm of one's own field. Like the letterhead for one's own agency or one's own studio. And like the splendidly composed New Year's greetings – that can even grow to the size of a poster. And the poster for one's own exhibition. Or a lecture. Or a seminar. They can be announced in like manner too. Naturally all one's colleagues, including friends from outside the design profession, benefit from the supportive genius graphicus: photographers with posters, advertisements, and catalogs; copywriters and modelling agencies with letterheads and invitations. One's own club mustn't be left out, of course. Posters and announcements of annual competitions all sport the insider label. □ The graphic industry – a distant relative after all – plays along. Typesetting computer hard-and-software-manufacturers, photo typesetters, printers, printing ink and paper manufacturers. The latter with breathtaking collections overflowing with creativity, and all appropriately geared up with the latest technical outfit. Publishers, publicizing graphic or photographic topics, anyhow – provide the whole show with a special budget. One is, after all, part of the scene. Graphic design schools, state subsidized or privately run, place their self-portrayal – whether posters, magazines or brochures – in professional hands. And all this takes place under the old boys' banner: "We know each other, we meet each other and we work with each other". □ Of course among the 10% of the selected works there are excellent pieces that stem from everyday business – even if there are limitations that are fundamentally imposed by national conditions and by the diverse requirements of the assignments. Such as in the USA, for instance, with its extremely clever and magnificently thought out sales promotions and self portrayals in brochure form – very gallantly dubbed in that country by the name of "Annual Reports". This glittering insight into alert Boards of Directors, swathed in their aluminum and steel-bullwarked fortresses – the USA does them uniquely proud. The letterheads are of similar quality – in a country that knows no typographic rules. Only very few other countries can keep up with that. □ Editorial art that once upon a time at its best was limited only to the USA, is now conquering other countries. It's strikingly evident here too that illustrators and photographers really do have an international effect. These are the special pages that so clearly reflect the special production. □ Poster art from Japan, with its many posters in silkscreen, indicates that the circulation must be limited. So still more studies? □ Competitions, from which annual exhibitions result, and which now include the yearly publications, annuals, show the "residual" ten percent that I've high-styled as exceptions to the rule. It would be nice if the ratio were the other way around and 90% were excellent graphic design and only 10% of the daily flood landed in the trashcan. But because this isn't the case there's only one thing left to be said: that good, outstanding graphic design is by no means a matter of course. It's still the exception. The something extraordinary that one so to speak achieves if one can afford it. □ Is graphic design then really something out of the ordinary? Far too few companies and institutions have recognized the value of graphic design as measure of their strategy and marketing, or as visual evidence. Unfortunately bad graphic design sells too, otherwise many products and companies wouldn't still be on their feet. So the dire need for more competitions, exhibitions, and annuals continues. It seems that we have a long way to go until graphic design will become a matter of course. □

Prof. Olaf Leu (born 1936) is proprietor of Olaf Leu Design & Partner, Frankfurt-on-the-Main, Germany.

Viele Male war ich in nationalen und internationalen Jurys tätig. Angesichts Tausender Einsendungen hingebungsvoller und einsendefreudiger Kollegen, wurde ich mir immer wieder der Tatsache bewusst, dass über 90% aller vorgelegten Arbeiten unberücksichtigt bleiben würden, dass nur maximal zehn Prozent der Einsendungen wirklich «ausgezeichnet» sind, sozusagen «reif für's Kabinett». Der Begriff «Kabinett» in seiner ursprünglichen historischen Bedeutung trifft insofern den Punkt, als dies als «besonderer Raum für Studien und für Kostbarkeiten» bezeichnet wurde. Tatsächlich hatten viele der ausgewählten Arbeiten die Qualität von Studien, zum Teil waren es wirklich Kostbarkeiten. □ Trotzdem beschleichen einen praxisbezogenen und - erfahrenen Juror leise Zweifel darüber, ob diese ausgewählten «Kabinett-Stücke» noch sehr viel mit dem Alltag zu tun haben. □ Es ist nicht zu übersehen, dass ein guter Teil der Arbeiten aus dem Bannkreis der eigenen Branche stammt: Die Briefausstattung für die eigene Agentur, das eigene Studio. Der splendid angelegte Neujahrsglückwunsch – er kann auch auf Poster-Grösse angewachsen sein. Das Plakat der eigenen Ausstellung, auch ein Vortrag oder ein Seminar kann so angekündigt sein. Selbstverständlich profitieren alle verwandten Kollegen, branchenfremde Freunde miteinbezogen, von dem tätigen Genius graphicus: Photographen mit Plakaten, Anzeigen und Katalogen, Texter und Modellagenturen mit Briefausstattungen und Einladungen. Auch der eigene Club darf nicht fehlen, Plakate und Ausschreibungen zu Jahreswettbewerben tragen das Insider-Signum. □ Die graphische Industrie, immerhin entfernter Verwandter, spielt mit: Satzcomputer-Hersteller für Hard- und Software, Photosetzereien, Druckereien, Farbenfabriken und Papierhersteller - letztere mit hinreissenden Kollektionen voller Kreativität und entsprechend grosszügiger technischer Ausstattung. □ Verlage, ohnehin ein graphisches oder photographisches Thema publizierend, geben der Ausstattung ein Sonder-Budget, letztlich fühlt man sich der Szene doch verpflichtet. Schulen für Graphik-Design legen ihre Selbstdarstellung – ob Poster, Magazin oder Broschüre – in professionelle Hände. Das geschieht alles unter dem Motto: Man kennt sich, man trifft sich, man arbeitet zusammen. □ Natürlich befinden sich unter den 10% der angenommenen Arbeiten auch exzellente Stücke, die sozusagen aus dem Alltagsgeschäft stammen, wenngleich ich hier eine Einschränkung anbringen muss, die, national bedingt, in den verschiedenen Auftragsverhältnissen und - bedürfnissen begründet liegt: So die USA mit ausgeklügelten und sehr grossartig angelegten Sales-Promotion-Aktionen und Selbstdarstellungen in Broschürenform, die in diesem Land sehr galant als «Annual Reports» bezeichnet werden, diese glänzende Sicht auf immer alerte Boards in aluminium- und edelstahlbewehrten Trutzburgen – so etwas zeigen die USA einmalig. Von gleicher Qualität sind die Briefausstattungen – in einem Land, das keine Normvorschriften der Beschriftung kennt – da kommen nur wenige andere Länder mit. □ Editorial Art, ursprünglich in seiner besten Anwendung lange Jahre auf die USA beschränkt, erobert jetzt auch andere Länder, auch hier fällt auf, dass Illustratoren und Photographen wahrhaft international wirksam werden – das sind dann die Sonderseiten, die deutlich die Sonderproduktion widerspiegeln. □ Poster Art aus Japan, hier auffällig viele Poster in Siebdrucktechnik, was darauf hindeutet, dass die Auflage limitiert sein muss – also doch mehr Studienobjekt? □ Wettbewerbe und die Jahrbücher zeigen die «übriggebliebenen» 10%, die ich jetzt hochstilisiert als Ausnahme von der Regel bezeichne. Schön wäre die Umkehrung der Verhältnisse: 90% exzellentes Graphik-Design und 10% der täglichen Flut für den Abfall. Weil es aber so nicht ist, lässt dies nur die Deutung zu, dass gutes, ausgezeichnetes Graphik-Design noch nicht «selbstverständlich» ist. Es gilt immer noch als Ausnahme, als Besonderheit – man leistet es sich, wenn man es sich leisten kann. □ Ist Graphik-Design also doch eine Besonderheit? Wenige, zu wenige Unternehmen und Institutionen haben den Wert, den Beitrag des Graphik-Designs als Massnahme ihrer Strategie, des Marketing, als visuelle Verkörperung erkannt. Leider verkauft auch schlechtes Graphik-Design – ansonsten dürfte es viele Produkte und Unternehmen gar nicht mehr geben. So bedarf es noch vieler Wettbewerbe, Ausstellungen und Jahrbücher. Graphik-Design sollte eine «Selbstverständlichkeit» werden. □

Prof. Olaf Leu (geb. 1936) ist Inhaber von Olaf Leu Design & Partner in Frankfurt am Main.

J'ai siégé de nombreuses fois au jury de concours nationaux et internationaux. Au vue des milliers d'envois émanant de collègues dévoués disposés à nous faire connaître leurs travaux, j'ai réalisé maintes fois que plus de 90% des envois allaient être écartés, qu'un grand maximum de 10% seraient considérés «excellents» et dignes d'être montés en épingle et de figurer au rang d'objets précieux méritant étude. Il est vrai qu'un grand nombre des œuvres retenues étaient dignes d'étude et qu'une partie pouvait même prétendre à la qualité d'objet précieux. □ Il n'en reste pas moins qu'un juré ayant réuni une certaine expérience professionnelle peut être amené à se demander si lesdits objets précieux ont encore grand-chose à voir avec la réalité de tous les jours. □ En effet, ce qui ne manque pas de surprendre, c'est qu'une bonne partie des travaux primés provient du cercle réservé de la branche sous forme d'entêtes d'agences ou de studios réalisés pour leurs propres besoins, ou de cartes de vœux de Nouvel An superbement conçues dans un format pouvant atteindre celui de l'affiche, ou encore d'affiches créées pour les conférences, expositions ou séminaires de leurs auteurs. Bien entendu, tous les amis, même s'ils n'ont rien à voir avec la profession, bénéficient du génie graphique des lieux: les photographes fournissent des affiches, annonces et catalogues, les rédacteurs et agences de modèles livrent des en-têtes et des invitations. Le club auquel on appartient fait également valoir ses droits, de sorte que ses affiches et appels d'envois pour les concours annuels portent la griffe de l'un de ses membres. □ L'industrie des arts graphiques, ce parent éloigné, est également dans le coup: fabricant de photocomposeuses (matérieles et logiciels), ateliers de photocomposition, imprimeries, fabriques d'encres, papetiers – ces derniers avec des collections époustouflantes de créativité dans une présentation technique impeccable. □ Les éditeurs voués de toute façon à une thématique graphique ou photographique accordent un budget spécial à la présentation, par devoir de solidarité. Les écoles de design graphique publiques ou privées confient leur publicité institutionelle (affiches, magazines, brochures) à des professionnels. Le tout procédant de ce constat: «On se connaît, on se voit, on travaille ensemble.» □ Bien entendu, les 10% de travaux retenus renferment des créations exceptionnelles surgies du tout-venant quotidien. A cet égard, je dois apporter une restriction de caractère national et qui concerne les différentes situations et besoins en matière de commandes. Ainsi, les Etats-Unis sont passés maîtres dans la mise au point de promotions et publications de prestige conçues avec flair et brillamment exécutés, baptisées galamment de «rapports annuels» et interprétant l'air héroïque des conseils d'administration superefficients à l'arbri de leurs châteaux forts d'aluminium et d'acier. Les en-têtes se hissent à des hauteurs comparables dans un pays qui ignore les normes régissant ailleurs les imprimés. Rares sont les pays à pouvoir égaler ces prouesses. □ L'art éditorial, jadis le fief incontesté des grands maîtres américains, fait désormais tache d'huile hors des USA. Là encore, on note que les illustrateurs et les photographes œuvrent à une échelle résolument internationale – ce qui nous donne des pages spéciales nettement représentatives d'une production spécialisée. □ Au Japon, l'affiche est très souvent sérigraphique ce qui constitue l'indice de tirages limités – l'affiche n'y serait-elle qu'un objet d'études. □ Les concours, les expositions annuelles qui en sont dérivées et les annuels qui leur sont consacrés servent à présenter les 10% «restants», que l'on peut qualifier d'exceptions à la règle en forçant un peu. Ce qui serait formidable, ce serait l'inversion de cette proportion: 90% de créations graphiques de tout premier plan contre 10% de déchet parmi le flot d'images qui nous envahit journellement. Pourtant, comme il n'en est pas ainsi, il nous faut bien admettre que le design graphique de très grande qualité n'est pas encore monnaie courante, mais constitue toujours l'exception, la singularité. □ D'où le caractère remarquable du design graphique, dont seul un nombre réduit d'entreprises et d'institutions sont déjà conscientes au point d'intégrer cette discipline dans leur stratégie, leur marketing et leur capital-image. Le design graphique de mauvaise qualité sert hélas aussi à vendre, sinon ce serait la disparition de nombreux produits et entreprises. Il faudra donc encore beaucoup de concours, d'expositions et d'annuels jusqu'à ce que le design graphique aille de soi dans la vie de la cité. □

Le Pr Olaf Leu (1936) est propriétaire de la société Olaf Leu Design & Partner de Francfort-sur-le-Main (RFA).*

Year after year this annual shows a collection of the best graphic design produced in the world in the preceding year. The selection of the material is based on entries sent by designers from all over the world, from different areas of graphic design. In selecting the material, two main factors intervene: the judgement of the reviewers and the nature of the material itself. □ We know that, historically, GRAPHIS has always attempted to be as objective as possible, beyond any current partisan position or trends. For this reason we believe the Annual Review to be a quite objective representation of what has been happening. The attentive eye of the editors has registered, with mercurial precision, every change of the creative body. New trends have been spotted and brought forward for us to decide their value. The task of the Annual is clear, correct and relevant. The Annual represents the most precious contribution to the history of graphic design. Through it we can follow the development of this young profession and all its ups and downs, and evaluate the depth of different approaches to communication design and the shallowness of trends. Trendiness is an infantile attitude which harvests talents year after year. □ The task of the Annual is also to register history so that we will learn how not to repeat it. But too often it backlashes and it serves as a real model for funky revivals, stylistic retro and onanistic complacences. As I see it, the Annual's main function is to bring forward emerging voices. The more I see unknown names doing great design, the better I feel. I actually pity the established protagonists of the world design stage striving for fifteen more minutes of limelight glitz. The Annual's liveliness does not depend on established positions but on the advancement of new ones. By the same token, it does not depend on trendy novelty, bizarre illustrations, scattered graphics, illegible typography, meaningless beauty, even if we see a lot of it. □ The task of the Annual, as I see it, is to raise the standards of our profession by showing the best efforts of our colleagues to solve usual problems in unusual ways and, therefore, expand our imagination, sensibility and knowledge. □ By showing us intelligent solutions, the Annual makes a positive contribution to our profession and to our culture. By showing us trendy solutions, it would lower the level of our profession. Today, more than ever, we are poisoned by a visual pollution of graphic material, as a projection of the current ethical values. More than ever, the continuous fight of all the conscious graphic designers to replace vulgarity with intelligence should be documented, to inspire others to improve our visual world. □ I believe that in graphics, word and image share equal value, no one being more important than the other, but both being good only when used appropriately. I belive the articulation of those two elements will always provide ground for excitement to intelligently portray the message, which, in the end, is indeed the only real reason for graphic design. □ This year's GRAPHIS DESIGN and those of the years to come will tell us. □

Born in Milan in 1931, Massimo Vignelli studied architecture in Milan and Venice. Since then he has worked with his wife, Lella, an architect. In 1971, they established the offices of Vignelli Associates and Vignelli Designs in New York and work for many of the leading American and European companies and institutions.

Jahr für Jahr zeigt dieses Jahrbuch eine Zusammenstellung des besten Graphik-Designs, das im vorangehenden Jahr in aller Welt produziert wurde. Es ist eine Auswahl von Arbeiten aus verschiedenen Bereichen, welche Designer von überall her einschicken. Bei der Jurierung spielen zwei Faktoren die grösste Rolle: Die Meinung der Juroren und die Qualität der Arbeit selbst. □ Ich weiss, dass GRAPHIS sich seit jeher bemüht hat, so objektiv wie möglich zu sein und keinem Land oder Trend den Vorzug zu geben. Deshalb glauben wir, dass dieser jährliche Rückblick eine recht objektive Darstellung des Geschehens ist. Das aufmerksame Auge der Redakteure hat, mit merkurischer Präzision, jegliche Änderung in der kreativen Szene wahrgenommen. Neue Trends wurden ausgemacht und uns zur Begutachtung ihres Wertes vorgelegt. Die Aufgabe des Jahrbuches ist eindeutig und wichtig. Es ist der wertvollste Beitrag zur Geschichte des Graphik-Designs, denn es ermöglicht uns, die Entwicklung dieses jungen Berufszweiges mit all den Höhen und Tiefen zu verfolgen, und uns über den Wert der verschiedenen Leistungen auf dem Gebiet des Kommunikations-Designs und über die Oberflächlichkeit von Trends klar zu werden. Jeden Trend mitzumachen bedeutet eine infantile Haltung, die Jahr für Jahr Talente ruiniert hat. □ Die Aufgabe des Jahrbuchs liegt im Aufzeichnen der Geschichte, so dass wir lernen, sie nicht zu wiederholen. Oft genug jedoch geht das schief, und es dient statt dessen als Vorlage für fade Neuaufgüsse, stilistische Rückschritte und Selbstbeweihräucherung. In meinen Augen ist die Hauptaufgabe eines Jahrbuchs, neuen Stimmen Gehör zu verschaffen. Je mehr unbekannte Schöpfer grossartiger Designs ich entdecke, desto besser fühle ich mich. Mir tun die etablierten Protagonisten der Design-Welt leid, wenn es wichtig für sie ist, ein paar Minuten länger im Rampenlicht zu stehen. Die Lebendigkeit des Jahrbuchs hängt sicher nicht von den etablierten Positionen ab, sondern von der Förderung neuer Wege. Sie hängt aber ebensowenig von modischen Neuheiten ab, von bizarren Illustrationen, wilden Graphiken, unleserlicher Typographie – auch wenn wir viel davon zu sehen bekommen. □ Die Aufgabe des Jahrbuchs ist, das Niveau in unserem Fachbereich zu steigern, indem es zeigt, wie unsere Kollegen alltägliche Probleme auf nicht alltägliche Weise hervorragend gelöst haben. Dadurch werden unsere Phantasie, unsere Sensibilität und unser Wissen gefördert. □ Durch das Aufzeigen intelligenter Lösungen leistet das Jahrbuch einen positiven Beitrag. Würden uns modische Trends präsentiert, hätte das allgemeine Niveau darunter zu leiden. Heute sind wir mehr denn je einer visuellen Verschmutzung durch graphisches Material, Spiegel der gegenwärtigen ethischen Werte, ausgesetzt. Mehr denn je sollte der ständige Kampf aller gewissenhaften Graphik-Designer für intelligente statt vulgäre Problemlösungen dokumentiert werden, um andere dazu anzuregen, zur Verbesserung der visuellen Umwelt beizutragen. □ Ich glaube, dass Wort und Bild die gleiche Bedeutung zukommt, wobei keines wichtiger als das andere ist, sondern beide gut sind, wenn sie richtig eingesetzt werden. Die richtige Handhabung dieser beiden Elemente wird immer Voraussetzung für Freude an der intelligenten Umsetzung einer Botschaft sein, um die es schliesslich im Graphik-Design einzig und allein geht. □ GRAPHIS DESIGN 90 und alle kommenden Bände werden uns dies beweisen. □

Massimo Vignelli wurde 1931 in Mailand geboren. Er studierte Architektur in seiner Geburtsstadt und in Venedig. Seit jener Zeit arbeitet er zusammen mit seiner Frau Lella, einer Architektin. 1971 gründeten sie die Firmen Vignelli Associates und Vignelli Designs in New York. Zu ihren Kunden zählen viele der führenden amerikanischen und europäischen Firmen und Institutionen.

MASSIMO VIGNELLI

D'année en année, le présent annuel regroupe un choix des meilleures productions de design graphique ayant vu le jour à travers le monde dans l'année écoulée. La sélection de ces matériaux s'effectue à partir des envois que les designers de tous pays font parvenir à l'éditeur. Deux facteurs interviennent dans l'opération: le jugement du jury et la nature du matériel expertisé. □ Nous savons depuis de longues années que GRAPHIS a toujours cherché à se montrer aussi objectif que possible, par-delà toute position ou orientation partisane. C'est ce qui nous porte à penser que le florilège réuni dans ce volume constitue une représentation tout à fait objective de ce qui s'est effectivement passé. L'œil attentif des rédacteurs n'a pas manqué d'enregistrer avec une précision alerte les changements les plus infimes qui ont affecté l'ensemble du corps créatif. Les tendances nouvelles ont été relevées de manière à nous faciliter une prise de position. La tâche impartie à cet annuel est claire, correcte, pertinente. Cette annuel incarne la contribution la plus précieuse qui soit à l'histoire du design graphique. Il nous permet de suivre pas à pas le développement de cette jeune profession, avec ses hauts et ses bas, et d'évaluer l'importance des différentes approches au design de communication. □ L'annuel a aussi pour tâche d'enregistrer l'histoire, de manière à nous éviter à l'avenir les déboires du passé. Il faut toutefois reconnaître qu'il en résulte trop souvent de surprenants retours de manivelle sous forme d'un culte de styles rétro et de satisfactions masturbatoires. A mes yeux, la fonction principale de l'annuel, c'est de faire entendre des voix qui ne font tout juste qu'émerger. Plus je vois des inconnus réaliser des grandes choses en matière de design, et mieux je me sens. Le présent annuel ne doit pas son caractère vivant aux positions déjà établies, mais à la conquête de positions nouvelles. Pareillement cette publication ne dépend pas de nouveautés dans le vent, d'illustrations bizarres, de compositions graphiques éparpillées, de typographies illisibles ou de beautés sans signification, même si notre environnement en est rempli. □ Pour moi, la mission de l'annuel, c'est de relever le niveau de qualité de notre profession en mettant devant nos yeux les efforts les plus réussis de nos collègues pour résoudre des problèmes usuels par des moyens inusuels, élargissant de cette façon notre imagination, notre sensibilité et nos connaissances. □ En nous présentant des solutions intelligentes, l'annuel apporte une contribution positive à notre profession et à notre culture. En nous montrant des solutions nées du goût du jour, on ne ferait qu'abaisser le niveau de notre profession. Aujourd'hui, nous sommes plus que jamais empoisonnés par une pollution visuelle de matériaux graphiques que sous-tendent les valeurs morales actuelles. Plus que jamais, le combat incessant que tous les graphistes conscients livrent pour substituer l'intelligence à la vulgarité a besoin d'être documenté, afin d'inspirer d'autres créateurs pour améliorer l'univers visuel où nous évoluons. □ Je crois qu'au sein de l'art graphique un rôle identique revient au mot et à l'image, sans qu'aucun puisse l'emporter sur l'autre, et que le mot ou l'image ne sont bons que lorsqu'on les emploie à bon escient. Je crois que l'articulation de ces deux éléments procurera toujours une source de stimulation extraordinaire en vue de parfaire un message intelligent lequel, en fin de compte, est la seule et unique raison de l'existence du design graphique. □ L'annuel GRAPHIS DESIGN de cette année et ceux des années à venir nous le confirmeront. □

Né à Milan en 1931, Massimo Vignelli a étudié l'architecture à Milan et à Venise. Depuis lors, il travaille avec sa femme Lella, qui est architecte. En 1971, ils installent à New York les bureaux de Vignelli Associates et de Vignelli Designs, avec pour clients de nombreuses sociétés de renom en Amérique et en Europe.

ADVERTISING

ANNONCES

ANZEIGEN

ANNONCES

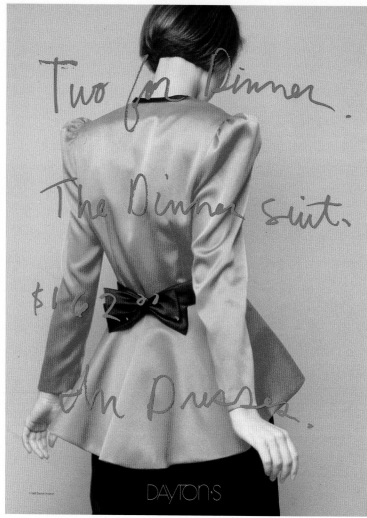

ART DIRECTOR:
AMY QUINLIVEN
DESIGNER:
AMY QUINLIVEN
PHOTOGRAPHER:
WILLIAM GARRETT
STYLIST:
MARY BERGTOLD
COPYWRITER:
VICKY ROSSI
AGENCY:
*DAYTON HUDSON DEPARTMENT
STORE/IN HOUSE*
CLIENT:
*DAYTON HUDSON DEPARTMENT
STORE*
■ 1, 2

ART DIRECTOR:
AMY QUINLIVEN
DESIGNER:
*AMY QUINLIVEN/
KAREN BROLON (TYPOGRAPHY)*
PHOTOGRAPHER:
WILLIAM GARRETT
COPYWRITER:
BARB READ
AGENCY:
*DAYTON HUDSON DEPARTMENT
STORE/IN-HOUSE*
CLIENT:
*DAYTON HUDSON DEPARTMENT
STORE*
►■ 3

■ 1-3 Magazine ads by the Dayton Hudson store for fall fashions by Issey Miyake, a festive deux-pièce and an ensemble with fashionable polka dots. (USA)

■ 1-3 Zeitschriftenanzeigen des Kaufhauses Dayton Hudson für Herbstmode von Issey Miyake, ein festliches Deux-Pièces und ein Ensemble mit modischen Tupfen. (USA)

■ 1-3 Annonces de magazines des grands magasins Dayton Hudson pour les modes d'automne d'Issey Miyake: deux-pièces élégant et ensemble à pois mode. (USA)

Let
Dots
Make
you
Point

Scarf-tie jacket
in black & white
rayon crepe, $110.
Rayon skirt $90.
J.M. by Shelli Segal.
Advanced Sportswear

DAYTON'S

ART DIRECTOR:
GRAHAM WATSON
PHOTOGRAPHER:
ELLIOTT ERWITT
COPYWRITER:
CHRIS HERRING
AGENCY:
BARTLE BOGLE HEGARTY LTD
CLIENT:
LEVI STRAUSS EUROPE SA
■ 4-6

■ 4-6 From a campaign on behalf of Levi Strauss. The texts are quotations from books in which the brand name *Levi's* is mentioned in the descriptions of clothes. (GBR)

■ 4-6 Aus einer Magazin-kampagne für Levi Strauss. Die Texte sind Zitate aus Büchern, in denen der Markenname *Levi's* in Beschreibungen von Kleidung erwähnt wird. (GBR)

■ 4-6 Exemples tirés d'une campagne de Levi Strauss. Les textes sont empruntés à des ouvrages où la marque *Levi's* est citée à propos de vêtements. (GBR)

501s

I reached in the pocket of my leather sheepherder's jacket, pulled out a black, passport-sized wallet, and put two dollars on the counter. In the dreary dawn of a hobo's breakfast at the Oxford Café, that wallet seemed as out of place as a diplomatic pouch or a pair of cashmere Levi's.

Hunter S. Thompson.
The Great Shark Hunt.

501s

And Billy, watching the brass brads on that woman's Levi's wink at him as she walked out of the day room, told Ellis to hell with that fisher of <u>men</u> business.

Ken Kesey.
One Flew Over The Cuckoo's Nest.

501s

Dean was wearing washed-out tight Levis and a T-shirt and looked suddenly like a real Denver character again.

Jack Kerouac.
On The Road.

ART DIRECTOR:
*BIRGITTA LAURELL/
NIKKO AMANDONICO*
PHOTOGRAPHER:
GUIDO HILDEBRAND
AGENCY:
*J. WALTER THOMPSON
ITALIA S.P.A.*
CLIENT:
BENETTON S.P.A.
■ 7

■ 7 From a series of magazine advertisements for *Sisley* fashion with a South American touch. (USA)

■ 7 Aus einer Serie von Zeitschriftenanzeigen für *Sisley*-Mode mit südamerikanischem Touch. (USA)

■ 7 Annonce de magazine figurant dans une série réalisée pour les modes *Sisley* dans le style d'Amérique du Sud. (USA)

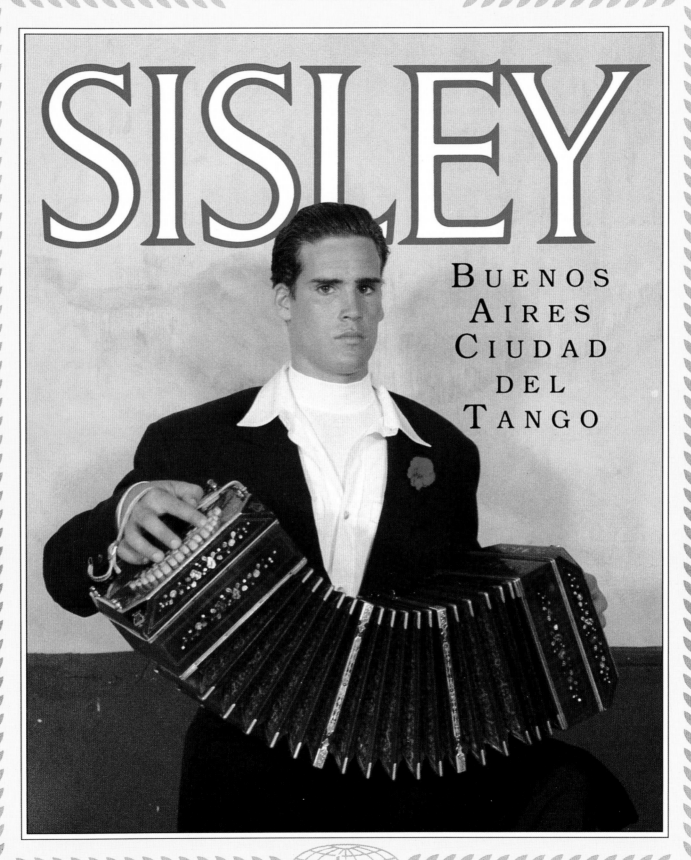

SPRING SUMMER 1988

SISLEY

BUENOS
AIRES
CIUDAD
DEL
TANGO

LOUIS FERAUD : MEN'S SUITS.

BASILE : MEN'S DESIGNER COLLECTIONS.

Suit £285.
Man's Shop, Ground Floor.

Suit £645.
Man's Shop, Ground Floor.

Harrods

GLAIRE DEDEYAN : YOUNG DESIGNERS.

WORKERS FOR FREEDOM : YOUNG DESIGNERS.

Jacket £395, Skirt £165.
Floor 1.

Linen Dress £245.
Floor 1.

Harrods

WORKING CLASS.

THE FINEST FALL CLOTHING AND ACCESSORIES FOR WORKING WOMEN
ARE AVAILABLE IN STORES LIKE TALBOT'S, ELÉGANCE, NATURALIZER
SHOES, AND BADINER'S JEWELRY AT IDS CRYSTAL COURT.

IDS CRYSTAL COURT

A SHORT COURSE IN THE CLASSICS.

AN EDUCATION FOR THOSE WHO DRESS FOR SUCCESS:
BROOKS BROTHERS, CHURCH'S ENGLISH SHOES, MERLE'S MENS STORE
AND BERMAN'S ARE LOCATED AT IDS CRYSTAL COURT.

IDS CRYSTAL COURT

ART DIRECTOR:
STEVE DUNN

PHOTOGRAPHER:
PETER LINDBERGH

COPYWRITER:
TIM DELANEY

AGENCY:
LEAGAS DELANEY

CLIENT:
HARRODS

◀■ 8, 9

ART DIRECTOR:
DEB MINER

PHOTOGRAPHER:
PETER LINDMAN

COPYWRITER:
CORINNE MITCHELL

AGENCY:
McCOOL & COMPANY

CLIENT:
BCE DEVELOPMENT

■ 10, 11

■ 8, 9 From an advertising campaign for various designers whose creations are available at the famous department store Harrods of London. (GBR)

■ 10, 11 Examples of newspaper advertisements from a campaign. The style creates awareness and underscores the image of a center offering classic clothing and accessories for men and women. (USA)

■ 8, 9 Aus einer Werbekampagne für verschiedene Designer, deren Kreationen im Londoner Kaufhaus Harrods erhältlich sind. (GBR)

■ 10, 11 Zeitungsanzeigen aus einer Kampagne für klassische Mode und Accessoires für Berufstätige. Der Stil dieser Werbung entspricht dem Angebot und dem gewünschten Image des Geschäftes. (USA)

■ 8, 9 Extraits d'une campagne publicitaire pour divers designers dont les créations sont disponibles aux grands magasins Harrods de Londres. (GBR)

■ 10, 11 Annonces de journaux pour une campagne en faveur de vêtements et accessoires classiques pour le travail. Le style de cette pub correspond à l'image que ce magasin entend donner de lui-même. (USA)

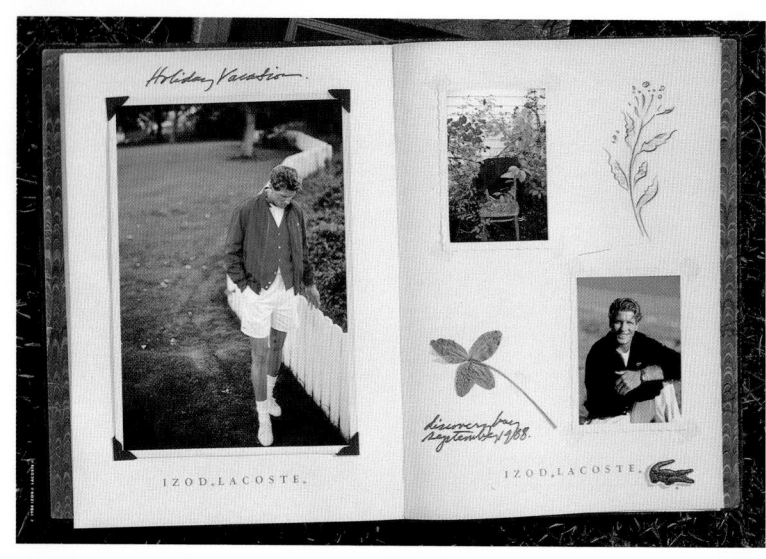

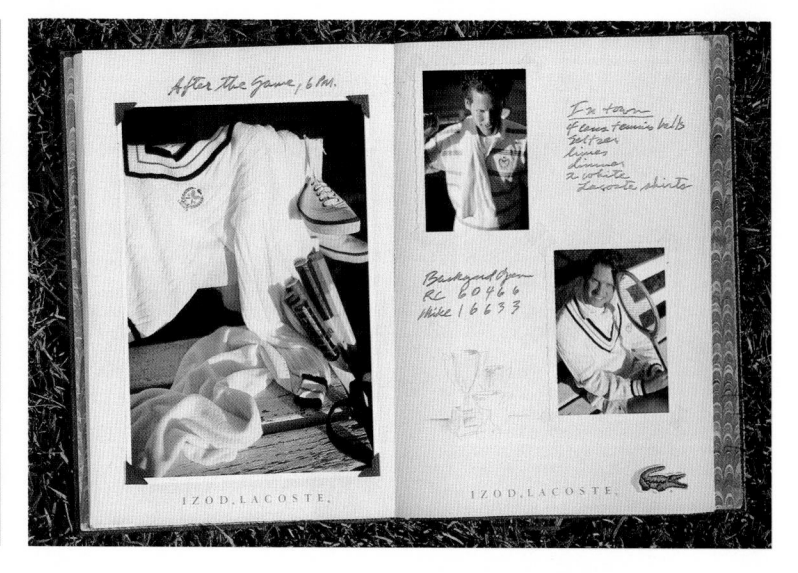

ART DIRECTOR:
David Edelstein/
Nancy Edelstein/
Lanny French/
Carol Davidson/
Rick Jost
DESIGNER:
David Edelstein/
Nancy Edelstein/
Lanny French/
Carol Davidson/
Rick Jost
PHOTOGRAPHER:
Peggy Sirota
▲■ 12,13

STYLIST:
Eric Castellano
COPYWRITER:
David Edelstein/
Lanny French
AGENCY:
Edelstein Associates
Advertising Inc.
CLIENT:
IZOD LaCoste Sportswear
▲■ 12 ,13

COOL WATER
Das Prinzip des Duftes

EAU DE TOILETTE

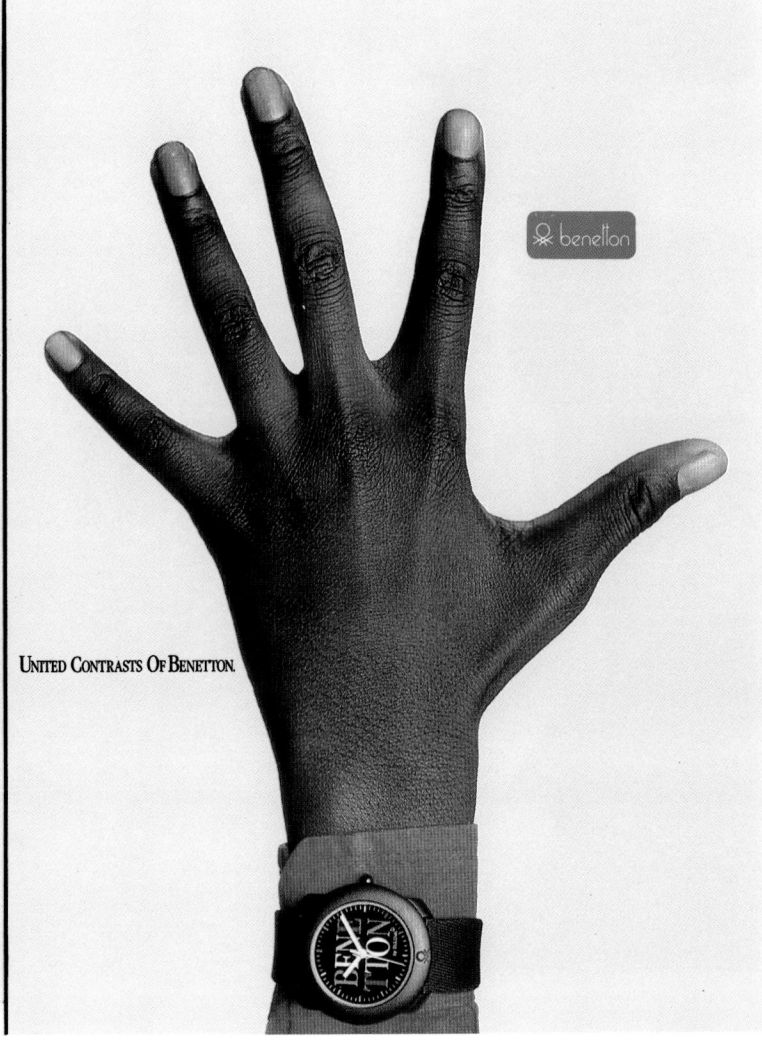

Art Director:
Roland Seeliger
Designer:
Christian Dennert
Photographer:
Jeanloup Sieff
Agency:
INEX Werbeagentur
Client:
Davidoff/Lancaster
◄■ 14

Art Director:
Bruno Sutter
Photographer:
Oliviero Toscani
Agency:
Eldorado
Client:
Benetton SpA
▲■ 15

■ 12, 13 Double-spread magazine ads for *LaCoste* sportswear. A snapshot album was the inspiration for this holiday campaign. (USA)

■ 14 Double-spread magazine ad for "Cool Water" – an eau-de-toilette by Davidoff. The advertisement is reduced to the visual interpretation of the product name. (GER)

■ 15 One version of the original slogan "United Colors of *Benetton*" for a double-spread magazine ad. (USA)

■ 12, 13 Doppelseitige Zeitschriftenanzeigen für *LaCoste*-Sportmode. Diese Ferien-Kampagne ist durch die Photoalbum-Idee geprägt. (USA)

■ 14 Ein auf die visuelle Interpretation des Produktnamens reduziertes, doppelseitiges Zeitschrifteninserat für «Cool Water» Eau de Toilette von Davidoff. (GER)

■ 15 Eine Variante des Slogans «United Colors of *Benetton*» für ein doppelseitiges Zeitschrifteninserat. (USA)

■ 12, 13 Annonces de magazines double page pour les modes sport de *LaCoste*. Cette campagne de vacances est axée sur l'idée des albums photo. (USA)

■ 14 Annonce de magazine double page pour «Cool Water», une eau de Toilette de Davidoff. Elle se réduit à une interprétation visuelle du nom du produit. (GER)

■ 15 Variante du slogan primitif «United Colors of *Benetton*» pour une annonce de magazine double page. (USA)

■ 16, 17 Advertisement from a magazine campaign in fall '88 for *Code Bleu* sportswear. (USA)

■ 18, 19 Examples from an advertising campaign for shoe creations by Charles Jourdan. (JPN)

■ 16, 17 Aus einer Zeitschriftenkampagne im Herbst 88 für *Code-Bleu*-Sportmode. (USA)

■ 18, 19 Beispiele aus einer Werbekampagne für Schuhkrea-tionen von Charles Jourdan. (JPN)

■ 16, 17 Campagne de magazines d'automne 1988 pour les modes sport *Code-Bleu*. (USA)

■ 18, 19 Exemples tirés d'une campagne publicitaire du chausseur Charles Jourdan. (JPN)

ART DIRECTOR:
DAVID EDELSTEIN/
LANNY FRENCH/
RICK JOST/
ANGELE WIGGIN
DESIGNER:
DAVID EDELSTEIN/
LANNY FRENCH/
RICK JOST/
ANGELE WIGGIN
PHOTOGRAPHER:
NICK VACCARO
STYLIST:
MICHAEL D'APICE
AGENCY:
EDELSTEIN ASSOCIATES
ADVERTISING INC.
CLIENT:
CODE BLEU SPORTSWEAR
▲■ 16, 17

CHARLES JOURDAN

CHARLES JOURDAN

Shoes 837521 ¥32,000

Shoes 837521 ¥32,000 Bag 4281 ¥58,000

ART DIRECTOR:
TSUYOSHI FUKUDA
DESIGNER:
MICHIHIRO ISHIZAKI/
MAIKO KARIYA
PHOTOGRAPHER:
TADAYUKI KAWAHITO/
YOSHIHIKO UEDA
AGENCY:
CHAMELEON INC.
CLIENT:
CHARLES JOURDAN
JAPAN BRANCH
▲■ 18, 19

■ 20 Double-spread magazine advertisement in the 30's style for Jean Paul Gaultier's men's fashionwear. (ITA)

■ 21 Magazine ad by the Japanese cosmetic company Shiseido for which photographer Serge Lutens not only took the shots but was also responsible for the make-up creations. (GER)

■ 22 One of the full-page magazine ads which are reduced to the visual statement and the designer name, for *Planet* fashions. (USA)

■ 20 Doppelseitiges Zeitschrifteninserat im Stil der 30er Jahre für *Gaultier*-Herrenmode. (ITA)

■ 21 Zeitschriftenanzeige des japanischen Kosmetikkonzerns Shiseido, für die der Photograph Serge Lutens nicht nur die Aufnahmen machte, sondern auch die Make-up-Farben kreierte. (GER)

■ 22 Ein auf die Bildaussage und den Designer-Namen reduziertes, ganzseitiges Zeitschrifteninserat für *Planet*-Modekreationen. (USA)

■ 20 Annonce de magazine double page, dans le style des années 30, pour les modes masculines *Gaultier*. (ITA)

■ 21 Annonce de magazine du groupe cosmétique japonais Shiseido pour lequel le photographe Serge Lutens ne s'est pas contenté de réaliser les photos: il a également créé la palette de maquillage. (GER)

■ 22 Annonce de magazine pleine page pour les créations de mode *Planet*. Elle est réduite à l'image et au nom du designer. (USA)

ART DIRECTOR:
JEAN PAUL GAULTIER/
FRANCIS MENUGE
DESIGNER:
THIERRY PEREZ
PHOTOGRAPHER:
JEAN PAUL GAULTIER
AGENCY:
JEAN PAUL GAULTIER
CLIENT:
JEAN PAUL GAULTIER
■ 20

ART DIRECTOR:
MARK BARRINGTON
PHOTOGRAPHER:
GLEN ERLER
AGENCY:
L.A. STYLE/IN HOUSE
CLIENT:
DOREEN DEMPSKI
■ 22

ART DIRECTOR:
SERGE LUTENS
DESIGNER:
SERGE LUTENS
PHOTOGRAPHER:
SERGE LUTENS
AGENCY:
EGGERT-DYR WERBEAGENTUR
CLIENT:
SHISEIDO
■ 21

ONCE AGAIN, PIRELLI MAKES A GENEROUS CONTRIBUTION
TO THE PERFORMING ARTS.

ART DIRECTOR:
Michael Arola
PHOTOGRAPHER:
Gastone Jung
COPYWRITER:
Carolyn Johnson
AGENCY:
AC&R/CCL
CLIENT:
Pirelli Tire Corporation
◀■ 23

DESIGNER:
Hans Christer Ericson
STUDIO:
H C Ericson
Grafiska Verkstaden
CLIENT:
Lammhults Möbel AB
■ 24, 25

■ 23 The Pirelli Tire Corporation underscores its expertise by making use of some of the world's most prominent automobile marques to promote its high quality tires which belong to the original equipment of these cars. (USA)

■ 24, 25 Examples of the full-page advertisements from a magazine campaign for *Lammhults* furniture. (SWE)

■ 23 Pirellis «grosszügige Unterstützung der darstellenden Künste», wie der Slogan ankündigt, besteht in der erstklassigen Qualität der *Pirelli*-Reifen, die zur Originalausstattung berühmter Automarken gehören. (USA)

■ 24, 25 Beispiele von ganzseitigen Anzeigen aus einer Zeitschriftenkampagne für *Lammhults*-Möbel. (SWE)

■ 23 Le slogan souligne «la générosité exemplaire de Pirelli pour les arts de spectacle», en fait la qualité exceptionnelle des pneus *Pirelli* qui font partie de l'équipement standard de marques de voitures célèbres. (USA)

■ 24, 25 Annonces pleine page pour une campagne de magazines en faveur des meubles *Lammhults*. (SWE)

■ 26, 27 Two newspaper advertisements for radios made by Japanese manufacturer National which were awarded the 1987 Asahi Advertising Prize in a contest of the large Japanese newspaper *Asahi Shimbun.* (JPN)

■ 28 Promotional ads for the camcorder (name for a video camera and recorder in one) made by Sanyo, claiming the advent of the new wave of Japanese technology. (GBR)

■ 29 Advertisement on behalf of Sanyo for portable radio/ cassette recorders. (GBR)

■ 26, 27 Zeitungsanzeigen für Radios des japanischen Herstellers National, die mit dem Asahi Werbepreis 1987, vergeben von der grossen japanischen Zeitung *Asahi Shimbun*, ausgezeichnet wurden. (JPN)

■ 28 «Auf den meisten Camcorders (Videokamera und Abspielgerät in einem) kam es aus dem Weltall. Auf unserem kam es über den Zaun.» Werbung für Sanyo. (GBR)

■ 29 «Der Prototyp hatte nur eine Besonderheit zuviel.» Anzeige für tragbare Audio-Geräte von Sanyo. (GBR)

■ 26, 27 Annonces de journaux pour les radios du fabricant japonais National. Elles ont été récompensées en 1987 du prix publicitaire Asahi fondé par le grand quotidien japonais *Asahi Shimbun.* (JPN)

■ 28 «Sur la plupart des camcorders (caméra vidéo avec magnétoscope), c'est venu de l'espace. Sur le nôtre, c'est venu par-dessus la clôture du voisin.» (GBR)

■ 29 «Le prototype avait juste une caractéristique de trop.» Annonce pour les appareils audio portables de Sanyo. (GBR)

■ 26, 27
CLIENT:
ASAHI SHIMBUN
COPYWRITER:
TOSHIHITO NAKANISHI
ILLUSTRATOR:
KEIJI NAKAGAWA
DESIGNER:
KATSUO MIZUGUCHI
ART DIRECTOR:
KATSUO MIZUGUCHI
CREATIVE DIRECTOR:
TOSHIHITO NAKANISHI

►■ 28, 29
CLIENT:
SANYO MARUBENI LTD.
AGENCY:
LEO BURNETT LTD.
COPYWRITER:
NICK SOUTER
PHOTOGRAPHER:
MARTIN THOMPSON
ART DIRECTOR:
STUART NEWMAN

ON MOST CAMCORDERS IT CAME FROM OUTER SPACE.

ON OURS IT CAME FROM OVER THE FENCE

VM-D5P. 3 HEAD SYSTEM. 6 SHUTTER SPEEDS (1/4000~1/50). DIGITAL AUTO FOCUS. 6X POWER ZOOM
WITH MACRO. DIGITAL MEMORY SUPER-IMPOSER. AUTO DATE IMPRINT. 5 LUX OPERATION. AND ONLY 1.2kg IN WEIGHT.

THE NEW WAVE IN JAPANESE TECHNOLOGY

SANYO

THE PROTOTYPE HAD JUST ONE FEATURE TOO MANY.

TWIN TAPE. HIGH SPEED DUBBING. CONTINUOUS PLAY. AUTO REVERSE.
4 BAND RADIO. SYNTHESISER TUNER. 20 PRESETS. LCD CLOCK AND AUDIO TIMER.

THE NEW WAVE IN JAPANESE TECHNOLOGY

SANYO

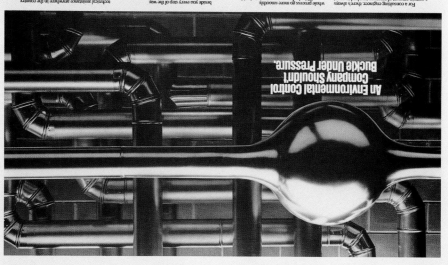

ART DIRECTOR:
PAUL LANG
PHOTOGRAPHER:
MARVY/MATTRE
COPYWRITER:
JO MARSHALL
AGENCY:
BBDO
CLIENT:
HONEYWELL
■ 30-32

■ 30-32 Advertising campaign for Honeywell. Each slogan emphasizes Honeywell's attitude toward the general environment – and the technical one they wish to create, e.g. providing solutions to relieve confusion, staying with the partner to alleviate tension, and supporting the consulting engineer to eliminate pressure. (USA)

■ 33 Advertising placed in public transport for JVC video recorders. (CAN)

■ 30-32 Beispiele aus einer Anzeigenkampagne für Honeywell: «Eine Firma für die Kontrolle der Umwelt sollte keine Umwelt der Verwirrung stiften»; «Eine Firma für die Kontrolle der Umwelt sollte nicht für viele Spannungen sorgen»; «Eine Firma für die Kontrolle der Umwelt sollte bei Druck nicht ausbeulen». (USA)

■ 33 Werbung für Video-Geräte der Marke JVC in Verkehrsmitteln. (CAN)

■ 30-32 Campagne d'annonces pour Honeywell: «Une société de contrôle de l'environnement ne devrait pas semer la confusion dans cet environnement»; «une société de contrôle de l'environnement ne devrait pas créer d'innombrables tensions»; «une société de contrôle de l'environnement ne devrait pas se gondoler sous la pression». (USA)

■ 33 Publicité pour les appareils vidéo JVC dans les moyens de transport. (CAN)

ART DIRECTOR:
PETER HOLMES
DESIGNER:
PETER HOLMES
PHOTOGRAPHER:
TIM SAUNDERS
COPYWRITER:
PETER HOLMES
AGENCY:
FRANKLIN DALLAS
CLIENT:
JVC CANADA INC.
■ 33

■ 34-36 Examples from an advertising campaign launched in the local press by a household wares store that offers information on the range of its stock – from kitchen utensils to tools. (USA)
■ 37-39 Examples from a magazine campaign for kitchen utensils marketed under the *Sunbeam* label. (USA)
■ 40 Full-page advertisement for an electric-appliances firm for its audio/video range. (GER)

■ 34-36 Aus einer in der lokalen Presse lancierten Werbekampagne für ein Haushaltswarengeschäft, das über den Umfang seines Warenangebotes – von Küchengeräten bis zu Werkzeugen – informieren möchte. (USA)
■ 37-39 Beispiele aus einer Zeitschriftenkampagne für Küchengeräte der Marke *Sunbeam*. (USA)
■ 40 Ganzseitiges Inserat eines Elektrogeschäftes für sein Audio-/Video-Angebot. (GER)

■ 34-36 Exemples d'une campagne publicitaire dans la presse locale pour un magasin d'articles ménagers qui entend présenter sa gamme entière, des appareils pour la cuisine à l'outillage. (USA)
■ 37-39 Exemples de magazines réalisées pour les ustensiles de cuisine *Sunbeam*. (USA)
■ 40 Annonce pleine page d'un magasin spécialisé en faveur de ses équipements audio et vidéo. (GER)

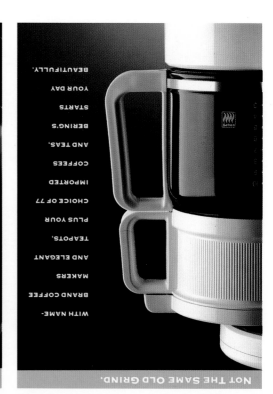

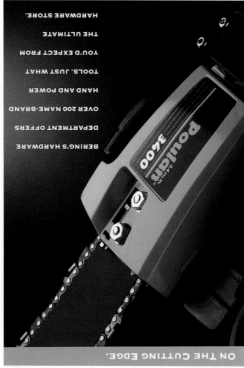

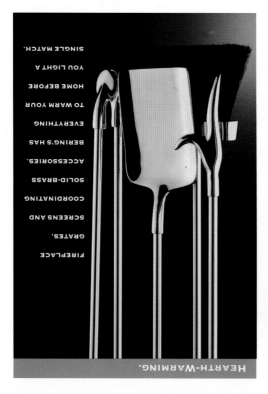

VERONICA diseñada por Afra y Tobia Scarpa   Casas - C. Milagro, 40 - 08028 Barcelona - Tel. (93) 3392800 - Telex 98387 MBIL E

CASAS

SEE AND
BE SEEN WITH

It was inevitable. As well as being urged to sport swatches and flaunt filofaxes here's an invitation to flash a suitable torch. Available in a variety of colours, the Ever Ready Personal Torch range takes torches out of musty cupboards and garden sheds and into the inside pockets of Armani suits and the inner recesses of Halliburton briefcases. And forget the old on-off switch, the Rota-light featured here comes on automatically when the head is rotated.

EVER READY

ART DIRECTOR:
EMILIO DE MADDALENA
DESIGNER:
FERRAN FREIXA/LLUIS CASALS
CLIENT:
CASAS
◄■ 41

CREATIVE DIRECTOR:
PAUL SMITH/MIKE EVERETT
ANDY COX
ART DIRECTOR:
ANDY COX
DESIGNER:
ANDY COX
PHOTOGRAPHER:
MIKE PARSONS
COPYWRITER:
STEVE BARKER
AGENCY:
ALLEN BRADY & MARSH
CLIENT:
EVER READY LTD.
■ 42

■ 41 Full-page magazine ad for designer furniture produced by the CASAS company in Barcelona. (SPA)

■ 42 Double-spread ads for torches by *Ever Ready* - that the firm claim are so elegant they can be tucked into pockets of designer-wear and in the best briefcases. (USA)

■ 41 Ganzseitiges Zeitschrifteninserat für Designer-Möbel des Hauses CASAS in Barcelona. (SPA)

■ 42 «Sehen und gesehen werden mit *Ever Ready*». Doppelseitiges Inserat für Taschenlampen in anspruchsvollem Design. (USA)

■ 41 Annonce de magazine pleine page pour le mobilier design de la société CASAS de Barcelone. (SPA)

■ 42 «Voir et être vu avec *Ever Ready*.» Annonce double page pour les lampes de poche de cette marque au design élaboré. (USA)

LONDON PALLADIUM.

Voor live muziek hoeft u voortaan de deur niet meer uit dankzij de DSP-1 van Yamaha. Een Digitale Sound Field Processor, waarmee u de sfeer die bij uw favoriete muziek past in huis haalt. U kunt 16 verschillende akoestieken oproepen. Een druk op de knop brengt u precies waar u zijn wilt. In een concertzaal of een kathedraal, een jazzclub of een stadion. De muziek klinkt alsof u er zelf bij bent. Kortom: met de Yamaha DSP-1 bent u uit in eigen huis.

DE YAMAHA DSP-1 MAAKT VAN UW HUISKAMER EEN CONCERTZAAL. ⬥ **YAMAHA**

Bel voor demonstratie-adressen J. Domp B.V. 02979 - 91600.

CARNEGIE HALL.

Voor live muziek hoeft u voortaan de deur niet meer uit dankzij de DSP-1 van Yamaha. Een Digitale Sound Field Processor, waarmee u de sfeer die bij uw favoriete muziek past in huis haalt. U kunt 16 verschillende akoestieken oproepen. Een druk op de knop brengt u precies waar u zijn wilt. In een concertzaal of een kathedraal, een jazzclub of een stadion. De muziek klinkt alsof u er zelf bij bent. Kortom: met de Yamaha DSP-1 bent u uit in eigen huis.

DE YAMAHA DSP-1 MAAKT VAN UW HUISKAMER EEN CONCERTZAAL. ⬥ **YAMAHA**

Bel voor demonstratie-adressen J. Domp B.V. 02979 - 91600.

ART DIRECTOR:
Rob Sluijs
PHOTOGRAPHER:
Ronald van Teunenbroek
AGENCY:
Kaspers, Koetse,
Burger & de Roos
CLIENT:
J. Domp B.V.
■ 43-45

CONCERT-GEBOUW.

Voor live muziek hoeft u voortaan de deur niet meer uit dankzij de DSP-1 van Yamaha. Een Digitale Sound Field Processor, waarmee u de sfeer die bij uw favoriete muziek past in huis haalt. U kunt 16 verschillende akoestieken oproepen. Een druk op de knop brengt u precies waar u zijn wilt. In een concertzaal of een kathedraal, een jazzclub of een stadion. De muziek klinkt alsof u er zelf bij bent. Kortom: met de Yamaha DSP-1 bent u uit in eigen huis.

DE YAMAHA DSP-1 MAAKT VAN UW HUISKAMER EEN CONCERTZAAL. ⬥ **YAMAHA**

Bel voor demonstratie-adressen of documentatie-materiaal J. Domp B.V. 02979 - 91600.

■ 43-45 Advertisements under the slogan "Yamaha makes a concert hall out of your living room". (NLD)

■ 46 Double-spread advertisement for the design firm Pro Industria, showing an Olsberg glazed-tile stove. (GER)

■ 43-45 Anzeigenkampagne unter dem Slogan «Yamaha macht aus Ihrem Wohnzimmer einen Konzertsaal.» (NLD)

■ 46 Doppelseitige Anzeige der Design-Firma Pro Industria mit einem Olsberg-Kachelkamin. (GER)

■ 43-45 Campagne d'annonces avec ce slogan: «Yamaha transforme votre salon en salle de concert». (NLD)

■ 46 Annonce double page de la société de design Pro Industria: poêle en faïence de la marque Olsberg. (GER)

ART DIRECTOR:
HANS GÜNTER SCHMITZ
DESIGNER:
CHRISTEL TÜRK/
HANS GÜNTER SCHMITZ
PHOTOGRAPHER:
FRANK EXNER
AGENCY:
HANS GÜNTER SCHMITZ,
GRUPPE FÜR VISUELLE KOMMU-
NIKATION
CLIENT:
PRO INDUSTRIA
■ 46

■ 47 Double-spread ad for "lightweight *Hush Puppies*." The living version of the brand name, on the scales, underscores this statement. (USA)

■ 48 From a series of ads for *Hasselblad* cameras with portrait shots by various photographers. Shown is Frank Zappa (pop singer) photographed by Lynn Goldsmith. (FRA)

■ 49 Just one more witty slogan by *Swatch* to promote their watches. Full-page advertisement. (USA)

■ 47 Doppelseitiges Inserat für «leichtgewichtige *Hush Puppies*». Unterstützt wird diese Aussage durch die lebendige Version des Markenzeichens auf einer Waage. (USA)

■ 48 Aus einer Anzeigenreihe für *Hasselblad*-Kameras mit Porträtaufnahmen verschiedener Photographen; hier Frank Zappa von Lynn Goldsmith photographiert. (FRA)

■ 49 «Vielleicht ist es Zeit, Ihre *Rolex* zu verkaufen.» Ganzseitige Anzeige für *Swatch*-Uhren. (USA)

■ 47 Annonce double page pour des «*Hush Puppies* extra-légers». Le message souligné par une version vivante de la marque trônant sur un plateau de balance. (USA)

■ 48 Portrait figurant dans une série d'annonces pour les appareils photo *Hasselblad* illustrées par divers photographes: ici, Frank Zappa interprété par Lynn Goldsmith. (FRA)

■ 49 «Peut-être le moment est-il venu de vendre votre *Rolex*.» Annonce pour les montres *Swatch*. (USA)

ART DIRECTOR:
JOHN HORTON
PHOTOGRAPHER:
KEN GRIFFITHS/
JEAN LUC BENARD
COPYWRITER:
RICHARD FOSTER
AGENCY:
ABBOTT MEAD VICKERS/
SMS LTD.
CLIENT:
BRITISH SHOE CORPORATION
■ 47

LIGHTWEIGHT HUSH PUPPIES

Take the weight off your feet with these sporty new ladies' casuals from Hush Puppies.

The leather is soft and supple, the soles light and flexible.

Skip down to your nearest Hush Puppies stockist and try a pair on.

Your feet won't know you're wearing them.

LEFT TO RIGHT: TRIGA II £19.99, QUARTZ £21.99, TRAYN II £24.99. FROM SAXONE, MANFIELD, LILLEY & SKINNER, ROLAND CARTIER, SELECTED FREEMAN HARDY WILLIS AND TRUEFORM, SELFRIDGES AND LEADING DEPARTMENT STORES.

Maybe It's Time To Sell Your Rolex.

swatch+ Holding steady at $35.

LYNN GOLDSMITH USED A HASSELBLAD TO SHOOT FRANK ZAPPA.

HASSELBLAD
Hasselblad France 5 A, Courcellor 1, 2 rue Curnonsky, 75017 Paris.

ART DIRECTOR:
PARRY MERKLEY
PHOTOGRAPHER:
FRANÇOIS GILLET
COPYWRITER:
KEVIN KELLY
AGENCY:
OGILVY & MATHER
CLIENT:
*NATIONWIDE MUTUAL
INSURANCE COMPANY*
■ 50, 51

■ 50, 51 Double-spread advertisements from a promotional campaign launched by the Nationwide Insurance whose central theme is preventive care. (USA)

■ 50, 51 Anzeigen aus einer Kampagne für die Versicherungsgesellschaft Nationwide Insurance, deren zentrales Thema Vorsorge ist. (USA)

■ 50, 51 Annonces pour une campagne de la compagnie d'assurances Nationwide Insurance, sur le thème de la prévoyance. (USA)

Presenting the
Eastside Lounge Chair
designed by
Ettore Sottsass.

Presenting the
you-know-what chair
designed by
you-know-who.

KnollStudio

Introducing the Eastside Lounge Chair by Ettore Sottsass. Re-introducing the 1929 Barcelona Chair by Mies van der Rohe. Two of the 87 new and classic designs that are now a new collection from Knoll.

Get it before The
Museum of
Modern Art does.

Too late.

KnollStudio

Introducing the Mandarin Chair by Ettore Sottsass. Re-introducing the 1929 MR Lounge Chair by Mies van der Rohe. Two of the 87 new and classic designs that are now a new collection from Knoll.

ART DIRECTOR:
GARY GOLDSMITH/
TRACY WONG
DESIGNER:
GARY GOLDSMITH/
TRACY WONG/
MIKE ROSEN
PHOTOGRAPHER:
GILLES LARRAIN
COPYWRITER:
DEAN HACOHEN
AGENCY:
GOLDSMITH/JEFFREY
CLIENT:
KNOLL INTERNATIONAL
■ 52, 53

■ 52, 53 In these advertisements for furniture makers Knoll, new creations by Ettore Sottsass (always left) are presented with classics from 1929 by Mies van der Rohe. (USA)

■ 52, 53 In diesen Anzeigen für Knoll werden neue Kreationen von Ettore Sottsass (jeweils links) zusammen mit Klassikern aus dem Jahre 1929 von Mies van der Rohe vorgestellt. (USA)

■ 52, 53 Dans ces annonces pour Knoll, on compare les créations d'Ettore Sottsass (à gauche) avec les réalisations classiques de Mies van der Rohe (1929). (USA)

Can you spot the Range Rover in this picture?

Goodbye road. Goodbye traffic. Goodbye 5 m.p.h.

A Range Rover does something far more impressive than get you through a traffic jam in air-conditioned, arm-chaired, stereo-surrounded comfort.

A Range Rover takes you where there are no jams. Because there is no traffic.

Through the woods. Along the beach. Across the desert. Range Rovers, after all, are so extraordinary, they drive for years in places

ordinary cars couldn't drive a quarter of a mile.

So it's not surprising that to many a Range Rover's most luxurious feature isn't its elegant interior, optional sunroof, or the

security of 24 hour roadside assistance.

Its most luxurious feature is its ability to provide an experience a bit more exhilarating than a highway to the suburbs at six p.m.

Why not call 1-800-FINE 4WD for the Range Rover dealer nearest you?

We won't deny that at somewhat above $34,000 a Range Rover is hardly inexpensive.

But after all the time you've spent in traffic like this, what could be nicer than going off on your own?

RANGE ROVER

2 Schneeketten
2 Paar Mietskis
4 Engadiner Teller
4 Zweierli Veltliner
5 Fünfuhr-Tees
2 Bündner Torten
7 Übernachtungen
2 Tankfüllungen

1 Karte

Die Karte, die in 170 Ländern über 6 Millionen mal problemloses Zahlen ohne Bargeld garantiert. Die Karte, die als einzige die Eheparturkarte immer gratis offeriert. Die Karte, die als einzige durch Bonus-System bei regelmässiger Benutzung günstiger wird. Die Karte, die als Partner die weltweit anerkannte MasterCard hat. Die Karte von Ihrer Schweizer Bank. Verlangen Sie dort das Antragsformular.

EUROCARD
SWITZERLAND

Die Weltkarte

ART DIRECTOR:
Roy Grace
DESIGNER:
Roy Grace
PHOTOGRAPHER:
Carl Furuta
COPYWRITER:
Diane Rothschild
AGENCY:
Grace & Rothschild
CLIENT:
Range Rover of North America, Inc.
■ 54

ART DIRECTOR:
Urs Fürer
DESIGNER:
Viola Zimmermann/ Magalie Schwaar
COPYWRITER:
Daniel Matter
AGENCY:
Adolf Wirz AG Werbeberatung
CLIENT:
Eurocard (Switzerland) S.A.
■ 55

■ 54 Ad for *Range Rover* in which the emphasis is on this vehicle's special feature - its performance in off-highway places such as the desert, and the beach, etc. (USA)

■ 55 Advertisement from an image campaign for Eurocard, with a long list of items and services relating to winter vacation which can be paid with this credit card. (SWI)

■ 56 Newspaper advertisement in the form of a cut-out coupon which entitles the reader to the free loan of a video-film cassette at a certain video dealer. (USA)

■ 57 Double-spread ad for *Porsche* using the name of the competition (*Mercedes*) in the slogan. (USA)

■ 54 «Können Sie den *Range Rover* in diesem Bild finden?» Eine Demonstration der besonderen Eigenschaften dieses Autos. (USA)

■ 55 Aus einer Image-Kampagne für die Eurocard, mit einer Liste von Dingen, die mit Winterferien verbunden sind und mit dieser Kreditkarte bezahlt werden können. (SWI)

■ 56 «Ausschneiden» - Zeitungsinserat in Form eines Coupons, der zum kostenlosen Ausleihen einer Video-Film-Kassette bei einem bestimmten Videohändler berechtigt. (USA)

■ 57 «Denken Sie an einen *Mercedes* mit *Tabasco*-Sauce». Doppelseitige Anzeige für *Porsche*. (USA)

■ 54 «Pouvez-vous découvrir la *Range Rover* sur cette image?» Démonstration des caractéristiques particulières de cette marque de voiture. (USA)

■ 55 Exemple tiré d'une campagne de prestige pour l'Eurocard utilisable pendant les vacances d'hiver pour une grande variété de biens et de services. (SWI)

■ 56 «A découper» - annonce de journal en forme de coupon donnant droit au prêt gratuit d'une vidéocassette dans un magasin vidéo désigné nommément. (USA)

■ 57 «Pensez à une *Mercedes*, à la sauce *Tabasco*». Annonce sur deux pages, pour *Porsche*. (USA)

ART DIRECTOR:
John-Seymour Anderson
DESIGNER:
John-Seymour Anderson
COPYWRITER:
Mike Gibbs
AGENCY:
McCool & Company
CLIENT:
Panorama Video
►■ 56

ART DIRECTOR:
Mark Johnson
DESIGNER:
Mark Johnson
PHOTOGRAPHER:
Jeff Zwart
AGENCY:
Fallon McElligott
CLIENT:
Porsche Cars North America
▼■ 57

"Cut!"

ONE FREE MOVIE RENTAL AT PANORAMA VIDEO.

Take one! Any film you like. Just bring this coupon in to any Panorama Video Family Superstore.
Limit one coupon per customer. Offer expires 2/29/88. Paper! Scissors! Action!

Park Square Center, 8026 Brooklyn Blvd., Brooklyn Park (Next to Rainbow Foods) 424-4343
Prairie View Center, 954 Prairie Center Dr., Eden Prairie (Next to Rainbow Foods) 934-1783
Rosedale Square, 1619 West County Rd. C, Roseville (Next to Byerly's) 631-2454
Open Sunday-Thursday 9AM-11PM Friday-Saturday 9AM-12AM

Think of it as a Mercedes with Tabasco sauce.

As with anything consumed in excess, a steady diet of luxury can become, after a time, somewhat bland.

At Porsche, we approach success and luxury from a wholly different point of view. The point of view that hard work and achievement should earn the right to acquire more excitement from life, rather than impose the expectation to avoid it.

The 928 S4 is a monument to that belief. It is, at once, a car designed to pamper the senses without dulling them. A library-quiet interior surrounds the driver with fine leather. Attention to ergonomic detail is so complete that the driver's seat and mirrors can be pre-programmed for three different people, then adjusted with the touch of one button.

Yet, this environment is coupled to all the power and engineering refinement necessary to make this car not only the ultimate transportation, but the ultimate entertainment.

As you would expect from a Porsche, speed is the initial hallmark against which that claim is measured. A 316 hp, 32 valve V-8 engine transports you from 0 to 60 mph in 5.7 seconds, and provides a top speed of 165 mph. Making the 928 S4 one of the three fastest production cars in existence.

All the while, however, a 50-50 weight distribution and our remarkable Weissach axle make the performance very predictable and responsive to the lightest touch.

And, so that you alone decide when you have reached a satisfactory level of sensory fulfillment, an incredibly sophisticated ABS braking system will bring you from 60 mph to 0 in a mere 154 feet.

If you've grown weary of living in the lap of luxury and find yourself repeating, "There has to be more," we suggest you try looking for it at your Porsche dealer.

The 928 S4 could be just the spice your life needs.

If you would like to receive a free full-color brochure detailing the Porsche 928 S4, simply give us a call at (800) 252-4444, extension 308.

PORSCHE

Jecklin

ART DIRECTOR:
SHINNOSUKE SUGISAKI
DESIGNER:
HIROKO TADA
PHOTOGRAPHER:
YASUNORI SAITO
COPYWRITER:
ICHIRO ITO
AGENCY:
DENTSU INC./
SHINNOSUKE INC.
CLIENT:
ACE CO. LTD.
■ 58

ART DIRECTOR:
WERNER SCHELLENBERG
DESIGNER:
MARIO FERRARA
COPYWRITER:
HANSPETER SCHWEIZER
AGENCY:
ADOLF WIRZ AG
WERBEBERATUNG
CLIENT:
JECKLIN & CO. AG
■ 59

■ 58 Promotional advertising for *Samsonite* cases. (JPN)

■ 59 Portrait of Igor Stravinsky from an image campaign promoting the classical-music department of the music store Jecklin. (SWI)

■ 60 In this advertisement an investment consultancy publicizes its services for special investment policies by using quotations by various American Presidents on the issue of taxes. (USA)

■ 61 Advertisement designed as an editorial page, issued on behalf of the World Financial Center in New York, in which the Grand Central building forms the topic. (USA)

■ 58 Anzeigenwerbung für *Samsonite*-Koffer. (JPN)

■ 59 Anzeige aus einer Image-Kampagne für die klassische Abteilung des Musikhauses Jecklin mit einem Porträt Igor Strawinskys. (SWI)

■ 60 «Wir sorgten für steuerfreie Anlagen. An Inspirationen fehlte es dabei nicht.» Mit den Aussagen verschiedener amerikanischer Präsidenten zum Thema Steuern wirbt ein Anlageberater für spezielle Anlagemöglichkeiten. (USA)

■ 61 Wie eine redaktionelle Seite gestaltetes Inserat für das World Financial Center in New York, in dem über das Gebäude, Grand Central, berichtet wird. (USA)

■ 58 Publicité pour les mallettes *Samsonite*. (JPN)

■ 59 Annonce pour une campagne de prestige du département classique du magasin de musique Jecklin, avec un portrait d'Igor Stravinski. (SWI)

■ 60 «Nous avons veillé à mettre en place des placements exonérés d'impôts. L'inspiration ne nous a pas fait défaut.» Un conseiller en placements s'inspire des déclarations de divers présidents américains sur le thème des impôts. (USA)

■ 61 Annonce conçue à la manière d'une page rédactionnelle pour le World Financial Center de New York logé dans le building Grand Central dont il est question ici. (USA)

Left advertisement

"I want taxes to be less."

"I favor tax reduction."

"I recommend tax reduction."

"Taxes must come down."

"I want an entirely new tax system."

"I urge tax reduction."

"I believe we can cut taxes."

"I will not raise taxes."

"I will not raise taxes."

WE CREATED TAX-FREE FUNDS. THEN AGAIN, WE HAD A LOT OF INSPIRATION.

Ever since World War I, when the modern income tax was introduced, administration after administration has been pledging to lower them.

Or, at least, not to raise them. Some were successful. And some weren't. But why should your investment income be subject to the ups and downs of economic policy?

In 1976, we went to Washington, D.C. and lobbied for a bill that allowed Dreyfus to offer people the first incorporated tax-exempt fund. Today we have fourteen different tax-exempt funds.

All protect your investment income from Federal taxes and, in some cases, state and local taxes as well.

Now you don't have to wait and see what happens with taxes during the new administration. Call us for a prospectus instead (1-800-645-6561, ext. 1211).

And start cutting your taxes yourself. Today.

Dreyfus
The right fund at the right time.

ART DIRECTOR:
LESLIE SWEET

DESIGNER:
LESLIE SWEET

COPYWRITER:
PAMELA SULLIVAN

AGENCY:
LEVINE, HUNTLEY, SCHMIDT & BEAVER

CLIENT:
DREYFUS CORP.
■ 60

Right advertisement

City Tales :
DESTINATIONS

Arrivals & Departures

by DANA GIOIA

photograph by Elizabeth Zeschin

Today most travel feels like commuting. Distant airline journeys begin and end by waiting in line. Cars find the traffic in exotic cities drearily familiar. The same bored faces look up from bus station benches from Antwerp to Alabama. There is no poetry in reaching a public garage, a bus stop or luggage carrousel. Just the flat, minimal prose of baggage claims and parking meters. But there is one commute that actually feels like travel—coming into Grand Central Terminal. Entering its vast main lobby either by descending from the noisy street or by rising from the steamy train platforms underground, one walks into Manhattan's greatest indoor public space, an area all the more exciting because unlike its closest contenders—Carnegie Hall, the Stock Exchange, the Palm Court at the Plaza— Grand Central is neither elitist nor exclusionary. In its democratic precincts investment bankers in snug italian suits line up for coffee behind Hawaiian-shirted street vendors and elderly nuns on a shopping spree share waiting room benches with honeymooners from Osaka. Stepping onto Grand Central's smooth marble floor is always like walking onstage but whether into a stark social drama or screwball screen comedy one can never quite tell in advance. Hundreds of lives hurry by, each one starring in its own compelling story. Charged by their sheer energy, one feels that particular rush of excitement that only great cities give. This almost delirious feeling that anything is possible represents the unacknowledged triumph of Grand Central's architecture. Utterly functional, this station is also truly grand. Its one vast central chamber stands impressively surrounded by teeming platforms, passageways, tunnels, balustrades, and antechambers, the air above crisscrossed by huge shafts of filtered sunlight rising to the high arched ceiling decorated astonishingly—as if to say that this one room is indeed its own universe—by the stars and constellations of the zodiac. Yet even to a gaping first-time visitor, a lone pedestrian clutching a battered suitcase on the swirling concourse below, all this grandeur seems not only unintimidating but inviting. This is a place which recognizes the importance of each arrival. Nervous, giddy, even inspired, one steps into the crowd ready to begin.

*Over 30 thousand people come to work or play at
The World Financial Center every day. They come by cars, boats, trains
and planes. Once they come, they stay till all hours.
Come and see what all the fuss is about.*

The World Financial Center

ART DIRECTOR:
STEPHEN DOYLE

DESIGNER:
STEPHEN DOYLE

PHOTOGRAPHER:
ELIZABETH ZESCHIN

COPYWRITER:
DANA GIOIA

AGENCY:
DRENTTEL DOYLE PARTNERS

CLIENT:
*OLYMPIA & YORK
COMPANIES (USA)/
THE WORLD FINANCIAL CENTER*
■ 61

Why just advertise to big business,
when 90% of New York business isn't big?

If you're just talking to big business, you're missing the biggest part of New York business.
The 190,000 small and mid-size companies that make up most of New York City.
So why not call Crain's at (212) 210-0259? Because unlike other business publications, we reach
New York's biggest businesses. As well as its smallest. Not to mention a few sizes in between.

CRAIN'S NEW YORK BUSINESS

Only those who've climbed to the top read Crain's.

Seventy-nine percent of our subscribers are Vice-Presidents, Presidents, CEOs
and Chairmen of their companies. If they sound like the kind of people you want to
talk to, call us at (212) 210-0259. We know where they can be reached.

CRAIN'S NEW YORK BUSINESS

ART DIRECTOR:
TRACY WONG/
GARY GOLDSMITH
DESIGNER:
TRACY WONG
COPYWRITER:
DEAN HACOHEN
AGENCY:
GOLDSMITH/JEFFREY
CLIENT:
CRAIN'S NEW YORK
BUSINESS PUBLICATION
■ 62, 63

■ 62, 63 The Chrysler Building and the Empire State Building in somewhat strange versions, in ads for the economic magazine *Crain's New York Business.* (USA)

■ 64 Double-spread ad for the *Apple Letraset* system. As the slogan implies and the text reads, the advertisement was produced in record time, by one person. (GBR)

■ 65 Double-spread advertisement for *Donghia* furniture and home textiles. (USA)

■ 62, 63 New Yorks Chrysler- und Empire-State-Gebäude in etwas verfremdeten Versionen in Inseraten für das Wirtschaftsmagazin *Crain's New York Business.* (USA)

■ 64 «Bei der Produktion dieser Anzeige in 2 Stunden blieb keine Zeit für den Satz.» Doppelseitige Anzeige für *Apple-Letraset*-Computer. (GBR)

■ 65 Doppelseitiges Inserat für *Donghia*-Möbel und Heimtextilien. (USA)

■ 62, 63 Version légèrement déformée des buildings Chrysler et Empire State de New York utilisée pour les annonces du magazine économique *Crain's New York Business.* (USA)

■ 64 «Lors de la production de cette annonce en seulement 2 heures, il a fallu se passer de la composition.» Annonce double page pour les ordinateurs *Apple Letraset.* (GBR)

■ 65 Annonce double page pour les ameublements et rideaux *Donghia.* (USA)

ART DIRECTOR:
GARY MARTIN
DESIGNER:
GARY MARTIN
COPYWRITER:
MARK GOODWIN
AGENCY:
BBDO
CLIENT:
APPLE COMPUTER UK, LTD.
■ 64

ART DIRECTOR:
SUSAN SLOVER
DESIGNER:
MARIO PULICE
PHOTOGRAPHER:
RAEANNE GIOVANNI
COPYWRITER:
SUSAN SLOVER
AGENCY:
SUSAN SLOVER DESIGN
CLIENT:
DONGHIA FURNITURE CO. LTD.
▼■ 65

We start out innocently enough. But all too soon, we start having to conform to the tyrannies of chairs that don't conform to us.

High chairs. School chairs. Office chairs that reflect a concern for our **The naked truth.** status at the expense of our stature.

Unfortunately for our bodies, you can't judge an office chair's conformance by its appearance. You have to undress it, check how it's built.

Do this, and you'll discover that one chair stands apart.

It features a one piece inner shell, for example, that's flexible in some places, inflexible in others.

How do you make a shell like this? Nothing to it. You simply instruct your engineers to invent a new technology.

Then you ask them to invent another that marries this shell to the internal mechanism in a way that gives support *and* freedom of movement.

Because the human body needs to be hugged and allowed to wiggle.

Then you ask them to invent a technology that bonds foam to fabric in a way that allows the chair to "breathe."

And to invent a low profile base that can accommodate a greater-than-ever height adjustment range without looking bulky.

Then you ask for snap-on casters and glides, replaceable cushions and changeable arms.

And before you know it, you've created a whole new kind of office chair that doesn't look like a whole new kind of office chair…until it's naked.

Sensor, from designer Wolfgang Müeller-Deisig and the inventive engineers and designers of Steelcase.

Steelcase
The Office Environment Company   *For more information, call 1-800-447-4700*

"From NBC radio station W-O-O-D come today's newlyweds…"

It was in April of 1947, in Grand Rapids, Michigan. A Tuesday morning.

Everybody in the chair plant at Metal Office (as Steelcase was called then) downed tools. Just shut down the machinery. **Romance halts production.** And tuned in a live radio broadcast of "Honeymoon in New York!"

They all knew Jim Sarnicola. When he and his new bride, Rose, won a honeymoon trip to New York to tell their unusual love story, no one at the plant wanted to miss a word of it.

"Jim's a welder on metal furniture, an ex-army aircorps gunner, 25 years old…His charming wife, Rose, is 19. She sat on his lap for the first time 12 years ago!"

Jim and Rose told a nationwide audience how he had looked after her when their

mothers went shopping together. When Jim went into the service, Rose was still a kid.

Four years later, when he got out, Rose asked him to a hayride. A couple of dates later, he proposed. "Well, she'd changed a lot!" Jim told the host of "Honeymoon in New York." *"You're a delightful young couple…happy honeymooning, today and everyday! Listen again tomorrow, friends!"*

With those words, everybody picked up their tools. Turned the machines back on. And the only employee-initiated work stoppage in the company's 75-year history was over.

Is it any wonder that 98% of all Steelcase orders are shipped on time?

Steelcase
The Office Environment Company   *For more information, call 1-800-447-4700*

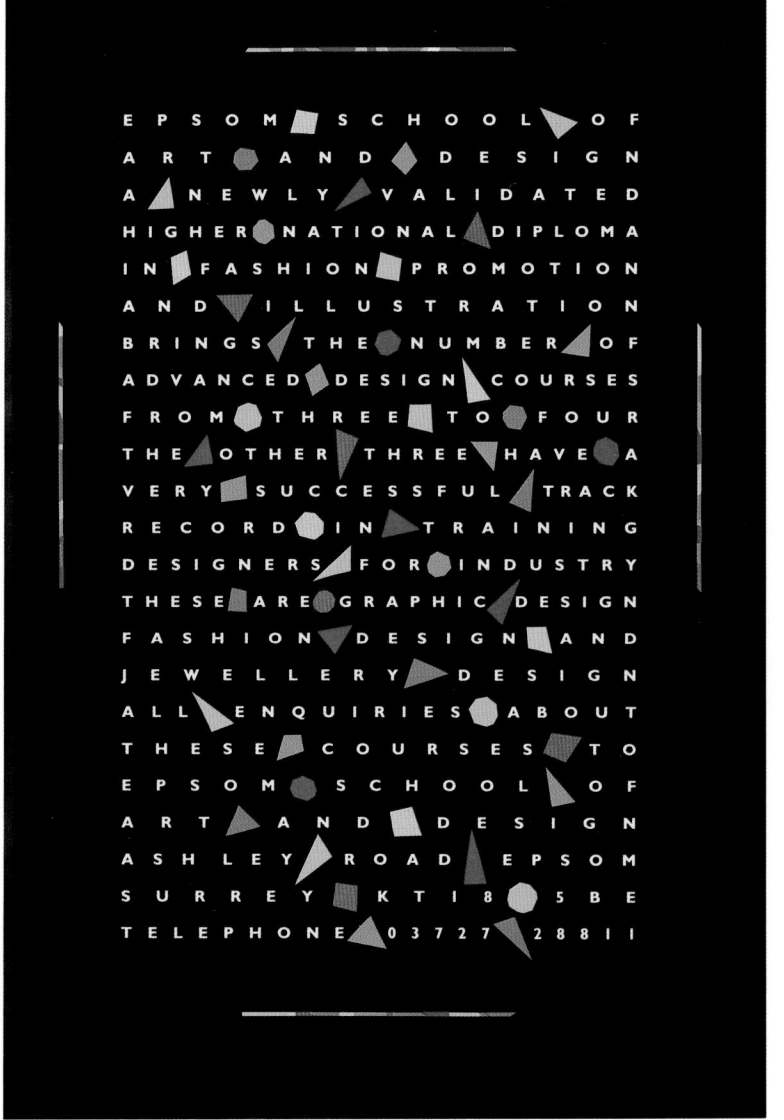

ART DIRECTOR:
CRAIG FRAZIER

DESIGNER:
CRAIG FRAZIER

PHOTOGRAPHER:
JACK MCDONALD 66
RUDI LEGNAME 67

COPYWRITER:
MICHAEL WRIGHT

AGENCY:
FRAZIER DESIGN

CLIENT:
STEELCASE. INC.

◄■ 66, 67

DESIGNER:
*EPSOM SCHOOL OF
ART & DESIGN*

AGENCY:
*EPSOM SCHOOL OF
ART & DESIGN*

CLIENT:
*EPSOM SCHOOL OF
ART & DESIGN*

■ 68

ART DIRECTOR:
SILAS H. RHODES

DESIGNER:
DAVID CONNOLLY

COPYWRITER:
DEE ITO

STUDIO:
VISUAL ARTS PRESS

CLIENT:
*SCHOOL OF VISUAL ARTS,
NEW YORK*

■ 69

■ 66, 67 Magazine advertisements for *Steelcase* office furniture. Each ad is accompanied by an extensive text; this one relates to the human body and job morale in connection with a love affair. (USA)

■ 68 Promotion for an art school. (GBR)

■ 69 Full-page newspaper ad for the School of Visual Arts listing the comprehensive selection of courses available and emphasizing the realization of ideas. (USA)

■ 66, 67 Doppelseitige Zeitschriftenanzeigen für *Steelcase*-Büromöbel. Jede Anzeige hat einen ausführlichen Text, hier über den menschlichen Körper und über Arbeitsmoral im Zusammenhang mit einer Liebesgeschichte. (USA)

■ 68 Werbung für eine Kunstschule. (GBR)

■ 69 Ganzseitiges Zeitungsinserat für die School of Visual Arts: «Auch eine grossartige Idee ist nur eine Idee bis man sie verwirklicht.» (USA)

■ 66, 67 Série d'annonces de magazine double page pour les meubles de bureau *Steelcase*. Chacune de ces annonces comporte un texte détaillé, ici sur le corps humain et le climat de travail en rapport avec une histoire d'amour. (USA)

■ 68 Publicité pour une école d'art. (GBR)

■ 69 Annonce de journal pleine page pour la School of Visual Arts: «Même une idée grandiose n'est qu'une idée, jusqu'au moment où elle est traduite dans les faits.» (USA)

ART DIRECTOR:
MIKE ROSEN
DESIGNER:
MIKE ROSEN
PHOTOGRAPHER:
STEVE HELLERSTEIN
COPYWRITER:
MIKE ROSEN
AGENCY:
GOLDSMITH/JEFFREY
CLIENT:
STEVE HELLERSTEIN
■ 70, 71

ART DIRECTOR:
LESLIE SMOLAN
DESIGNER:
ERIC A. PIKE
AGENCY:
CARBONE SMOLAN ASSOCIATES
CLIENT:
FPG INTERNATIONAL
■ 72, 73

■ 70, 71 From an advertisement campaign in magazines for photographer Steve Hellerstein. (USA)

■ 72, 73 For a photo agency – ads that relate to a specific category, like – as shown here – the fifties and historical photographs. (USA)

■ 70, 71 Aus einer Anzeigenkampagne in Zeitschriften für den Photographen Steve Hellerstein. (USA)

■ 72, 73 Anzeigen einer Photoagentur, die jeweils auf eines der Sachgebiete anspielen, hier die 50er Jahre und historische Aufnahmen. (USA)

■ 70, 71 Campagne d'annonces de magazines pour le photographe Steve Hellerstein. (USA)

■ 72, 73 Exemples d'annonces d'une agence photo avec références à des sujets précis, ici les années 50 et les photo historiques. (USA)

IF THIS GOES,
EVERYTHING ELSE
GOES WITH IT.

MS MULTIPLE
SCLEROSIS

WITHOUT YOUR HELP IT'S INCURABLE

THE MULTIPLE SCLEROSIS SOCIETY, 25 EFFIE RD, FULHAM, LONDON SW6 1EE. TEL: (01) 736 6267.

ART DIRECTOR:
NANCY STEPHENS
PHOTOGRAPHER:
BRUCE NICHOL
COPYWRITER:
CRAIG JACKSON
AGENCY:
BMP DAVIDSON PEARCE INC.
CLIENT:
MULTIPLE SCLEROSIS SOCIETY
◄■ 74

ART DIRECTOR:
TRACY WONG
DESIGNER:
TRACY WONG
PHOTOGRAPHER:
STEVE HELLERSTEIN
COPYWRITER:
TRACY WONG
AGENCY:
GOLDSMITH/JEFFREY
CLIENT:
*NEW YORK LUNG
ASSOCIATION*
▼■ 75-77

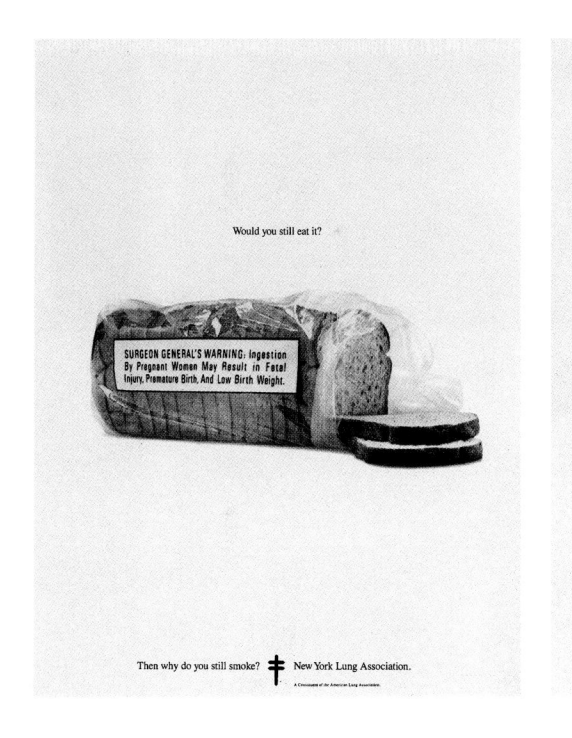

■ 74 From a campaign calling for the general public's assistance in helping sufferers of multiple sclerosis. (GBR)

■ 75-77 Advertisements from a newspaper campaign devised to bring the public's attention to the dangers of smoking, issued by the New York Lung Association (member of the American Lung Association). (USA)

■ 74 «Wenn sie hier zuschlägt, ist alles aus.» Aus einer Kampagne für die Unterstützung von MS-Patienten. (GBR)

■ 75-77 Anzeigen aus einer Kampagne gegen das Rauchen. Die Lebensmittel sind mit Warnungen gekennzeichnet, die sich auf Zigaretten beziehen. Die Fragen: «Würden Sie das noch essen? Würden Sie das noch trinken?» (USA)

■ 74 «Si elle frappe ici, c'est la fin de tout. » Campagne sollicitant de l'aide pour la sclérose en plaques. (GBR)

■ 75-77 Annonces pour une campagne de journaux contre la tabagie. Les aliments sont assortis de mises en garde contre la cigarette. Questions: «Est-ce que vous mangeriez encore ça? Est-ce que vous boiriez encore ça?» (USA)

Maggie is first to arrive with the newest fashions.

Bert Brüggemann schießt blaue Schleifchen so!

city light poster

Bert Brüggemann 040/48 20 55, Kunde: Deutsche Städte-Reklame, Agentur: Springer & Jacoby, AD: Thomas Ritter
Headline: Wer dem citylightposter die Schau stehlen will, muß schon was bieten!

PHOTOGRAPHER:
STEPHEN WILKES
AGENCY:
JOHN EMMERLING ASSOCIATES
CLIENT:
MAGAZINE PUBLISHERS' OF
AMERICA
■ 78

ART DIRECTOR:
THOMAS RITTER/
BERT BRÜGGEMANN
DESIGNER:
JÖRG BARTEL/
BERT BRÜGGEMANN
PHOTOGRAPHER:
BERT BRÜGGEMANN
COPYWRITER:
JÖRG BARTEL/
THOMAS RITTER
AGENCY:
SPRINGER & JACOBY
WERBEAGENTUR GMBH/
THE MAYDAY COMPANY
CLIENT:
BERT BRÜGGEMANN
■ 79

■ 78 From a promotional campaign issued by the Magazine Publishers of America. (USA)

■ 79 "This is how Bert Brüggemann shoots blue ribbons." Self-promotion by photographer Bert Brüggemann, with an ad for citylightposter. (GER)

■ 80 Newspaper advertisement for *The Wall Street Journal* – with an amusing emphasis on the subscriber's title. (USA)

■ 78 «Maggie kommt als Erste mit der neuen Mode an.» Werbekampagne der Magazine Publishers of America. (USA)

■ 79 Eigenwerbung des Photographen Bert Brüggemann mit einem Inserat, das im Auftrag der Deutschen Städte Reklame für citylightposter entstand. (GER)

■ 80 «Einige sehr erfolgreiche Leute abonnieren das *Wall Street Journal*.» Zeitungsanzeige für diese Zeitung. (USA)

■ 78 «Maggie est la première à incarner la nouvelle mode.» Campagne des Magazine Publishers of America. (USA)

■ 79 Autopromotion du photographe Bert Brüggemann au moyen d'une annonce pour citylightposter: «Bert Brüggemann tire ses rubans bleu comme ça.» (GER)

■ 80 «Certaines personnes qui ont fait leur chemin sont abonnées au *Wall Street Journal*.» Annonce. (USA)

ART DIRECTOR:
BOB BARRIE
COPYWRITER:
JAMIE BARRETT
AGENCY:
FALLON MCELLIGOTT
CLIENT:
WALL STREET JOURNAL
■ 80

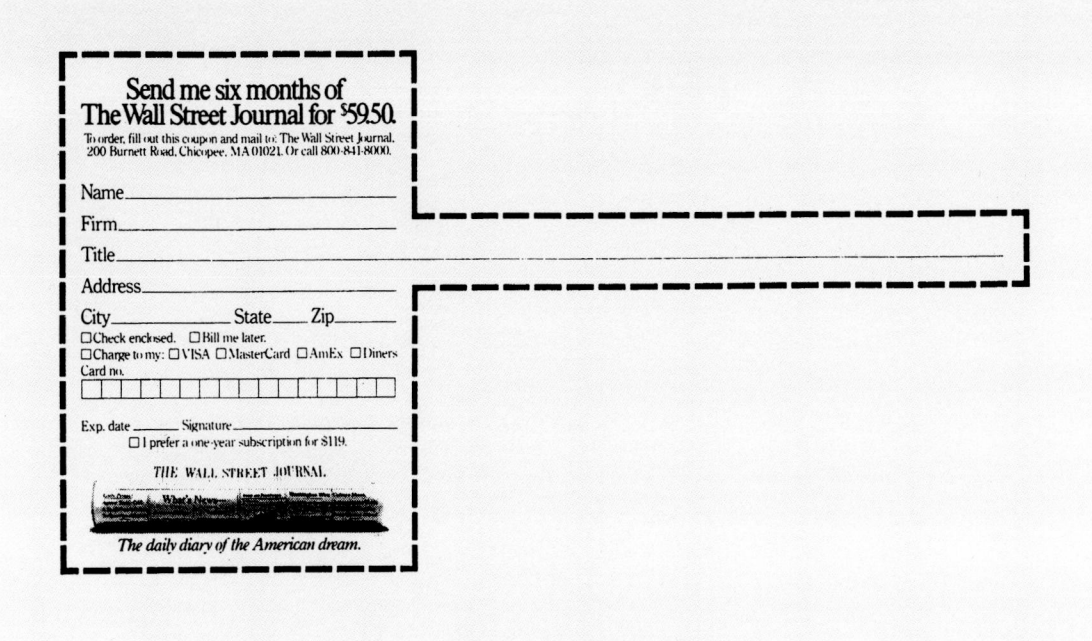

(Some very successful people subscribe to The Wall Street Journal.)

PREVENT LIFE AND DEATH ALL IN ONE SHOT.

CONDOM

It's virtually impossible to know if someone is carrying the AIDS virus simply by looking at their face.
But by wearing a condom during sex, you can prevent both yourself and your partner from contracting the AIDS virus.
Because right now the only cure for AIDS is not to get it in the first place. If you have any questions or would
like more information, please give us a call. We're here to listen, we're here to help. **HERO**

Baltimore Metro 945-AIDS ■ DC Metro 251-1165 ■ Elsewhere in MD 1-800-638-6252

Not Everything You Inherit From Your Family Is Worth Keeping.

Let's face it, given the chance, many of us would change some of what we inherited from our families.
And a lot of people are doing just that. In fact, last year over 477,000 surgeries were performed for cosmetic reasons.
Today, at North Cosmetic Surgery Center, we're changing a lot of family traditions for the better. Noses, eyes, ears, chins, necks, breasts, stomachs, legs. Just about every part of the body.

And it's not just the rich and famous who are doing the remodeling.
People of all ages and income levels are having cosmetic surgery because it helps them look and feel better about themselves.
As part of North Memorial, one of the leading medical centers in the region, we have the advanced medical technology, experience, and expertise needed for successful cosmetic surgery.

Of course, the thought of cosmetic surgery poses a lot of questions. That's why we have a full-time cosmetic consultant to explain the procedures, results, risks, recovery, even financing.
So if you want to reevaluate what you've inherited, call 520-5954 for a free consultation and brochure.

NORTH COSMETIC SURGERY CENTER

ART DIRECTOR:
Sal DeVito

DESIGNER:
Sal DeVito

COPYWRITER:
Sal DeVito

AGENCY:
Levine Huntley Schmidt & Beaver

CLIENT:
Health Education Resource Organization
■ 81

ART DIRECTOR:
David Fox

PHOTOGRAPHER:
Tom Berthiaume

COPYWRITER:
Jerry Fury

AGENCY:
Clarity Coverdale Rueff Advertising

CLIENT:
North Memorial Medical Center
■ 82

ART DIRECTOR:
Kevin Thomas

PHOTOGRAPHER:
Graham Ford

AGENCY:
TBWA

CLIENT:
Central Office of Information
►■ 83, 84

■ 81 From a campaign to advise the use of condoms during sex to prevent contracting the AIDS virus. (USA)

■ 82 For the North Cosmetic Surgery Center, Minneapolis, giving the various remodeling operations available. (USA)

■ 83, 84 Double-spread ads from an AIDS campaign in which the danger of infection by syringe is stressed. (USA)

■ 81 «Verhüte gleichzeitig Leben und Tod.» Aus einer Kampagne für die Verwendung von Kondomen. (USA)

■ 82 «Nicht alles, was man von der Familie erbt, sollte erhalten bleiben.» Werbung für kosmetische Chirurgie. (USA)

■ 83, 84 Aus einer AIDS-Kampagne, in der die Ansteckungsgefahr durch Spritzen angesprochen wird. (USA)

■ 81 «Prévenez le vie et la mort à la même occasion.» Campagne pour l'usage du préservatif. (USA)

■ 82 «Pas tout ce qu'on hérite de sa famille ne vaut la peine d'être conservé.» Pub de chirurgie cosmétique. (USA)

■ 83, 84 Annonces pour une campagne sur le SIDA où il est question des risques d'infection par seringue. (USA)

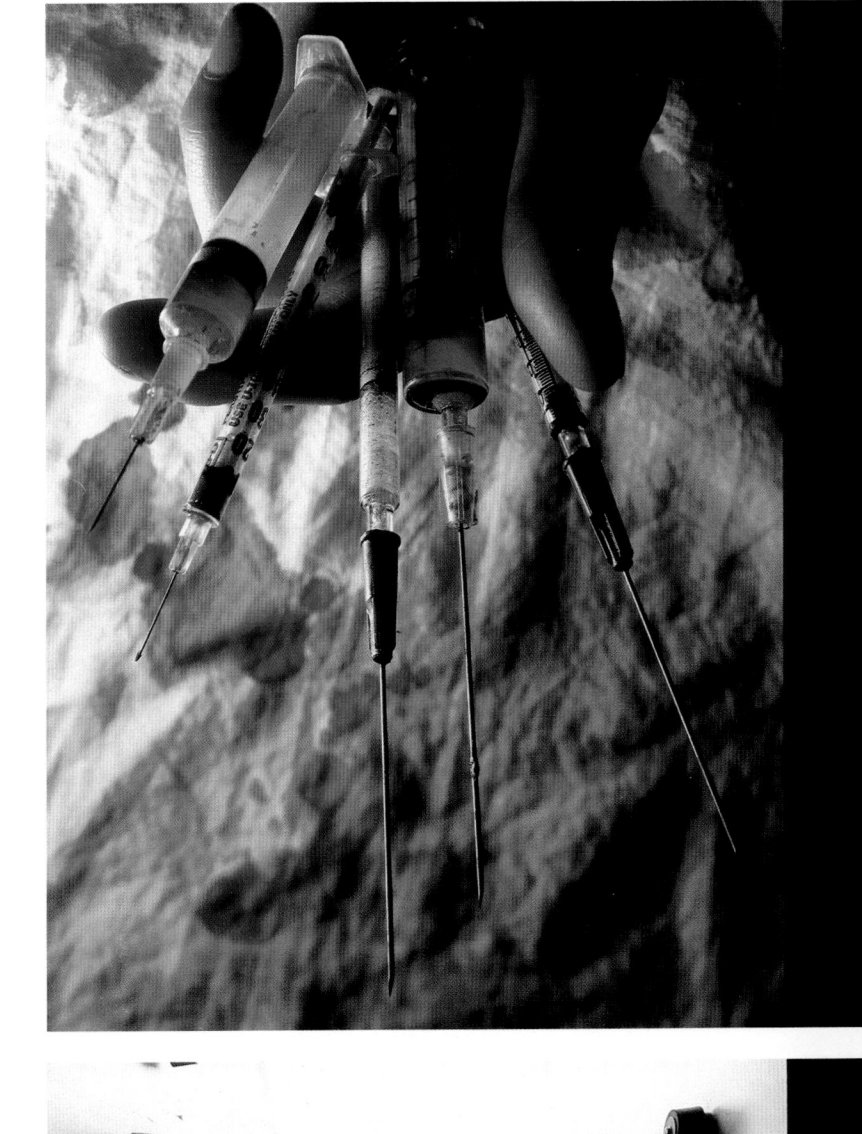

Only one of these
needles is free from AIDS.

Take your pick.

This is your first fix.

You've already smoked heroin quite a bit (and probably done yourself quite a bit of damage).

But you've never actually planned to inject.

So you're about to borrow someone else's needle.

The AIDS virus can live on dirty needles and works and just one fix can put it straight into your blood.

You can't tell by looking at a needle or syringe if they're infected.

You can't even tell by looking at their owner. (Besides, how do you know where else they've been?)

Go on. Take your pick.

DON'T INJECT AIDS

For further advice, phone 0800 567 123, free of charge.

Just one fix can get you
totally wasted.

To anyone who smokes smack, death can seem a long way away.

(Even though smoking it still does a lot of damage.)

But to anyone who injects, death is a lot closer.

Nobody who smokes it thinks they'll ever inject, yet people still do it.

If they don't have needles of their own, they share other people's.

But the AIDS virus can live on dirty needles and works.

Sharing is the easiest way to put the virus straight into your bloodstream.

And just one fix is all it takes.

DON'T INJECT AIDS

For further advice, phone 0800 567 123, free of charge.

ART DIRECTOR:
PETER WIBROE
ILLUSTRATOR:
JOE PETAGNO
AGENCY:
*SAATCHI & SAATCHI
ADVERTISING A/S*
CLIENT:
THE CARLSBERG BREWERIES
■ 85, 86

ART DIRECTOR:
CHRIS BOURNE
PHOTOGRAPHER:
PAUL BEVITT
COPYWRITER:
TOBY MESSER
AGENCY:
KHBB
CLIENT:
THE CARLSBERG BREWERIES
►■ 87

■ 85, 86 "*Carlsberg* agrees with everybody." Examples from a promotional campaign with posters and full-page ads for *Carlsberg* beer. (DEN)

■ 87 Full-page magazine advertisement for *Carlsberg* beer – with no text. (GBR)

■ 85, 86 «Jeder kann ein *Carlsberg* vertragen.» Beispiele aus einer Werbekampagne mit Plakaten und ganzseitigen Anzeigen für *Carlsberg*-Bier. (DEN)

■ 87 Ganzseitiges Zeitschrifteninserat für *Carlsberg*-Bier, ohne jeglichen Text. (GBR)

■ 85, 86 «Tout le monde aurait besoin d'une *Carlsberg*.» Exemples tirés d'une campagne d'affiches et d'annonces pleine page en faveur de la bière *Carlsberg*. (DEN)

■ 87 Annonce de magazine pleine page pour la bière *Carlsberg*, sans aucun texte. (GBR)

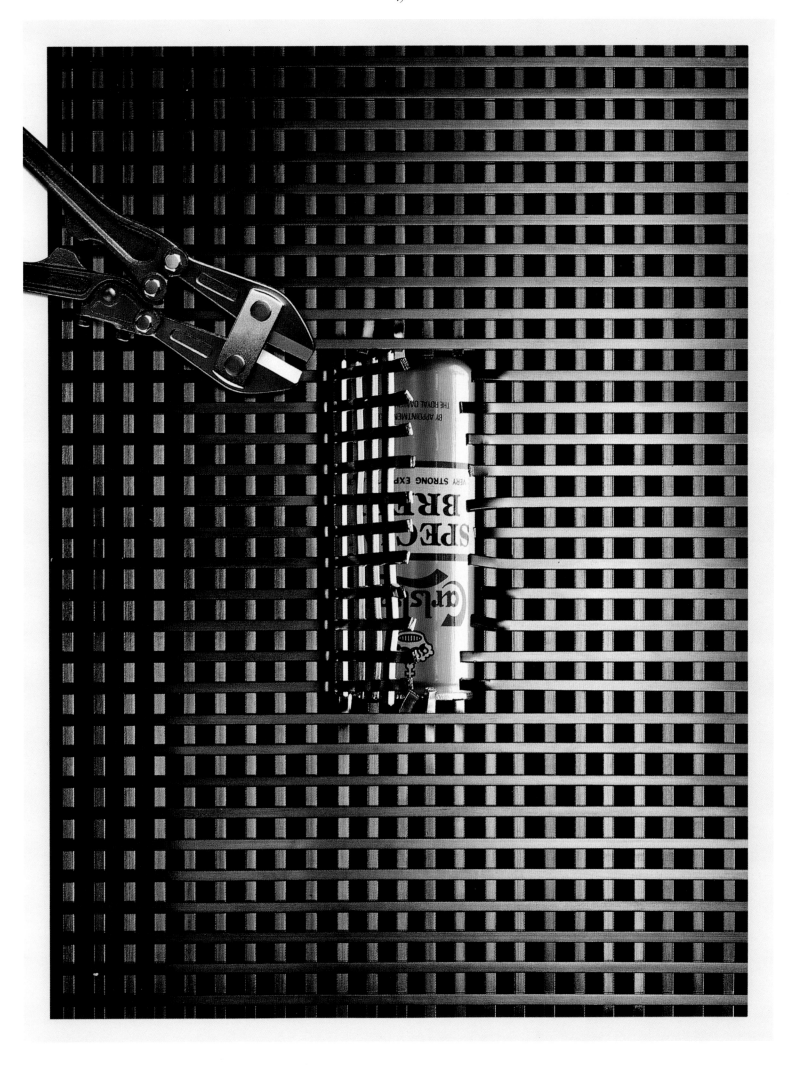

THE AUSTRALIAN FOR STRENGTH

FOSTER'S EXPORT STRENGTH LAGER

...IN THE COOL OF THAT SAME EVENING...

EARLIER IT HAD BEEN 112°. IN THE SHADE. SOMEHOW THAT NOW SEEMED IRRELEVANT...

■ 88

ART DIRECTOR:
IAN DUCKER
PHOTOGRAPHER:
ASHLEY JOUHAR
COPYWRITER:
WILL FARQUHAR
AGENCY:
BMP DAVIDSON PEARCE
CLIENT:
COURAGE LTD.

■ 88 A cool beer in the evening makes you forget the heat of the day – double-spread magazine advertisement for the Australian beer *Foster's Lager*. (GBR)

■ 89 A reminder of a Christmas gone by – with a scene of skaters in Central Park, New York. From a Christmas promotional campaign for *Chivas Regal* whisky. (USA)

■ 90 Full-page magazine advertisement for *Jim Beam* – the Kentucky bourbon whiskey. (USA)

■ 88 Das kühle Bier am Abend lässt die Hitze des Tages vergessen – doppelseitiges Zeitschrifteninserat für das australische Bier *Foster's Lager*. (GBR)

■ 89 Eislaufen im New Yorker Central Park, ca. 1890 – ein weihnachtliches Bild vergangener Zeiten aus einer Weihnachts-Werbekampagne für *Chivas-Regal*-Whisky. (USA)

■ 90 «Oh nein! Er hat einen *Jim Beam* bestellt.» Magazinanzeige für *Jim-Beam*-Whiskey. (USA)

■ 88 Une bière fraîche le soir venu fait oublier la chaleur de la journée – annonce de magazine double page pour la bière australienne *Foster's Lager*. (GBR)

■ 89 Scène de patinage sur la glace du Central Park de New York, vers 1890 – un tableau évoquant les Noëls de jadis. Campagne de Noël pour le whisky *Chivas Regal*. (USA)

■ 90 «Oh non! Il a commandé un *Jim Beam*.» Annonce de magazine pour le whisky *Jim Beam*. (USA)

Christmas past.

Skating in Central Park, New York City, c. 1890. Courtesy of the New York Historical Society.

Christmas present.

Visit your local retailer, or call 1-800-238-4373 to send a gift of Chivas anywhere in the U.S. Void where prohibited.

WHAT ARE YOU SAVING THE CHIVAS FOR?

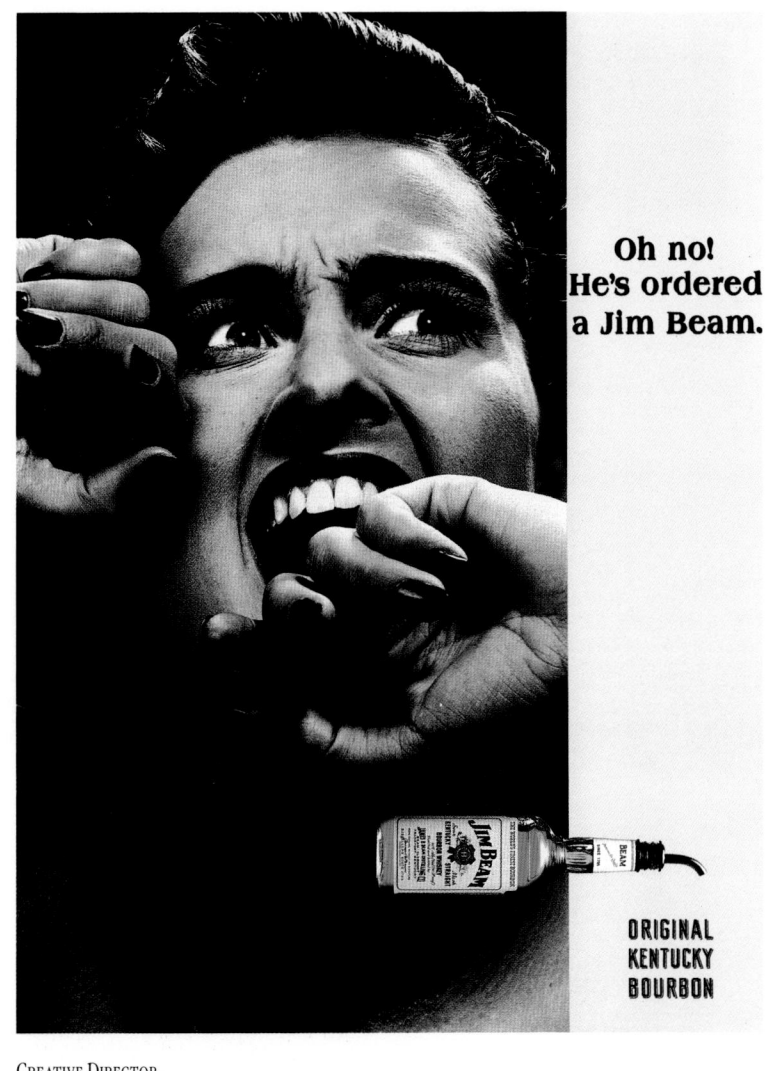

Oh no!
He's ordered
a Jim Beam.

ORIGINAL
KENTUCKY
BOURBON

ART DIRECTOR:
SHONY RIVNAY
DESIGNER:
SHONY RIVNAY
COPYWRITER:
ELIZABETH GEIGER
AGENCY:
DDB NEEDHAM
CLIENT:
SEAGRAM
■ 89

CREATIVE DIRECTOR:
GEORGE THEO
ART DIRECTOR:
MARY GODWAD
PHOTOGRAPHER:
STUART REDLER
COPYWRITER:
MICK PEARCE
AGENCY:
MARSHALL ADVERTISING LTD.
CLIENT:
WHYTE & MACKAY
■ 90

French ad (left):

Une vieille passion redécouverte: les fromages irlandais.

Ici commence une des plus belles régions de fromages d'Europe.

A l'extrême ouest de l'Europe, un petit bout de terre, une île faite de prairies bordées de sombres rochers et l'océan atlantique qui vient là s'époumoner. Qui aurait pu penser que ce somptueux paysage abritait une des plus riches traditions de fromage du vieux continent? Pas grand monde sans doute. Tout le monde ne peut pas en effet deviner que ces verts pâturages gonflés d'arômes sont baignés toute l'année par une douceur quasi méditerranéenne venue du gulfstream, tout le monde ne peut pas savoir que les vaches y paissent toute l'année au grand air et que leur lait est à la mesure de ces conditions de vie exceptionnelles. En découvrant le St. Killian, vous retrouverez toutes les merveilles de cette nature irlandaise. St. Killian, un fromage moelleux, doux au palais, tout en nuances et qui très vite vous apparaîtra comme une invitation à aller découvrir cette terre où fleurent bon les grands fromages d'Irlande.

St. KILLIAN
IRISH FARMHOUSE CHEESE
FROMAGE DE LA FERME
IERSE HOEVE-KAAS
M.G. 56% VOL. 250 g

Dutch ad (right):

Een nieuwontdekte passie is terug: Ierse kaas.

Wil je Ierland leren kennen, proef dan eens Ierse Cheddar.

Wellicht hebt u enkel krachtig Iers bier, Folk Songs en het ruwe, hartverwarmende Ierse karakter voor ogen. Aan dat beeld kan u rustig een lekkernij toevoegen, en dat ze Iers is mag niet eens verwondering wekken. Het is kaas, heerlijke kaas. Nergens anders in Europa zijn de voorwaarden om dit produkt te vervaardigen zo perfekt vervuld als in Ierland. Het klimaat is er mild mediterraan, de koeien grazen er heel het jaar door en kruiden maken de weilanden bijzonder aromatisch. Dat proef je in de melk, dat proef je in de kaas. Van de talrijke kaassoorten die naar aloude traditie vervaardigd worden, hebt u hier een wel bijzonder verfijnd exemplaar: de Ierse Cheddar. Vast, kompakt en kruidig pikant, is hij de ster van elke kaasschotel. En mocht u geen Ierse Guinness bij de hand hebben, dan kan een glaasje Bordeaux wonderen doen: een droom van een kombinatie met deze klassieke Ier.

IRISH CHEDDAR

ART DIRECTOR:
Helmut Rottke
DESIGNER:
Brigitte von Haehling
COPYWRITER:
Reinhold Scheer
AGENCY:
Rottke Werbung
CLIENT:
Irish Dairy Board
■ 91-93

Une vieille passion redécouverte: les fromages irlandais.

Shannon Vale. Ici le temps s'est arrêté pour goûter un poème de fromage.

"J'ai endormi le langage" avait dit un jour James Joyce, célèbre écrivain irlandais. 'Endormi le langage, endormi les palabres, endormi pour mieux laisser parler sans doute ces goûts particuliers des fromages du pays d'Irlande. Ce pays, si loin des gens de Dublin où paissent, depuis toujours à travers ces immenses bocages somptueusement verts les vaches irlandaises, sous un climat quasi méditerranéen. Ce pays où bien avant Joyce, on appréciait déjà le goût délicatement fumé du Shannon Vale, ce goût qu'ont les fromages bien pleins, bien ronds qui vous donne dès la découverte l'envie d'endormir votre discussion pour laisser parler votre plaisir. Et quand vous saurez que ce plaisir n'est pas unique, que les fromages en Irlande sont aussi variés que les accents du langage, il vous prendra sans doute l'envie de devenir poète pour les présenter à vos amis.

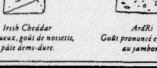

Irish Cheddar
Onctueux, goût de noisette, pâte demi-dure.

ArdRi
Goût prononcé et relevé, au jambon.

St. Killian
Moelleux, doux, pâte molle.

Cashel
Goût prononcé et piquant, à la coupe.

Shannon Vale
Goût fumé, pâte demi-dure.

Tipperary
Doux, goût de noisette, pâte molle.

Oak-Smoked
Shannon Vale
SMOOTH NATURAL IRISH CHEESE
kerrygold

God Morgon är vår finaste juice. Mejerierna.

ART DIRECTOR:
OLLE MATTSSON
PHOTOGRAPHER:
FABIO GALLI
COPYWRITER:
MIKAEL HJÄRTSJÖ
AGENCY:
HALL & CEDERQUIST
CLIENT:
SMR
■ 94

■ 91-93 "An old passion rediscovered: cheese from Ireland."
Examples from an advertising campaign for various Irish
cheeses. (BEL)

■ 94 A market place in the night and in the early morning
sets the scene for the advertising of *God Morgon* (Good
Morning) orange juice. (SWE)

■ 91-93 «Eine alte Leidenschaft wiederentdeckt: Käse aus
Irland.» Beispiele aus einer Werbekampagne für verschiedene irische Käsesorten. (BEL)

■ 94 Ein Marktplatz in der Nacht und den frühen Morgen-
stunden als Werbung für *God Morgon* (Guten Morgen)
Orangensaft. (SWE)

■ 91-93 «Une ancienne passion redécouverte: le fromage
irlandais.» Exemples tirés d'une campagne publicitaire pour
divers fromages d'Irlande. (BEL)

■ 94 Ces scènes d'une place de marché la nuit et au petit
jour sert à la publicité du jus d'orange *God Morgon* (bon-
jour!). (SWE)

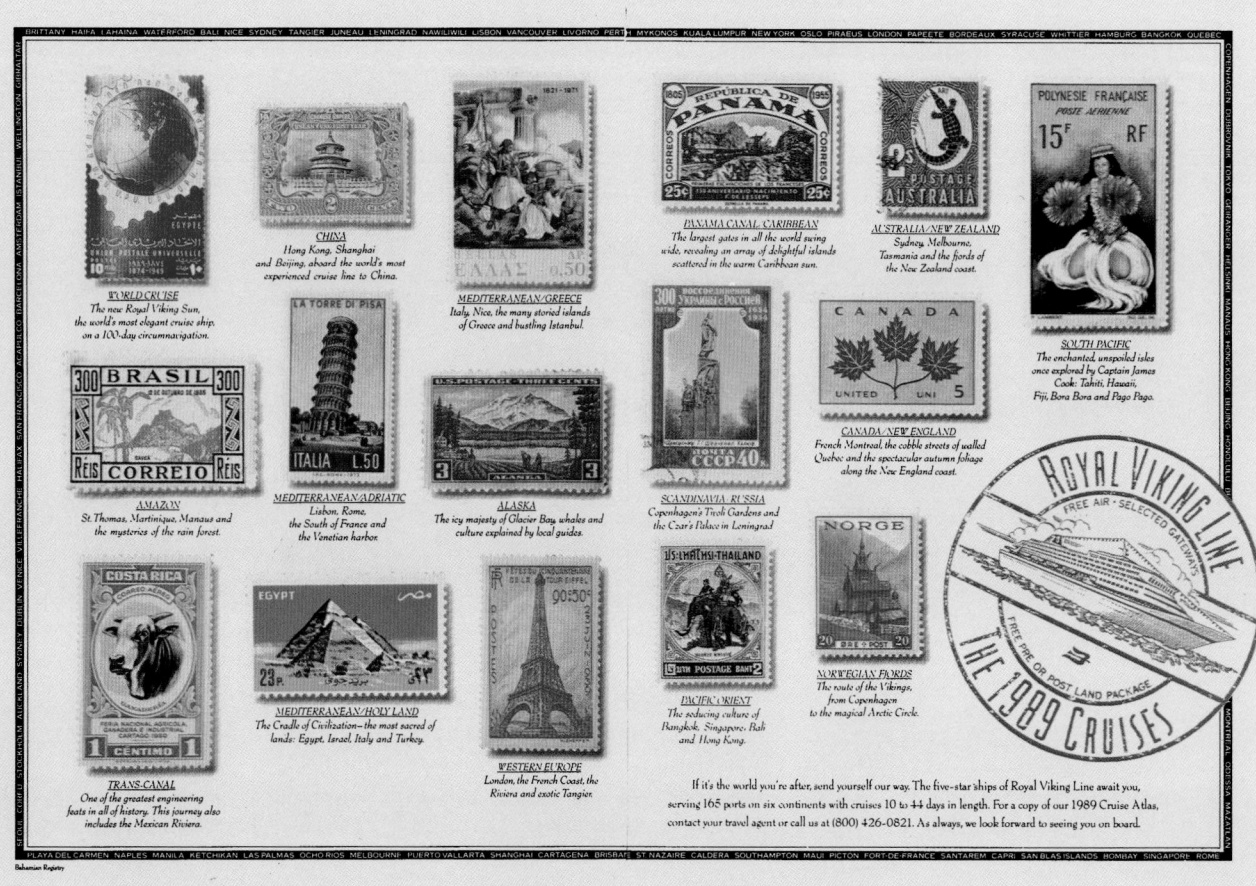

CREATIVE DIRECTOR:
JEFFREY GOODBY/
RICH SILVERSTEIN
ART DIRECTOR:
JEREMY POSTAER 95, 98
RICH SILVERSTEIN/
BETSY ZIMMERMAN 96, 97
DESIGNER:
MICHAEL MABRY 97
ILLUSTRATOR:
JEREMY POSTAER 95
PHOTOGRAPHER:
HARVEY LLOYD/
HANK BENSON 95
GERRY BYBEE 96
JAY MAISEL 98
COPYWRITER:
AMY KROUSE 95, 96
ROB BAGOT 98
AGENCY:
GOODBY, BERLIN & SILVERSTEIN
CLIENT:
ROYAL VIKING LINE
■ 95-98

■ 95-98 Examples from a magazine campaign for cruises with the Royal Viking Line. (USA)

■ 95-98 Beispiele aus einer Zeitschriftenkampagne für Kreuzfahrten mit der Royal Viking Line. (USA)

■ 95-98 Exemples figurant dans une campagne de magazines pour les croisières de la Royal Viking Line. (USA)

ART DIRECTOR:
John Seymour-Anderson
DESIGNER:
John Seymour-Anderson
PHOTOGRAPHER:
Mike Haberman
COPYWRITER:
Mike Gibbs
AGENCY:
McCool & Company
CLIENT:
Penn Athletic Products
■ 99, 100

ART DIRECTOR:
David Dalley
PHOTOGRAPHER:
Duncan Sim/
Peter Seaward
COPYWRITER:
Chrissie Feagins
AGENCY:
Young & Rubicam Ltd.
CLIENT:
Jamaica Tourist Board
►■ 101, 102

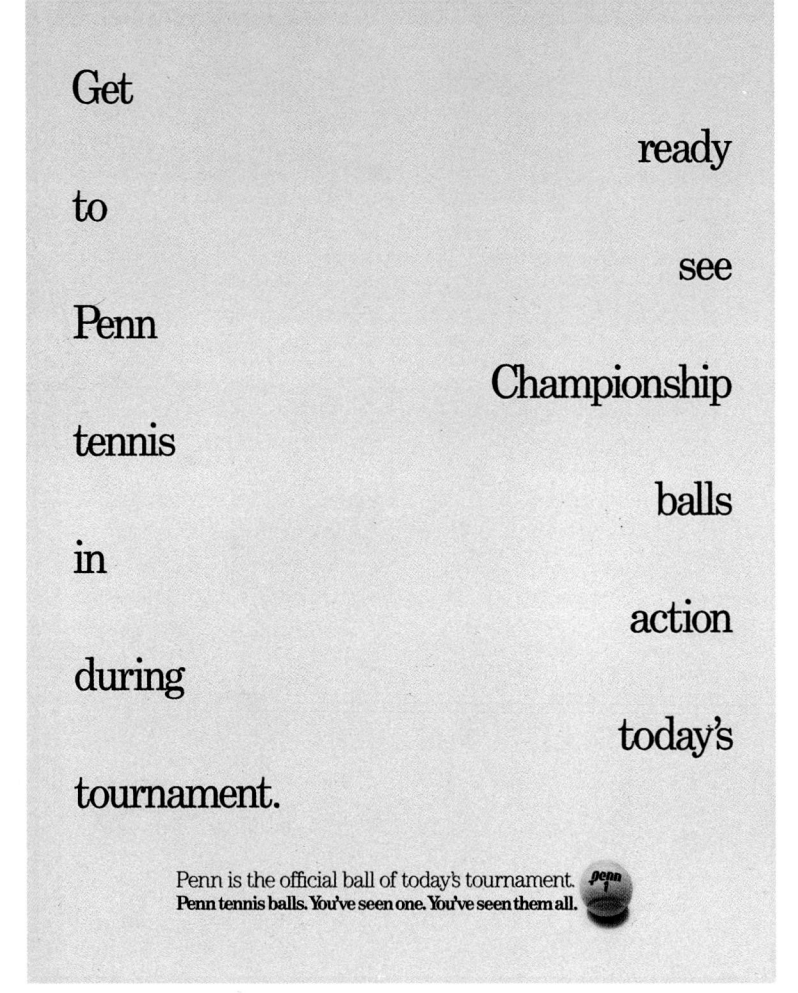

Get to Penn tennis in during tournament.

ready see Championship balls action today's

Penn is the official ball of today's tournament.
Penn tennis balls. You've seen one. You've seen them all.

■ 99, 100 From a series of advertisements for *Penn* tennis balls which appeared in the programs of the tournaments at which these balls are used. (USA)

■ 101, 102 Ads for the Jamaica Tourist Board in London mentioning two famous people who at some time lived on the Caribbean island – Noël Coward and Ian Fleming. (The real James Bond wrote a book on West Indian birds, and ornithology was also Ian Fleming's hobby.) (GBR)

■ 99, 100 Diese Anzeigen für *Penn*-Tennisbälle erschienen in Programmheften anlässlich bestimmter Turniere, bei denen diese Bälle verwendet wurden. (USA)

■ 101, 102 Anzeigen für das Jamaica Tourist Board in London. «Noël Cowards Zimmer mit Aussicht. Unsere war auch nicht übel.» «Spürte Bonds Versteck auf. Verbrachte den Nachmittag möglichst unauffällig» – Beide Autoren lebten zeitweise auf Jamaica. (GBR)

■ 99, 100 Ces annonces en faveur des balles de tennis *Penn* ont paru dans les programmes publiés à l'occasion de divers tournois ayant recours à ces balles. (USA)

■ 101, 102 Pour l'Office jamaïcain du tourisme à Londres. «La chambre avec vue de Noël Coward. La nôtre n'était pas mal non plus.» «Ai déniché la cachette de James Bond. Ai passé l'après-midi sans me faire remarquer» – Les deux écrivains ont jadis vécu en Jamaïque. (GBR)

JAMAICA

NOEL COWARD'S ROOM WITH A VIEW.

OURS WASN'T BAD EITHER.

We'd arrived at our hotel after dark. So I really wasn't prepared for it.

The next morning I stumbled over to open the wooden shutters.

And there it was. The view. Our view. Oh my. Just looking at it was good for the soul.

And every morning after that one, and most evenings we'd just sit there. We'd listen to the birds and the quiet between their calls and take in the view.

On Tuesday we drove to Noel Coward's house. 'Firefly Hill'. A surprisingly modest house for a chap with such a grand manner.

And then I saw his view.

For our free Information Pack, call 01-499 1707 or 01-493 3647 or write to Jamaica Tourist Board, 63 St. James's Street, London SW1A 1LY.

JAMAICA

TRACKED DOWN BOND'S HIDEAWAY.

SPENT THE AFTERNOON LYING LOW.

We bumped slowly down the narrow lane. Suddenly we came across two imposing old gateposts. This was it. Ian Fleming's house 'Goldeneye'. The place that inspired the world's most famous secret agent.

'Do you know where he got the name for 007 from?' Sally asked, in her best trivial pursuits manner.

'Tell me.' I said. I switched off the engine and looked down the drive to the house. It was quiet. To our left, through the undergrowth I could see a small private cove with white sand and the Caribbean rhythmically lapping at its edge. The *real* James Bond wrote an ornithological classic, 'Birds of the West Indies', in 1936. It was Ian Fleming's hobby, and the book was on his desk when he was thinking of a suitable name for his hero.

The very idea kept me amused all afternoon. Bond named after a real bird watcher.

Well done, Mr Fleming.

For our Information Pack, call 01 499 1707 or write to Jamaica Tourist Board, 63 St. James's Street, London SW1A 1LY.

■ 103-105 Ads for the Victoria & Albert Museum. The initials V and A are points of departure for all the slogans. The objects from the collection shown here are: French hairpin in the form of a skull, 1867; men's snakeskin platform shoes, with 2³/₄" heel, 1972; an anti-British Sultan's plaything consisting of a tiger over a screaming Briton. (GBR)

■ 106, 107 Examples from a promotional campaign for Scharnow Tours in which the advantages of apartments and bungalows are presented. (GER)

■ 103-105 Aus einer Anzeigenserie für das Victoria & Albert Museum. Die Initialen V und A sind Ausgangspunkt aller Schlagworte. Die gezeigten Gegenstände der Sammlung: Französische Haarnadel in Schädelform, 1867; Männerschuhe aus Schlangenleder, mit Absatz, 1972; Spielzeug eines Sultans mit Tiger über schreiendem Briten. (GBR)

■ 106, 107 Beispiele aus einer Anzeigenkampagne für Scharnow-Reisen, in denen die Vorteile von Appartements und Bungalows hervorgehoben werden. (GER)

■ 103-105 Annonces pour le Victoria & Albert Museum. Les initiales V et A ont été choisies comme point de départ de tous les slogans. Objets de collection présentés ici: aiguille à cheveux française en forme de crâne de mort, 1867; chaussures d'homme en croco, 1972; jouet de sultan, montrant un tigre assaillant un Britannique épouvanté. (GBR)

■ 106, 107 Exemples d'annonces dans une campagne des Voyages Scharnow: «Appartements de vacances pour cuisine et grillades»; «appartements avion compris». (GER)

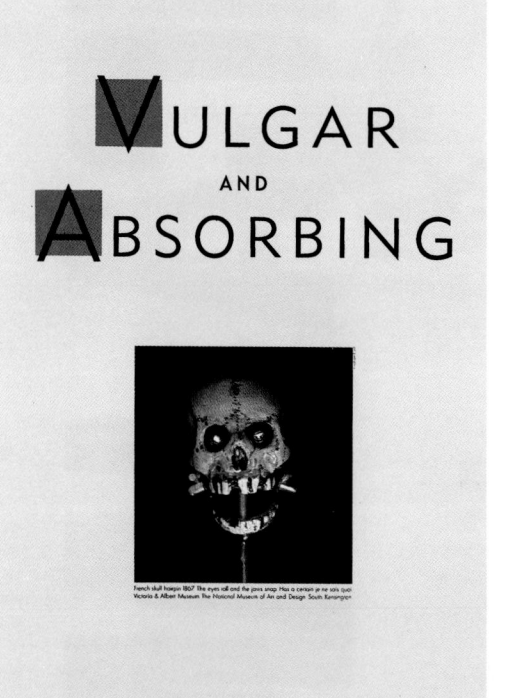

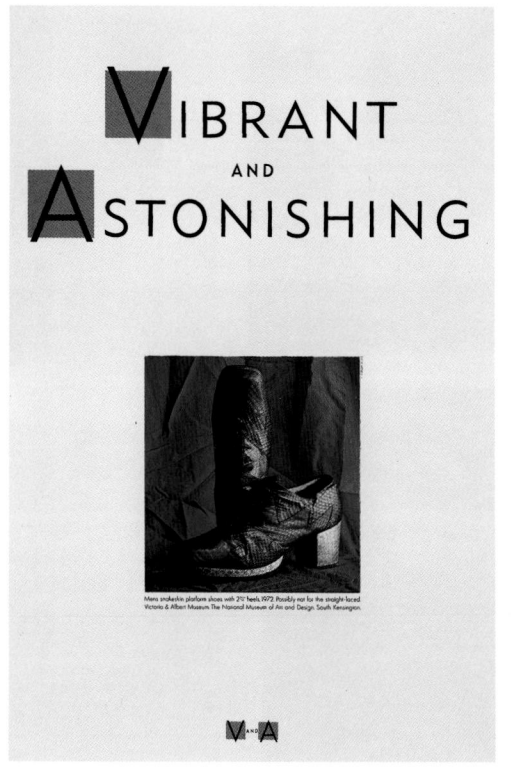

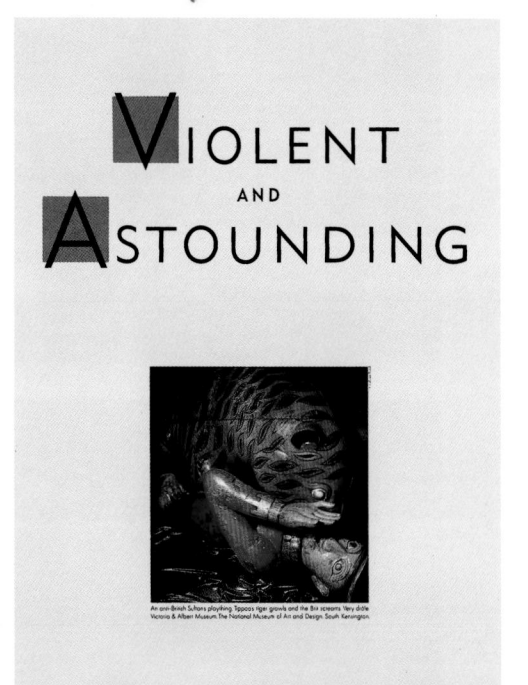

ART DIRECTOR:
CHRIS GREGORY
PHOTOGRAPHER:
GRAHAM FORD
AGENCY:
SAATCHI & SAATCHI
CLIENT:
VICTORIA & ALBERT MUSEUM
■ 103-105

ART DIRECTOR:
HARTMUT PFLÜGER/
STEFAN STEGERS
PHOTOGRAPHER:
UWE DÜTTMANN
COPYWRITER:
GERD SIMON
AGENCY:
HILDMANN, SIMON,
REMPEN & SCHMITZ/SMS
CLIENT:
TOURISTIK UNION
INTERNATIONAL
►■ 106, 107

Ferien-Appartements zum Kochen und Braten.

Sie fliegen in den Süden, wohnen privat und sind unter netten Freunden.

Ist das ein Leben: Ein „eigenes" Appartement im milden Klima der Kanarischen Inseln, in dem Sie tun und lassen können, was Sie wollen. Schlafen, essen oder in der Sonne braten, ganz nach Ihrem Geschmack. Zum Beispiel auf **Lanzarote** in den **Appartements Lanzaplaya,** 2 Wochen pro Person ab **DM 1072,–**. Oder auf **Teneriffa** in den **Appartements Park Club Europe,** 2 Wochen pro Person ab **DM 1248,–**. Einschließlich Flug, ohne Verpflegung. Ihr TUI-Reisebüro hat für Ihren privaten Urlaub mit Scharnow noch viele andere heiße Tips.

SCHARNOW
Urlaub privat.

Statt in Pension zu gehen.

Die Ungezwungenheit eines Ferienhauses – kein Bedarf nach Vollpension.

Wenn Sie statt Halb- oder Vollpension lieber die Individualität eines „eigenen" Ferienhauses suchen, sollten Sie „Urlaub privat" mit Scharnow machen. In Ihrem TUI-Reisebüro finden Sie mit Sicherheit ein Feriendomizil ganz nach Ihren Wünschen, wo Sie Ihre Urlaubstage so gestalten können, wie Sie es selbst wollen.

Sie sind Ihr eigener Herr – zum Beispiel in einem **Herrenhaus** (Foto) aus dem 11. Jahrhundert in der **Toskana.** Eine geräumige Wohnung für 4 Personen ab **DM 556,–** pro Woche. Oder, wer nicht in die Ferne schweifen will, in einem **Satteldachhaus** im **Seepark Kirchheim** im **Hessischen Bergland,** für 6 Personen ab **DM 400,–** pro Woche. Bei eigener Anreise, versteht sich. Wer einmal die Freiheit eines solchen Ferienhauses genossen hat, wird sobald nicht in Pension gehen.

SCHARNOW
Urlaub privat.

Advertisement 1

EUROPEANS KNOW HOW TO LEAD US INTO TEMPTATION.

Advertisement 2

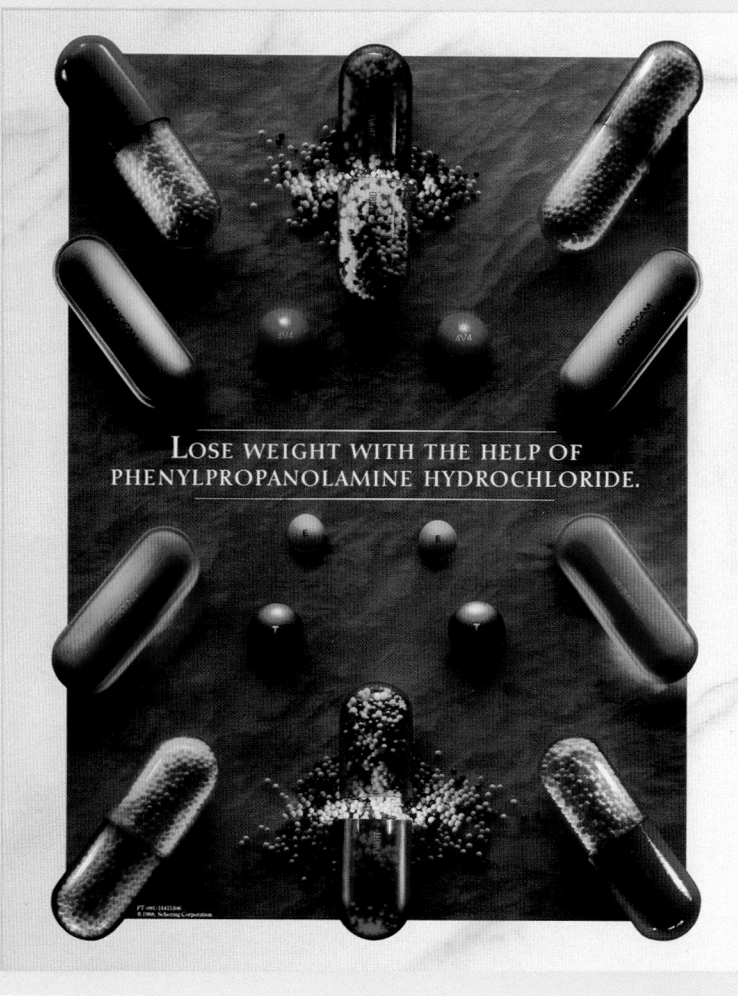

LOSE WEIGHT WITH THE HELP OF PHENYLPROPANOLAMINE HYDROCHLORIDE.

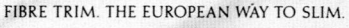

■ 108, 109 From an advertising campaign for *Fibre Trim* diet plan. *108* is for effervescent tablets that make sparkling fruit-flavored drinks and *109* is for a natural fiber food which, the advertisement claims, helps to take weight off and keep it off – without drugs. (USA)

■ 110 "To tell the truth I'm not here by chance. Neither am I, to be honest." From a campaign for *Piper-Heidsieck* champagne. (FRA)

■ 108, 109 Aus einer Werbekampagne für *Fibre-Trim*-Diät-nahrung. «Die Europäer wissen, wie man uns in Versuchung führt. Sie helfen, uns davon zu erlösen.» «Man kann mit Hilfe von Phenylpropanolamin Hydrochlorid abnehmen. Oder mit Hilfe von natürlichen Fasern.» (USA)

■ 110 «Um die Wahrheit zu sagen, ich bin nicht zufällig hier. – Ich auch nicht, um ehrlich zu sein.» – Aus einer Kampagne für *Piper-Heidsieck*-Champagner. (FRA)

■ 108, 109 Campagne publicitaire pour l'alimentation de régime *Fibre-Trim*. «Les Européens savent comment nous induire en tentation. Ils nous aident à y échapper.» «A l'aide de phénylpropanolamine hydrochloride, on peut mincir. On peut aussi le faire à l'aide de fibres naturelles.» (USA)

■ 110 Campagne publicitaire en faveur du champagne d'origine français *Piper-Heidsieck*. Annonce de magazine double page. (FRA)

▶ 108, 109
FIBRE TRIM
CLIENT:
OGILVY & MATHER
AGENCY:
DAVID APICELLA
COPYWRITER:
AARON JONES
PHOTOGRAPHER:
TRACY WONG
ART DIRECTOR:

■ 110
PIPER-HEIDSIECK
CLIENT:
DOYLE DANE BERNBACH
AGENCY:
ERIC HOLLANDER
COPYWRITER:
PETER LINDBERGH (PORTRAIT)
PAUL GOIRAND (CHAMPAGNE)
PHOTOGRAPHER:
DESIGNER:
CHRISTIAN VINCE
ART DIRECTOR:

A vrai dire, je ne suis pas là par hasard.

A dire vrai, moi non plus.

ART DIRECTOR:
Franz Merlicek
DESIGNER:
Franz Hochwarter
ILLUSTRATOR:
Jürgen Mick
COPYWRITER:
Angelo Peer
AGENCY:
Demner & Merlicek
CLIENT:
*Evidenzbüro Österreichi-
scher Zuckerfabriken*
■ 111

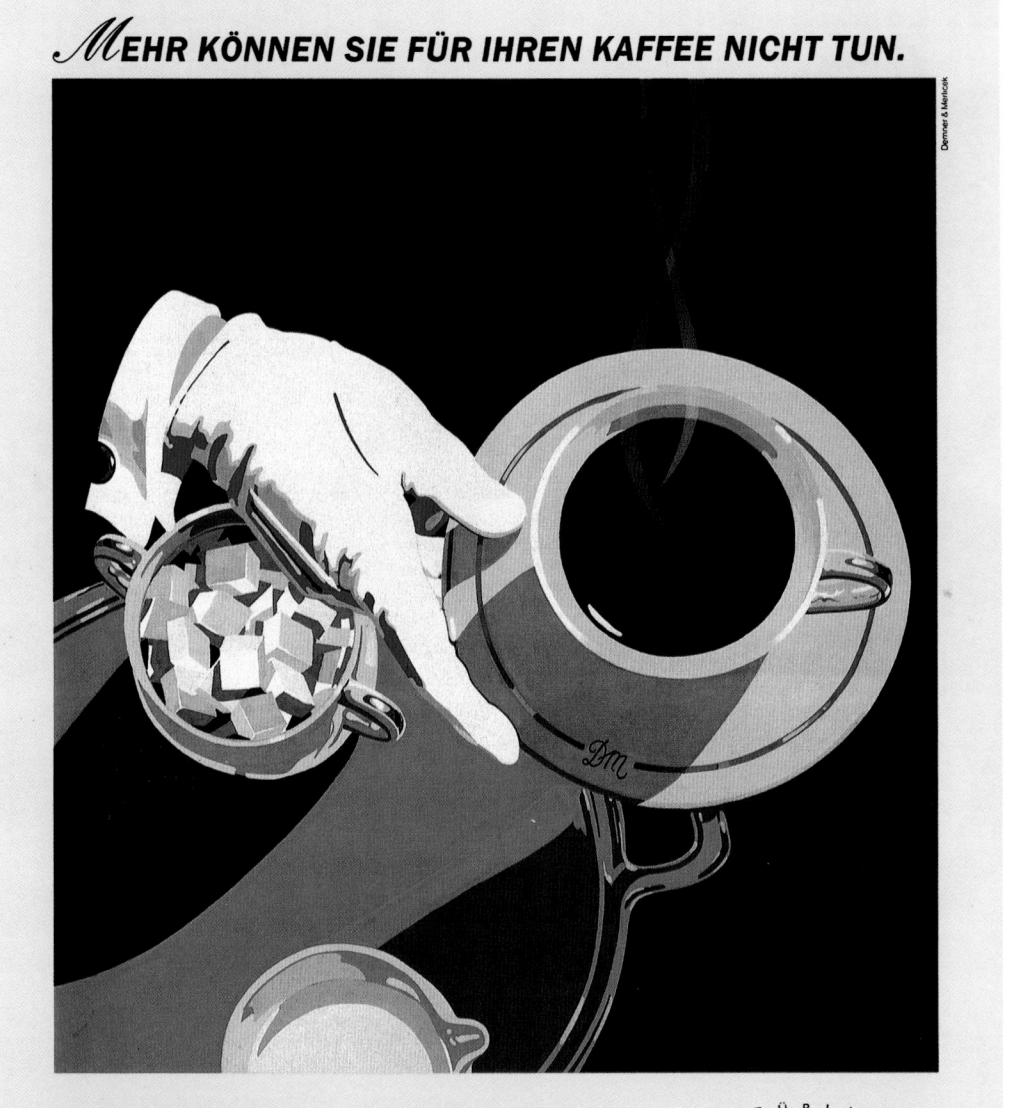

MEHR KÖNNEN SIE FÜR IHREN KAFFEE NICHT TUN.

1683: die Türken haben die Schlacht um Wien verloren, den Siegern fallen 500 Säcke mit Kaffeebohnen in die Hände.

Für seine Dienste als geheimer Bote, die zur Befreiung der Stadt entscheidend beitrugen, überläßt Wien dem Georg Franz Kolschitzky neben der Ehrenbürgerschaft die seltsamen braunen Bohnen, die man für Kamelfutter gehalten hatte.

In seinem Kaffeehaus „Zur blauen Flasche" mußte Kolschitzky zunächst aber die Wiener an das fremdartige Getränk gewöhnen: er paßte die türkische Art der Zubereitung ihrem Geschmack an. Durch ein Sieb befreite er den Kaffeetrank von seinem Satz, gab ihm Milde durch eine kleine Zugabe von Milch und Rahm und nahm ihm die Herbheit durch Zusatz von Honig.

An dieser Zubereitung hat sich seit drei Jahrhunderten nichts geändert. Nur das Süßen wurde noch feiner – natürlich mit Zucker. Und jetzt ist es auch noch praktischer geworden: mit dem neuen kleinen Moccawürfel können Sie Ihren Kaffee ganz genau so süß machen, wie Sie ihn gerne haben wollen.

NATÜRLICH
ZUCKER

■ 111 One of a series of advertisements from an image campaign for sugar. The text tells about the history of coffee and its preparation. (AUT)

■ 111 Beispiel aus einer Image-Kampagne für Zucker. Der Text berichtet über die Geschichte des Kaffees und seiner Zubereitung. (AUT)

■ 111 Exemple de campagne d'image sur le thème du sucre: «Vous ne pouvez faire davantage pour votre café.» Histoire du café et de sa préparation. (AUT)

BROCHURES

BROSCHÜREN

BROCHURES

■ 112 Cover of a catalog for men's sportswear marketed under the Savane label. (USA)
■ 113-116 Pages from a catalog for Kafka fashions. (ITA)

■ 112 Umschlag eines Katalogs für sportliche Herrenmode der Marke Savane. (USA)
■ 113-116 Seiten aus einem Katalog für Kafka-Mode. (ITA)

■ 112 Couverture d'un catalogue de modes masculines sport, marque Savane. (USA)
■ 113-116 Pages d'un catalogue des modes Kafka. (USA)

ART DIRECTOR:
*David Edelstein/
Lanny French*
DESIGNER:
*David Edelstein/
Lanny French/
Rick Jost*
PHOTOGRAPHER:
Veronica Simm
COPYWRITER:
Kathy Cain
AGENCY:
*Edelstein Associates
Advertising Inc.*
CLIENT:
Farah
◄■ 112

ART DIRECTOR:
Ciriano Zanon
PHOTOGRAPHER:
Alberto Facchi
STYLIST:
Roberto Trovati
AGENCY:
*Zan On Design
Communication*
CLIENT:
Kafka S.R.L.
▼■ 113-116

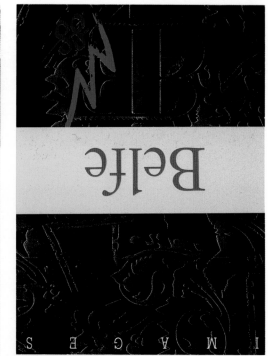

ART DIRECTOR:
JAN & LAURIE ELLIS
DESIGNER:
JAN & LAURIE ELLIS
PHOTOGRAPHER:
MARK TUCKER
STYLIST:
KYLE TAYLOR
COPYWRITER:
MARTHA DUBOSE
STUDIO:
JAN ELLIS DESIGN
CLIENT:
KYLE TAYLOR
■■ 117, 118 ▲

▲■ 121
CLIENT:
HALEKO – HANSEATISCHES
LEBENSMITTELKONTOR GMBH
AGENCY:
NOLTE WERBEAGENTUR GMBH
COPYWRITER:
RANDOLPH NOLTE
PHOTOGRAPHER:
OLAF KRONKE
DESIGNER:
JAN MERKEL
ART DIRECTOR:
RANDOLPH NOLTE

◄■ 119, 120
CLIENT:
BELFE S.PA.
AGENCY:
ZAN ON DESIGN
COMMUNICATION
PHOTOGRAPHER:
CLAUDIO MAINARDI
ART DIRECTOR:
CIRIANO ZANON

Six

Number 2/1988

■ 122-128 Covers and double spreads from two issues of a regularly appearing catalog for the fashion label *Comme des Garçons* under the title "Sixth Sense". (JPN)

■ 122-128 Umschläge und Doppelseiten von zwei Ausgaben der regelmässig erscheinenden Kataloge für Mode der Marke *Comme des Garçons* unter dem Titel «Sixth Sense» (6. Sinn). (JPN)

■ 122-128 Couvertures et doubles pages de deux éditions des catalogues publiés périodiquement pour les modes *Comme des Garçons* sous le titre de «Sixth Sense». (JPN)

ART DIRECTOR:
TSUGUYA INOUE

DESIGNER:
TSUGUYA INOUE

PHOTOGRAPHER:
KARL BLOSSFELDT (COVER)
PETER LINDBERGH
PIERRE BOUCHER

AGENCY:
COMME DES GARÇONS/
SERVICE DE PUBLICITÉ

CLIENT:
COMME DES GARÇONS

■ 122-128

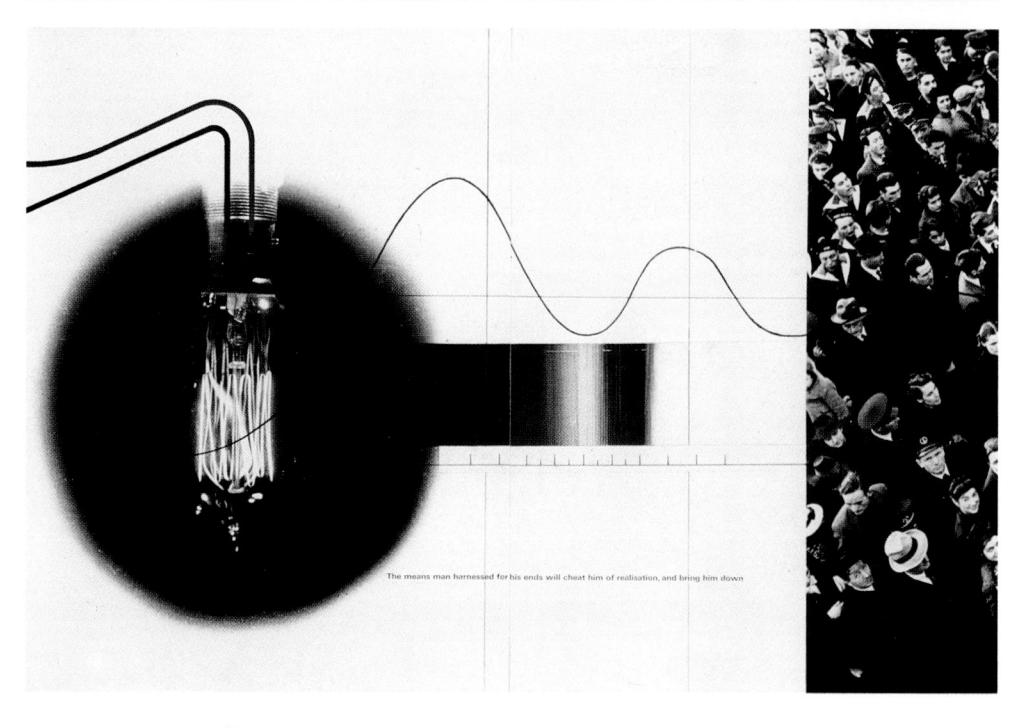

ART DIRECTOR:
Debra Herdman
DESIGNER:
Debra Herdman
PHOTOGRAPHER:
José Picayo
STYLIST:
Liz Roemer
COPYWRITER:
Vicky Rossi
AGENCY:
Dayton Hudson/In House
CLIENT:
Dayton Hudson Department Store Co.
◄■ 129

ART DIRECTOR:
Malcolm Garrett
DESIGNER:
Malcolm Garrett
PHOTOGRAPHER:
Simon Fowler
STYLIST:
Judy Blame
AGENCY:
Assorted Images Ltd.
CLIENT:
BOY
►■ 130-133

■ 129 Example of the direct mail advertising in poster form for the Dayton Hudson store. This fashionwear can also be ordered by telephone. (USA)

■ 130-133 Cover and double spreads from an order catalog for fashion by BOY of London. (GBR)

■ 129 Beispiel der Direct-Mail-Werbung des Kaufhauses Dayton Hudson in Plakatform. Diese Mode kann auch per Telephon bestellt werden. (USA)

■ 130-133 Umschlag und Doppelseiten aus einem Bestellkatalog für Mode von BOY, London. (GBR)

■ 129 Exemple de publicité directe de la part des grands magasins Dayton Hudson sous forme d'affiche. Ces vêtements se commandent aussi par téléphone. (USA)

■ 130-133 Couverture et doubles pages d'un catalogue de v.p.c. des modes BOY de Londres. (GBR)

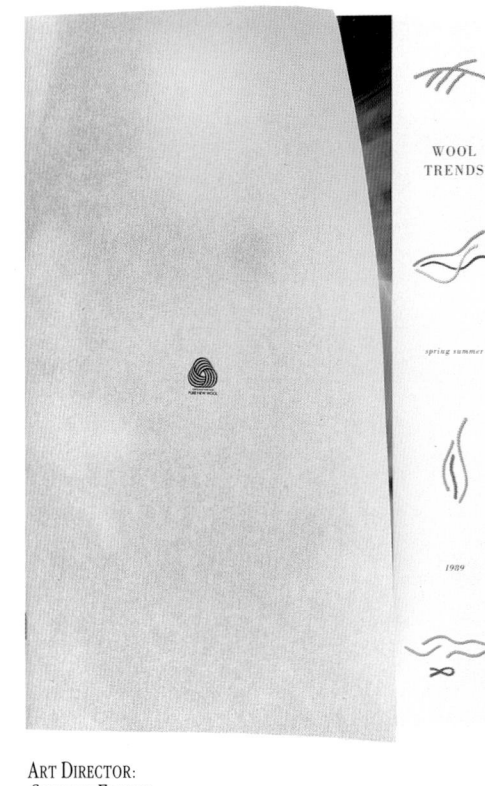

ART DIRECTOR:
STEPHEN FRANKS
DESIGNER:
JUSTIN BANKS
PHOTOGRAPHER:
JEAN-LUC FOURNIER/
MIKE OWEN
AGENCY:
COLEY PORTER BELL
CLIENT:
INTERNATIONAL WOOL
SECRETARIAT
■ 134-136

■ 134-136 Cover with parchment foil and two double spreads from the spring/summer catalog for fashions with the wool seal. (GBR)

■ 137-139 Baseball star Babe Ruth, famous onetime player with the Boston Red Sox, who was sold to the New York Yankees, as symbol for a Boston menswear store. Shown is a full-page photograph and double spreads from a catalog to make *Louis, Boston* known in New York. (USA)

■ 134-136 Umschlag mit Pergamentfolie und zwei Doppelseiten aus dem Frühjahrs/Sommerkatalog für Mode mit dem Wollsiegel. (GBR)

■ 137-139 Baseball-Star Babe Ruth, ehemaliger Spieler bei den Boston Red Sox, der an die New York Yankees verkauft wurde, als Symbol für ein Bostoner Herrenmodegeschäft. Aufnahme und Doppelseiten aus einem Katalog, der *Louis, Boston* in New York bekanntmachen soll. (USA)

■ 134-136 Couverture avec parchemin et deux doubles pages du catalogue de modes printemps/été orné du fameux emblème de la laine. (GBR)

■ 137-139 Un magasin de modes masculines de Boston a choisi pour symbole la vedette du base-ball Babe Ruth qui a joué jadis pour le Boston Red Sox avant de passer aux New York Yankees: photo pleine page et doubles pages d'un catalogue destiné à la publicité de *Louis, Boston*. (USA)

ART DIRECTOR:
Tyler Smith
DESIGNER:
Tyler Smith
PHOTOGRAPHER:
*John Goodman/
Chris Maynard/Myron*
COPYWRITER:
Lee Nash
AGENCY:
Tyler Smith
CLIENT:
Louis, Boston
■ 137-139

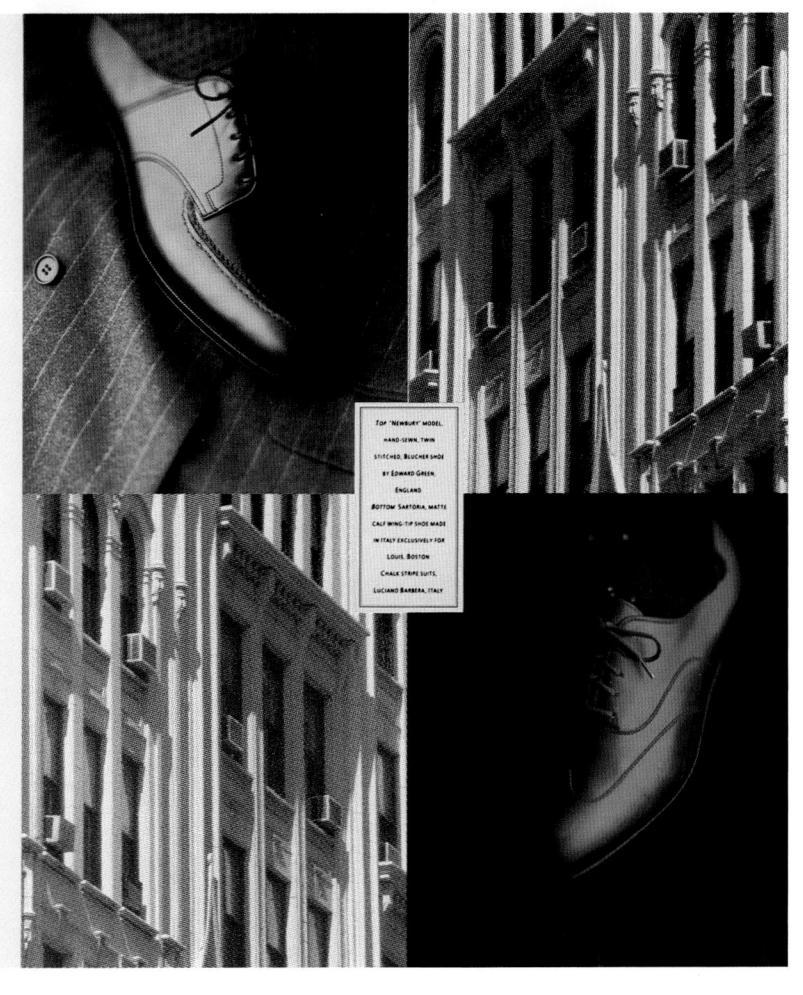

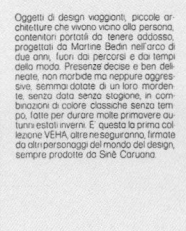

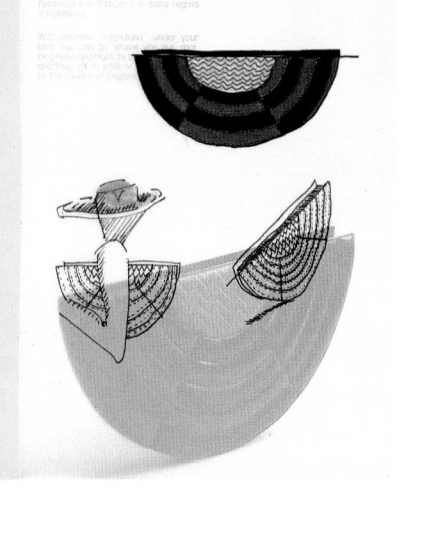

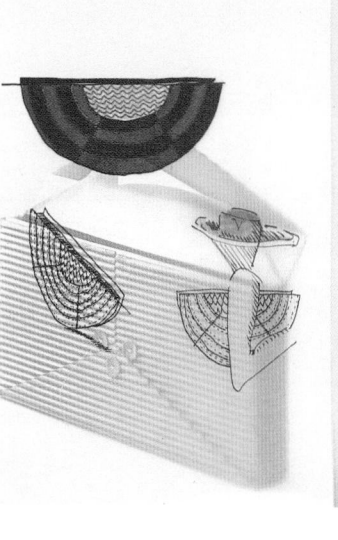

ART DIRECTOR:
ADELAIDE ACERBI

DESIGNER:
ADELAIDE ACERBI

PHOTOGRAPHER:
MARIAROSA BALLO

AGENCY:
ADELAIDE ACERBI

CLIENT:
VEHA DI SINÈ CARUANA
■ 140-143

ART DIRECTOR:
MONTE DOLACK

DESIGNER:
MONTE DOLACK

ILLUSTRATOR:
MONTE DOLACK

STUDIO:
MONTE DOLACK GRAPHICS

CLIENT:
THE GHURKA COLLECTION
►■ 144

■ 140-143 Brochure for *Veha* handbags: Cover, the flap with the first page, and double spreads, with a photograph of the cardboard packaging, sketches on parchment paper and the illustration of a handbag model. (ITA)

■ 144 Poster, stickers in various sizes, and stamps, as promotion for cases and bags in the classic style. (USA)

■ 140-143 Broschüre für *Veha*-Handtaschen. Umschlag, die Klappe mit der ersten Seite, und Doppelseiten, die aus einer Aufnahme der Kartonverpackung, Skizzen auf Pergamentpapier und der Abbildung eines Modells bestehen. (ITA)

■ 144 Plakat, Aufkleber und Briefmarken als Werbung für Koffer und Taschen im klassischen Stil. (USA)

■ 140-143 Brochure pour les sacs à main *Veha:* couverture, rabat avec la première page, exemples des doubles pages. On y voit une photo de l'emballage carton, des croquis sur parchemin et un modèle de sac à main. (ITA)

■ 144 Affiche, autocollants et timbres-poste publicitaires pour des valises et sacs de style classique. (USA)

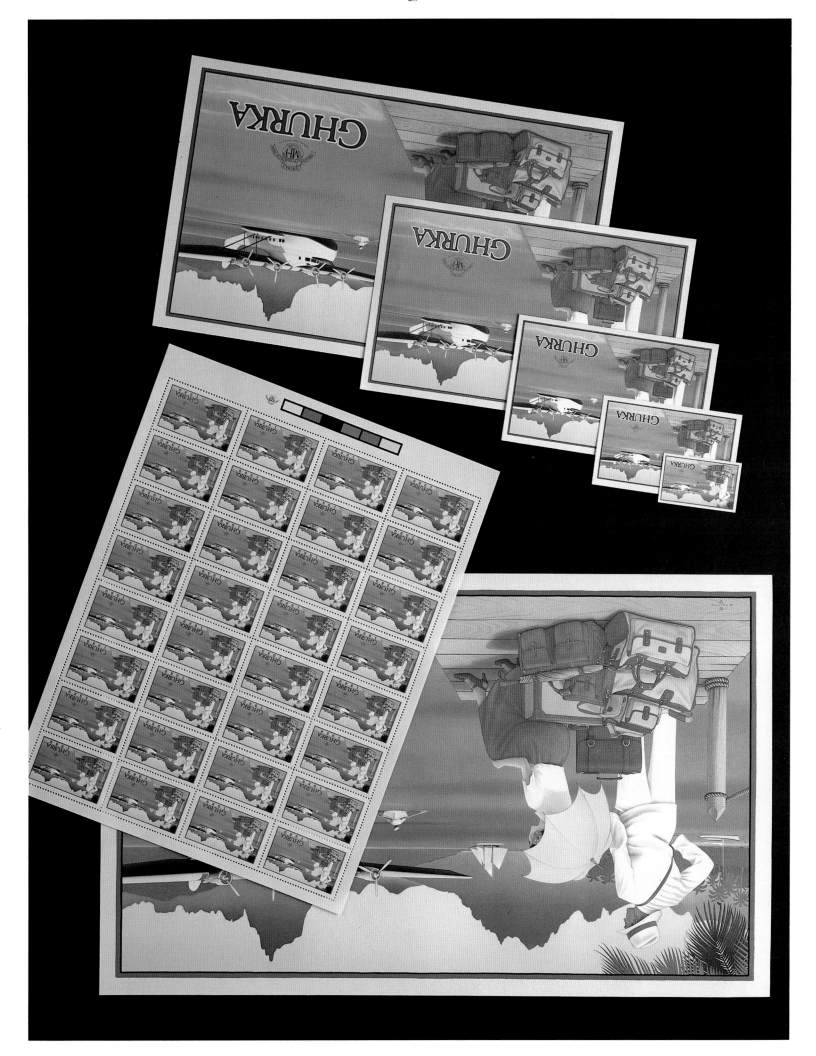

ART DIRECTOR: *JOE DUFFY*
DESIGNER: *JOE DUFFY/ CHARLES S. ANDERSON/ HALEY JOHNSON*
ILLUSTRATOR: *CHARLES S. ANDERSON/ JAN EVANS/ LYNN SCHULTE*
PHOTOGRAPHER: *JEFF ZWART*
COPYWRITER: *CHUCK CARLSON*
AGENCY: *THE DUFFY DESIGN GROUP*
CLIENT: *PORSCHE CARS OF NORTH AMERICA*
▶ ■ 147-149

ART DIRECTOR: *JOEL FULLER*
DESIGNER: *MARK CANTOR/JOEL FULLER*
PHOTOGRAPHER: *BO HYLEN*
COPYWRITER: *FRANK CUNNINGHAM*
STUDIO: *PINKHAUS DESIGN*
CLIENT: *AUSTIN ROVER CARS OF NORTH AMERICA*
■ 145, 146

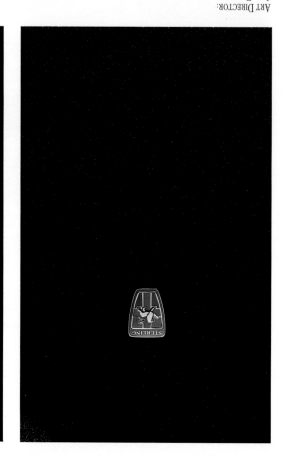

■ 145, 146 Cover and double spread from a brochure for the *Sterling 827 SL*. Only a limited number of this car model was produced. (USA)
■ 147-149 From a brochure for the *Porsche 928 S4* in North America. (USA)

■ 145, 146 Umschlag und Doppelseite aus einer Broschüre für den *Sterling 827 SL*, von dem nur eine begrenzte Anzahl hergestellt wurde. (USA)
■ 147-149 Aus einer Broschüre für den *Porsche 928 S4* in Nordamerika. (USA)

■ 145, 146 Couverture et double page d'une brochure pour la *Sterling 827 SL* produite en un nombre limité d'exemplaires. (USA)
■ 147-149 Extraits d'une brochure pour la présentation de la *Porsche 928 S4* en Amérique du Nord. (USA)

Porsche
A Car A Company A Family

The 928 S4 delivers an eloquent message about Porsche quality in its design, its engineering, and in the rigorous testing done at each step of its development. But one of the most important points the 928 S4 makes is what Dr. Ferry Porsche refers to as loving care. We build the 928 S4 mostly by hand. The human control, judgment, and finesse that go into it help make the 928 S4 our finest car. It communicates quality to driver and passenger in the "handwriting" that is unmistakably Porsche.

SAFETY IS AN EQUALLY IMPORTANT PART OF PORSCHE PERFORMANCE.

In the previous pages focusing on the heritage, luxury, performance, and durability of the Porsche 928 S4, you can see that safety pervades its design and manufacture. The 928 S4 is a safe car because it is a Porsche, because it offers comfort and convenience, because it is a smooth handling and superb cornering sports car, and because it offers reliable, trouble-free driving. In short, safety is top-of-mind in all Porsche does. More pointedly, it is the sole purpose of our large crash test facility, where we test the safety of Porsches as well as provide safety testing and development for other carmakers. Although Porsche safety may be less well-known than Porsche performance and racing success, safety brings us our greatest victories.

THREE DESIGN FEATURES HELP LESSEN THE CHANCE OF INJURY DURING A COLLISION. THE FIRST TO COME INTO PLAY ARE FRONT AND REAR "CRUSH ZONES" BUILT TO ABSORB ENERGY AS THEY COLLAPSE. THE OFFSET, JOINTED STEERING COLUMN DEFLECTS IMPACT FORCE DOWNWARD BENEATH THE CAR. THE STRUCTURAL INTEGRITY OF THE 928 S4 BODY AND CHASSIS IS REINFORCED BY THE TORQUE TUBE DRIVE SHAFT CONNECTING THE FRONT-MOUNTED ENGINE TO THE REAR-MOUNTED TRANS-AXLE. IT PROVIDES A SECOND MEASURE OF ENERGY ABSORPTION AND STRENGTH AGAINST FRONT OR REAR COLLISIONS. THE 928 S4 ULTRA-RIGID, UNITIZED BODY BENEFITS FROM SEAM WELDING PERFORMED BY SKILLED CRAFTSMEN. THE STRENGTH OF THE STEEL PASSENGER COMPARTMENT PROVIDES A THIRD LINE OF DEFENSE TO ABSORB ENERGY FROM FRONT, REAR, SIDES, TOP, AND BOTTOM IMPACTS. THE FRONT AND REAR ENDS OF THE 928 S4 FUNCTION AS BUMPERS, FORMED OF FLEXIBLE, CHIP-RESISTANT POLYURETHANE. THEY ARE THE EXTERIOR PORTION OF AN ALUMINUM-BEAM/HYDRAULIC STRUT ENERGY ABSORPTION SYSTEM THAT IS SELF-RESTORING AFTER LOW SPEED IMPACT.

All controls are designed not only for aesthetics and solid feel but are recessed or deformable for safety. All interior materials, including the abundant leather, are flame-resistant and, as on the storage shelf facing, thickly bolstered wherever possible. The 928 S4's maneuverability helps make driving safer. The power-assisted rack-and-pinion steering is accurate and razor-sharp, yet handling is smooth and predictable. The force-sensitive power assist allows for steering ease in low-speed cornering and optimum "road feel" at higher speeds and on slippery surfaces.

A high-pressure spray system provides on-the-road cleaning for the 928 S4's large, retracting halogen headlights. In conjunction with the fog lights beneath them, they allow bright, well-patterned illumination for night and inclement weather driving.

Since Porsche believes that to be a safe, capable driver you must first be comfortable, the 928 S4's orthopedically designed seats and steering wheel/instrument cluster adjust precisely and over a wide range so put you in an ergonomically correct driving position.

Side mirrors on the 928 S4 can be adjusted electrically by a remote control button on the driver's door or through the Positrol electronic seat/mirror memory system. Activating the rear window defroster also heats the side mirrors to clear them of moisture, frost, or ice.

To encourage you and your passengers to wear the 3-point lap and shoulder belts provided for all seats, we've designed them for comfort and easy fastening and release. They're thick to resist twisting and an inertia reel system keeps them snug while allowing freedom of movement. Large, well-placed windows allow excellent visibility. A two-stage heating system and rear wiper keep the rear window clear. In addition to the regular windshield washer with heated nozzles, a secondary high-pressure system removes bugs and accumulated grime.

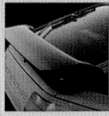

Automotive safety results from exercising good judgment while driving a car and in purchasing one. The Porsche 928 S4 rewards on both accounts. It offers active safety features to help you avoid accident situations and passive safety features to lessen the chance of injury should a collision occur. By nature and philosophy, Porsche is cautious and conservative. Through our safety research and testing and racing experience, we continuously seek ways to build safety into our cars.

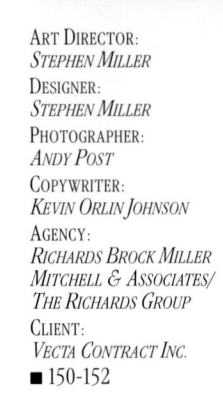

WILKHAHN 540   DESIGN BY KLAUS FRANCK

ART DIRECTOR:
STEPHEN MILLER
DESIGNER:
STEPHEN MILLER
PHOTOGRAPHER:
ANDY POST
COPYWRITER:
KEVIN ORLIN JOHNSON
AGENCY:
RICHARDS BROCK MILLER
MITCHELL & ASSOCIATES/
THE RICHARDS GROUP
CLIENT:
VECTA CONTRACT INC.
■ 150-152

■ 150, 151 Cover and double spread from a narrow brochure for *Vecta* office furniture. (USA)

■ 152 Cover of a catalog for the introduction of a stackable chair in the *Vecta* range. (USA)

■ 150, 151 Umschlag und Doppelseite aus einer schmalen Broschüre für *Vecta*-Büromöbel. (USA)

■ 152 Umschlag eines Katalogs für die Einführung eines stapelbaren Stuhls aus dem *Vecta*-Programm. (USA)

■ 150, 151 Couverture et double page d'une brochure étroite pour les meubles de bureau *Vecta*. (USA)

■ 152 Couverture du catalogue de lancement d'une chaise empilable du programme *Vecta*. (USA)

Vecta
ASSISA CHAIRS

■ 153, 154 From a small manual about technology and use of the *Morrison* office furnishing system by Knoll. (USA)

■ 155, 156 Wooden pages, illustrated with stuck on wood-cuts, from the catalog for G&S furniture. (AUT)

■ 157-160 From a catalog issued to mark the fiftieth anniversary of Knoll International. (USA)

■ 153, 154 Aus einem kleinen Handbuch über Technik und Einsatz der *Morrison*-Büromöbel von Knoll. (USA)

■ 155, 156 Holzseiten, illustriert mit aufgeklebten Holz-schnitten, aus dem Katalog für G&S-Möbel. (AUT)

■ 157-160 Aus einem Katalog zum 50jährigen Bestehen von Knoll International. (USA)

■ 153, 154 Extraits d'un petit manuel expliquant la techni-que et l'utilisation des meubles de bureau *Morrison.* (USA)

■ 155, 156 Pages en bois, illustrées de bois collés, dans un catalogue de meubles G&S. (AUT)

■ 157-160 Extraits d'un catalogue publié pour le 50e anni-versaire de Knoll International. (USA)

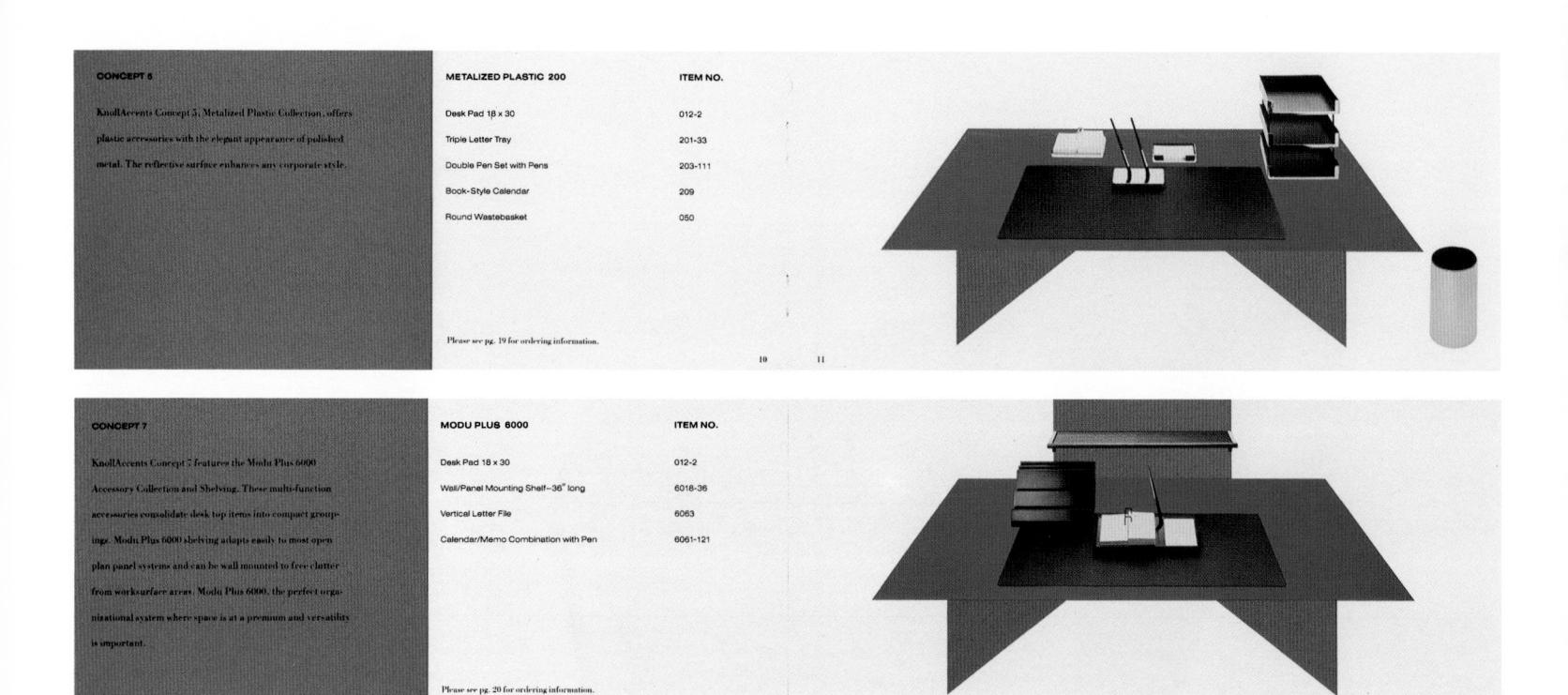

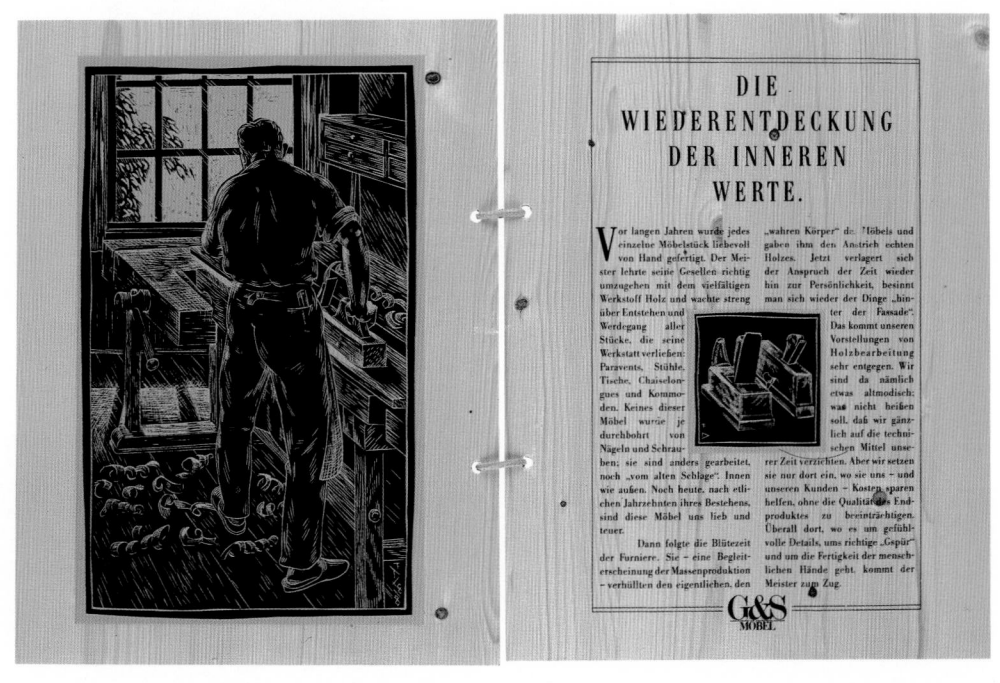

92

Now there is KnollOffice

KnollStudio

Knoll is

KnollTextiles

and KnollAccents.

ART DIRECTOR:
ALISON CHOATE
DESIGNER:
ALISON CHOATE
PHOTOGRAPHER:
MIKIO SEKITA
AGENCY:
KNOLL GRAPHICS
CLIENT:
KNOLL INTERNATIONAL
◀■ 153, 154

ART DIRECTOR:
ERWIN SCHMÖLZER
DESIGNER:
KRISTIN KONIAREK
ARTIST:
FRANZ DURST
COPYWRITER:
ISOLDE OZLBERGER
AGENCY:
CREATEAM LINZ
CLIENT:
GRUBER & SCHLAGER
◀■ 155, 156

ART DIRECTOR:
GARY GOLDSMITH
DESIGNER:
GARY GOLDSMITH/
TRACY WONG
COPYWRITER:
DEAN HACOHEN
AGENCY:
GOLDSMITH/JEFFREY
CLIENT:
KNOLL INTERNATIONAL
▶■ 157-160

■ 161-164 Cover and double spreads from a catalog for a new product by the Brillantleuchten company: "DASDAS" – a clock combined with a light, in different versions. (GER)

■ 165-176 Cover and double spreads from a narrow product brochure for the "Piretti Collection" – a new series of ergonomic chairs. (USA)

■ 161-164 Umschlag und Doppelseiten aus einem Katalog für ein neues Produkt der Brillantleuchten AG: «DASDAS», eine Uhr, kombiniert mit einer Leuchte. (GER)

■ 165-176 Umschlag und Doppelseiten aus einer schmalen Produktbroschüre für die «Piretti Collection», eine neue Serie ergonomischer Stühle. (USA)

■ 161-164 Couverture et doubles pages du catalogue d'un nouveau produit de la société Brillantleuchten AG: la lampe-pendule «DASDAS» en diverses exécutions. (GER)

■ 165-176 Couverture et doubles pages d'une brochure de produit étroite pour la «Piretti Collection», une nouvelle gamme de sièges ergonomiques. (USA)

ART DIRECTOR:
Harald Schweers
DESIGNER:
Atelier Haase & Knels
ILLUSTRATOR:
Dieter Kahl
COPYWRITER:
Lutz Augustin
AGENCY:
Atelier Haase & Knels
CLIENT:
Brillantleuchten AG
■ 161-164

ART DIRECTOR:
Massimo Vignelli
DESIGNER:
Massimo Vignelli
PHOTOGRAPHER:
Piero Casade
AGENCY:
Vignelli Associates
CLIENT:
Krueger International
■ 165-176

presents

The Piretti Collection®

a conceptual preview of a seating collection based on responsive ergonomics, designed by Giancarlo Piretti.

Krueger Inernational

Plia
designed by Giancarlo Piretti
manufactured by Castelli
distributed by KI

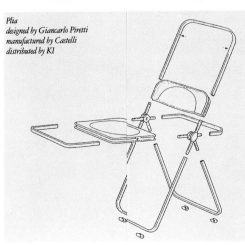

95

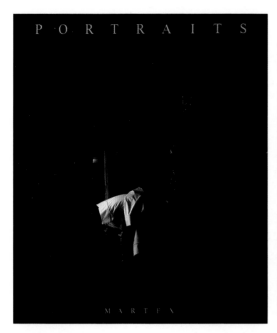

ART DIRECTOR:
JAMES SEBASTIAN
DESIGNER:
JAMES SEBASTIAN/
JUNKO MAYUMI
INTERIOR DESIGNER:
WILLIAM WALTER
PHOTOGRAPHER:
BRUCE WOLF
AGENCY:
DESIGNFRAME INC.
CLIENT:
MARTEX/
WEST POINT PEPPERELL
■ 177-181

■ 177-181 Cover of a catalog
for *Martex* home textiles
bearing the title "Special
Places" and pages from the
catalog "Portraits" for the
introduction of a new product in the *Martex* home
textile range. (USA)

■ 177-181 Umschlag eines
Katalogs für *Martex*-Heim-
textilien mit dem Titel
«Besondere Orte» und Sei-
ten aus dem Katalog «Por-
träts» für die Einführung
eines neuen Produktes im
Martex-Heimtextiliensorti-
ment. (USA)

■ 177-181 Couverture d'un
catalogue des tissus décoratifs *Martex* intitulé «Sites
particuliers» et des extraits
d'un autre catalogue intitulé
«Portraits», pour le lancement d'un nouveau produit
dans la gamme *Martex* des
tissus décoratifs. (USA)

Triton Container International Limited

With a new fleet built after 1980 to proprietary specifications, Triton benefits customers with the newest container technology for durability and lower repair costs.

We founded Triton in 1980 with one unswerving mandate: to benefit international ocean carriers with better leasing solutions and more innovative options.

So at a time when carriers paid a premium to accommodate the geographic container imbalance, we challenged that practice. At Triton, we returned to the fundamentals of service by matching our equipment availability to the trade patterns of carefully selected customers. And we continue to strengthen that availability by retaining flexible manufacturer relationships for more units in the world's high-demand areas— whether the demand is for high service master-interchange leases, long-term leases, or for emergency "spot" requirements. We also offer the industry's youngest fleet in a mix of dry vans, high cubes, open top, and refrigerated containers — all commissioned to our own designs that exceed ISO specs, all adhering to a single high-quality equipment standard. As a result, carriers enjoy the benefits of reliability, stability, damage resistance, and lower repair costs through Triton's leasing expertise.

3000 BC:
Metal coins begin to replace barley as legal tender in Sumeria.

552:
Travelers bring back silkworms from China and Ceylon to begin the European silk industry.

900:
Vikings develop the art of shipbuilding.

1191:
Tea arrives in Japan from China.

ART DIRECTOR:
Jamie Davison
DESIGNER:
Jamie Davison/
Rita Damore
PHOTOGRAPHER:
Henrik Kam
STYLIST:
Liz Ross
COPYWRITER:
Lindsay Beaman
AGENCY:
Jamie Davison Design, Inc.
CLIENT:
Triton Container
International Ltd.
■182, 183

ART DIRECTOR:
Leslie Smolan
DESIGNER:
Beth Bangor
ILLUSTRATOR:
Mark Penberthy
COPYWRITER:
John Goldman
AGENCY:
Carbone Smolan Associates
CLIENT:
Merrill Lynch
▼■ 184, 185

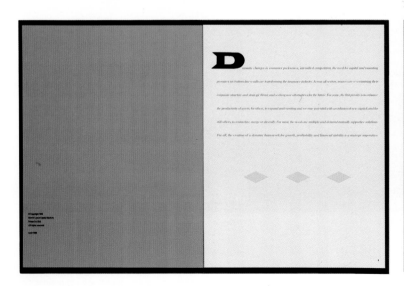

■ 182, 183 The contribution to world trade made by Triton Container International (worldwide leasers of a variety of marine cargo containers) is highlighted in the company brochure. Shown are the cover and a double spread. (USA)

■ 184, 185 Spreads from a brochure exploring services for insurers by Merrill Lynch's insurance group. The circus imagery supports the text in a novel juxtapositioning. (USA)

■ 186 Front of an overview brochure to hold literature used in trade fairs for the Westfield Company - specialists in the building and leasing of shopping centers. (USA)

■ 187 Cover of a folder to promote the lease of light-industrial and office space in an industrial park. (USA)

■ 182, 183 Der Beitrag der Schiffsmaklerfirma Triton Container International zum internationalen Handel ist das zentrale Thema der Firmenbrochüre. Hier der Umschlag und eine Doppelseite. (USA)

■ 184, 185 Doppelseiten aus einer Broschüre über die Versicherungs-Gruppe der Firma Merrill Lynch. Die Zirkusbilder unterstützen den Text auf spezielle Weise. (USA)

■ 186 Vorderseite einer Faltmappe für Werbematerial der Firma Westfield, spezialisiert auf den Bau und die Vermietung von Einkaufszentren. (USA)

■ 187 Umschlag einer Faltmappe für Dokumentationsmaterial über Mietobjekte in einem Industriepark. (USA)

■ 182, 183 Cette brochure d'entreprise a pour thème la contribution des courtiers maritimes Triton Container International au commerce international. On voit ici la couverture et une double page. (USA)

■ 184, 185 Doubles pages d'une brochure consacrée au groupe d'assurances de la société Merrill Lynch. Les illustrations de cirque viennent à l'appui du texte. (USA)

■ 186 Recto d'un dossier pliant pour la documentation publicitaire de la société Westfield spécialisée dans la construction et la location de centres commerciaux. (USA)

■ 187 Couverture d'un dossier avec une documentation sur les locaux à louer au sein d'un parc industriel. (USA)

ART DIRECTOR:
JOSH FREEMAN
DESIGNER:
GREG CLARKE
ILLUSTRATOR:
GREG CLARKE
COPYWRITER:
BESS DeBECK
AGENCY:
JOSH FREEMAN/ASSOCIATES
CLIENT:
WESTFIELD, INC.
■ 186

ART DIRECTOR:
THOMAS FRANCISCO
DESIGNER:
THOMAS FRANCISCO
PHOTOGRAPHER:
THOMAS FRANCISCO
AGENCY:
*NORTHLIGHT VISUAL
COMMUNICATIONS GROUP, INC.*
CLIENT:
*NATIONAL REALTY &
DEVELOPMENT CORP.*
■ 187

712 Fifth Avenue

The focal point of Fifth Avenue between 55th and 56th Streets, 712 Fifth Avenue rises above one of the most respected international centers of commerce.

712 Fifth Avenue is surrounded by the world's most distinguished and powerful corporations. In fact, many of New York's "Fortune 500" firms are within walking distance of the office tower as are branches or headquarters of virtually every major bank in the world.

The neighborhood is also celebrated for its internationally-acclaimed shops, hotels, and restaurants.

Luxurious accommodations are available nearby at the majestic Plaza Hotel, the Pierre, and the St. Regis-Sheraton; while the most sumptuous dining attainable can be experienced at La Cote Basque, La Grenouille, The Four Seasons and Le Cygne.

712 Fifth Avenue is served by New York's comprehensive network of transportation, communication and financial services. Tenants traveling from anywhere in New York City can arrive at 712 Fifth Avenue via subway through station at 53rd and 59th Streets at Fifth Avenue, Rockefeller Center, and 57th Street at the Avenue of the Americas. The Lexington Avenue and Broadway subway lines are also close by. Grand Central Station with connections to Times Square and commuter trains are just a few minutes away, and tenants departing for JFK International Airport can catch the "Train to the Plane" at 57th Street and the Avenue of the Americas.

Six downtown bus routes follow Fifth Avenue and stop within two blocks of 712 Fifth Avenue. Uptown bus lines for transit to the Upper East and Upper West Sides are one block away on Avenue of the Americas and Madison Avenue.

ART DIRECTOR:
MASSIMO VIGNELLI
DESIGNER:
MICHAEL BIERUT/
MICHAEL LEONE
ILLUSTRATOR:
BRIAN BURR
PHOTOGRAPHER:
NATHANIEL LIEBERMAN/
REVEN T.C. WURMAN
AGENCY:
VIGNELLI ASSOCIATES
CLIENT:
SOLOMON EQUITIES
■ 188-191

■ 188-191 Hard cover and double spreads from a brochure about a new skyscraper (53 floors) on Manhattan's Fifth Avenue in which offices are to let. The brochure gives information about all the aspects of the new building, including the building materials, as well as giving a history of this famous address. (USA)

■ 188-191 Fester Umschlag und Doppelseiten einer Broschüre über einen neuen Wolkenkratzer (53 Stockwerke) an der Fifth Avenue in Manhattan, in dem Büroraum zu vermieten ist. Die Broschüre informiert über alle Aspekte des neuen Gebäudes, einschliesslich der Baumaterialien, sowie über die Geschichte dieser Adresse. (USA)

■ 188-191 Couverture rigide et doubles pages d'une brochure consacrée à un nouveau gratte-ciel de 53 étages sur la 5e Avenue de New York où des bureaux sont en location. On y détaille les divers aspects du building en explicitant les matériaux de construction, et on fait l'historique du site fameux. (USA)

DESIGNER:
MICHAEL MABRY
COPYWRITER:
LINDA PETERSON
AGENCY:
MICHAEL MABRY DESIGN
CLIENT:
STRATHMORE PAPER COMPANY
■ 193-199

ILLUSTRATOR:
MICHAEL MABRY 197
ANTHONY RUSSO 199
PHOTOGRAPHER:
JEURGEN TELLER 194
JEFFERY NEWBURY 195 -199

■ 193-199 Catalog cover with slipcase for "Esprit" paper by Strathmore, and cover with double spreads of a further company brochure for the paper "Rhododendron". Each brochure is devoted to one topic: "Esprit" - the spirit of creativity, "Rhododendron" - stress. (USA)

■ 193-199 Katalogumschlag mit Schuber für die Papiersorte «Esprit» von Strathmore und Umschlag mit Doppelseiten einer weiteren Broschüre der Firma für «Rhododendron». Jede Broschüre ist einem Thema gewidmet: «Esprit» dem Geist der Kreativität, «Rhododendron» dem Stress. (USA)

■ 193-199 Couverture de catalogue sous emboîtage pour la qualité de papier «Esprit» de Strathmore; couverture et doubles pages d'une autre brochure pour le papier «Rhododendron». Chaque brochure est axée sur un sujet bien déterminé: la créativité (Esprit), le stress (Rhododendron). (USA)

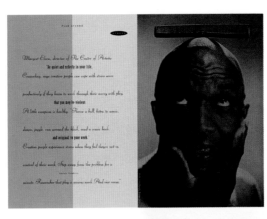

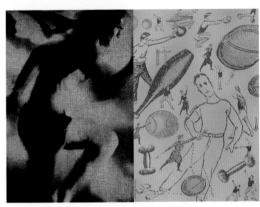

ART DIRECTOR:
MALCOLM WADDELL

DESIGNER:
MALCOLM WADDELL/
MERCEDES ROTHWELL

ILLUSTRATOR:
JAN WADDELL/
KATE WADDELL

PHOTOGRAPHER:
THE IMAGE BANK
OF CANADA

COPYWRITER:
B.W. POWE/GEORGE HOUK

AGENCY:
ESKIND WADDELL

CLIENT:
MEAD PAPER/
EMPRESS GRAPHICS INC.

■ 200-203

■ 200-203 Front and examples of the contents of a portfolio for the product launch of a new paper by Mead. This reference portfolio for graphic designers demonstrates the paper's ability to enhance a multiplicity of film and printing techniques. (USA)

■ 200-203 Vorderseite und Beispiele aus dem Inhalt einer Mappe für die Lancierung einer neuen Papierqualität von Mead. Sie ist an Graphik-Designer gerichtet und soll die Eignung des Papiers für verschiedenste Anforderungen der Litho- und Drucktechnik demonstrieren. (USA)

■ 200-203 Recto et spécimens du contenu d'un dossier pour l'introduction d'une nouvelle qualité de papier Mead. Destinée aux graphistes, cette documentation entend leur apporter la preuve de l'utilité du nouveau papier pour la reprographie et l'impression. (USA)

ART DIRECTOR:
CHRIS LOWER
DESIGNER:
ROSANNA BIANCHINI/
ANDREW BARKER
PHOTOGRAPHER:
JOHN CLARIDGE
AGENCY:
DESIGN HOUSE
CONSULTANTS LTD.
CLIENT:
DESIGN HOUSE
CONSULTANTS LTD.
■ 204-206

■ 204-206 Cover and double spreads from a self-promotional brochure for the Design House Company, with a selection of wine labels – designed for the Victoria Wine Company – stuck on the pages. (GBR)

■ 207-211 "Signature" is the name of a paper and it is being promoted by *Mead* in this catalog. (USA)

■ 204-206 Umschlag und Doppelseiten aus einer Eigenwerbungsbroschüre der Firma Design House, mit einer Auswahl der für die Victoria Wine Company entworfenen Weinetiketts, die auf die Seiten aufgeklebt sind. (GBR)

■ 207-211 «Signature» (Unterschrift) ist der Name einer Papiersorte, für die Mead mit diesem Katalog wirbt. (USA)

■ 204-206 Couverture et doubles pages d'une brochure autopromotionnelle de la société Design House, avec un choix d'étiquettes réalisées pour les bouteilles de vin de la Victoria Wine Company, collées à même les pages. (GBR)

■ 207-211 La qualité de papier présentée dans ce catalogue Mead a été baptisée «Signature». (USA)

Make Your Mark on Signature from Mead

ART DIRECTOR:
John Van Dyke
DESIGNER:
John Van Dyke
PHOTOGRAPHER:
Terry Heffernan
STYLIST:
Holly Stewart
COPYWRITER:
Jon Bell
AGENCY:
Van Dyke Company
CLIENT:
Mead Paper Company
■ 207-211

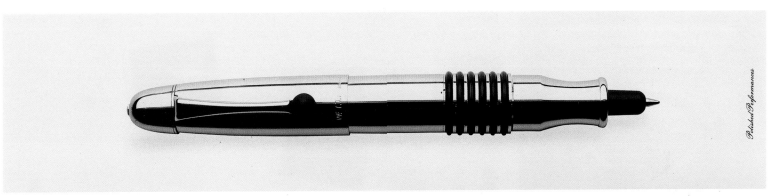

Polished Performance

Through the looking gloss. As you can see, Signature's higher gloss provides more intense contrast. Colors have more brilliance and snap, shaded areas are richer, and varnishes more satiny. It's not just the paper; it's the system we created to meet our own standards. Our new blade coating process ensures more uniform gloss from side to side and from run to run. Just one more reason why Signature is going to help you make your mark.

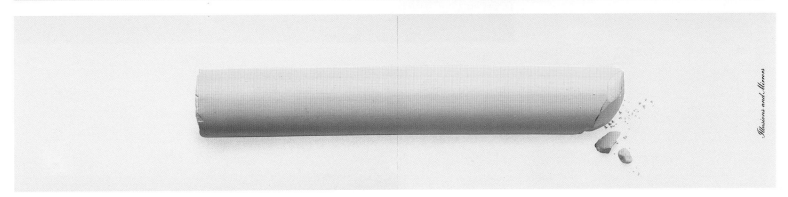

Illusions and Mirrors

Textures captured on a mirror-bright surface. Ironic, isn't it? Signature's mirror-like surface captures the nubby texture of this chalk and eraser with superb clarity. Equipment advances account for Signature's consistent rawstock smoothness, while our new coating system creates smoother surfaces. Together they produce halftone dots that fairly jump off the page and textures you have to feel to disbelieve.

■ 212-214 Cover and double spreads of a brochure for *Polaroid* film cartridges that serve for test shots, and are suitable for various cameras. (USA)

■ 215-221 From a small advertising brochure for *Mead* and *Gilbert* papers relating to September: the death of Mao Tse Tung in 1976; a "Bad is Beautiful" convention; September is supposed to be the best time for wood-chopping; the birth of author O. Henry; Henry Hudson enters the river which bears his name; the William Tell Festival in New Glarus; President William McKinley is shot in Buffalo, New York, in 1901. (USA)

■ 212-214 Umschlag und Doppelseiten einer Broschüre für *Polaroid*-Film-Kassetten, die für Testaufnahmen dienen und für verschiedene Kameras passen. (USA)

■ 215-221 Aus einer kleinen Werbebroschüre für *Mead* und *Gilbert*-Papiere über den Monat September: Tod Mao Tse-tungs, 1976; eine «Kahl-ist-schön»-Demonstration; September soll die beste Zeit zum Holzfällen sein; Geburtstag von O. Henry; Henry Hudson geht in den nach ihm benannten Fluss; Wilhelm-Tell-Festival in New Glarus; 1901 wird der 25. Präsident der Vereinigten Staaten, William McKinley, in Buffalo, New York, erschossen. (USA)

■ 212-214 Couverture et doubles pages d'une brochure sur les films *Polaroid* en cassettes servant aux essais, et qui sont disponibles pour divers types d'appareils. (USA)

■ 215-221 Extraits d'une petite brochure publicitaire pour les papiers *Mead* et *Gilbert* où il est question du mois de septembre: la mort de Mao Zedong en 1976; une manifestation en faveur des chauves; le mois idéal pour le bûcheronnage; l'anniversaire d'O. Henry; Henry Hudson s'aventurant dans le fleuve qui porte son nom; le festival Guillaume Tell à New Glarus; l'assassinat du président William McKinley à Buffalo, New York, en 1901. (USA)

ART DIRECTOR:
VARTUS ARTINIAN
DESIGNER:
VARTUS ARTINIAN
PHOTOGRAPHER:
STEVE MARSEL
STYLIST:
STACY KOCH
COPYWRITER:
BRIAN FLOOD
AGENCY:
POLAROID
CLIENT:
POLAROID/NBC PHOTO DIV.
■ 212-214

September 1976: 9 Death of Mao Tse Tung

September 1988: 'Bald is Beautiful' 10 Convention, Morehead, North Carolina

ART DIRECTOR:
PETER HARRISON

DESIGNER:
SUSAN HOCHBAUM

ILLUSTRATOR:
ANDREZEJ DUDZINSKI 219
HENRIK DRESCHER 220

COPYWRITER:
JOHN BERENDT

AGENCY:
PENTAGRAM DESIGN

CLIENT:
MEAD PAPER COMPANY

■ 215-221

According to the Farmer's Almanac, early September is the optimum time to begin logging.

September 1862: 11 O. Henry born

September 1609: Henry Hudson 12 enters the river which bears his name

September 1988: William Tell 5 Festival, New Glarus, Wisconsin

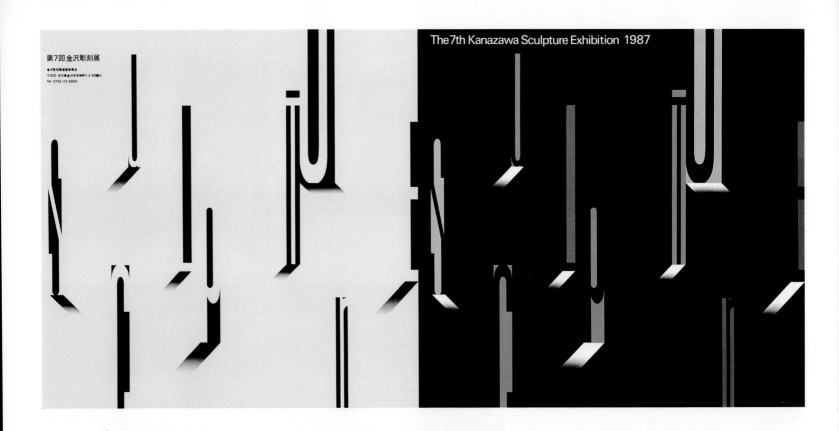

第7回 金沢彫刻展

金沢彫刻展運営委員会
〒920 石川県金沢市天神町1-2-59離れ
Tel 0762-22-8965

The 7th Kanazawa Sculpture Exhibition 1987

PROOST PAPIER

■ 222 Complete catalog cover for a sculpture exhibition in the Japanese city of Kanazawa. (JPN)

■ 223 Folders with information on paper and cardboard made by the Dutch company Proost en Brandt. (NLD)

■ 224, 225 From a promotional mailing by the French Paper Company. Shown is the cover of one of the brochures collected in a slipcase, showing the various paper qualities, and a double spread. (USA)

■ 222 Vollständiger Katalogumschlag für eine Skulptur-Ausstellung in der japanischen Stadt Kanazawa. (JPN)

■ 223 Informationsmaterial für die Papier- und Kartonqualitäten der holländischen Firma Proost en Brandt. (NLD)

■ 224, 225 Aus einer Werbesendung der French Paper Company. Hier der Umschlag einer der in einem Schuber zusammengefassten Broschüren für die verschiedenen Papierqualitäten und eine Doppelseite. (USA)

■ 222 Couverture complète du catalogue d'une exposition de sculpture dans la ville japonaise de Kanazawa. (JPN)

■ 223 Des brochures d'information concernant les papiers et cartons de la sociéte néerlandaise Proost en Brandt. (NLD)

■ 224, 225 Extraits d'un envoi publicitaire de la French Paper Company: couverture de l'une des brochures réunies sous emboîtage; double page. Chaque brochure documente une qualité de papier. (USA)

ART DIRECTOR:
Minoru Niijima
DESIGNER:
Minoru Niijima/
Chiaki Aiba
STUDIO:
Minoru Niijima
Design Studio
CLIENT:
Kanazawa Sculpture
Exhibition Comittee
◀■ 222

ART DIRECTOR:
Hans Versteeg
DESIGNER:
Hans Versteeg
AGENCY:
Shape
CLIENT:
Proost en Brandt
◀■ 223

ART DIRECTOR:
Charles S. Anderson
DESIGNER:
Charles S. Anderson
ILLUSTRATOR:
Charles S. Anderson/
Lynn Schulte
COPYWRITER:
Chuck Carlson
AGENCY:
The Duffy Design Group
CLIENT:
French Paper Co.
■ 224, 225

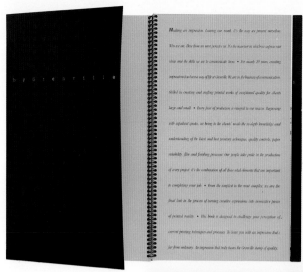

ART DIRECTOR:
CARMEN DUNJKO
DESIGNER:
CARMEN DUNJKO/
JENNIFER COGHILL
ILLUSTRATOR:
JOE BIOFORE 228
BILL BOYKO 229
PHOTOGRAPHER:
LIAM SHARP 227
DEBORAH SAMUEL 230
COPYWRITER:
ELLIOTT COLLINS/
RITA YUNGER LINDER
AGENCY:
CARMEN DUNJKO ASSOCIATES
CLIENT:
GRENVILLE PRINTING
■ 226-230

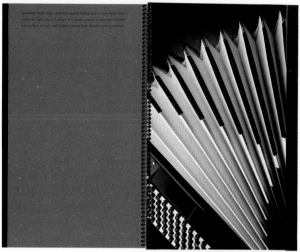

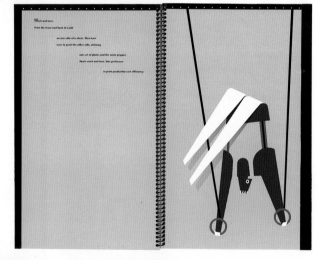

■ 226-230 Opened up dustjacket showing the introductory page and double spreads from a spiral-bound brochure issued by the Grenville Printing Company. *227* relates to the various folding methods, *228* to "work-and-turn", *229* to color match, and *230* to positive/negative print. (CAN)

■ 226-230 Aufgeklappter Schutzumschlag mit der einleitenden Seite und Doppelseiten aus einer ringgehefteten Broschüre. *227* bezieht sich auf verschiedene Falttechniken, *228* auf den Schön- und Widerdruck, *229* auf die Farbabstimmung, *230* auf Negativ/Positiv-Druck. (CAN)

■ 226-230 Jaquette ouverte, page initiale et doubles pages d'une brochure à reliure spirale de l'imprimerie Grenville Printing. *Fig. 227:* diverses techniques de pliage, *228:* impression recto-verso, *229:* harmonisation des couleurs, *230:* impression négative/positive. (CAN)

Negative/Positive
Black/White
Left/Right
Right/Wrong
Stop/Go
In/Out
Shadows/Highlights
Opposites that attract.
Positive/Negative,
Negative/Positive.
Where dark and light
tonal values are the same
as the original,
that's positive.
Negative is where
tonal values of the
original image
are reversed.
Dark appears light.
And vice versa.

ART DIRECTOR:
Pat & Greg Samata
DESIGNER:
Pat & Greg Samata
PHOTOGRAPHER:
*Dennis Dooley/
Mark Joseph*
COPYWRITER:
Janet Blank
STUDIO:
Samata Associates
CLIENT:
Mead Paper Company
■ 231-233

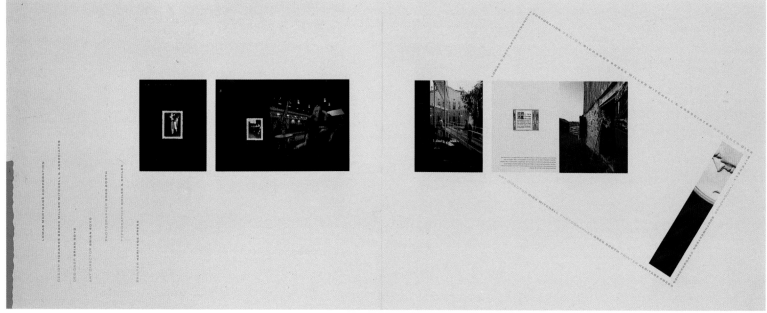

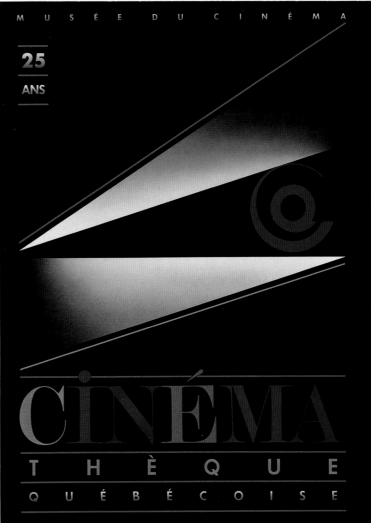

DESIGNER:
NENAD MARTIĆ
ILLUSTRATOR:
NENAD MARTIĆ
CLIENT:
AUTORSKA AGENCIJA
■ 234

ART DIRECTOR:
NELU WOLFENSOHN
DESIGNER:
LISE CHARBONNEAU-GRAVEL/
LUC PARENT
AGENCY:
LAVALIN GRAPHISME
CLIENT:
CINÉMATHÈQUE QUÉBÉCOISE
■ 235

■ 231-233 Cover and double spreads of a brochure in which Mead presents the award-winning works of the Mead Competition for the Design of Annual Reports. (USA)

■ 234 For the catalog of a Croatian authors' agency. (YUG)

■ 235 Cover of a catalog issued on the occasion of the 25th anniversary of the Cinématèque Québécoise. (CAN)

■ 231-233 Umschlag und Doppelseiten einer Broschüre, in der die im Mead-Wettbewerb für die Gestaltung von Jahresberichten prämierten Arbeiten vorgestellt werden. (USA)

■ 234 Für den Katalog einer Autoren-Agentur. (YUG)

■ 235 Katalog, der zum 25jährigen Bestehen der Cinemathek von Quebec herausgegeben wurde. (CAN)

■ 231-233 Couverture et doubles pages d'une brochure où le jury du concours Mead présente les travaux couronnés lors du concours du meilleur rapport annuel. (USA)

■ 234 Pour le catalogue d'une agence littéraire croate. (YUG)

■ 235 Couverture d'un catalogue publié pour le 25e anniversaire de la Cinémathèque Québécoise. (CAN)

■ 236-238 From an advertising brochure sent out at Christmas by the printers Heritage Press. Various designers, who are numbered among the printer's clients, recall the Christmas wishes of their childhood. (USA)

■ 239-242 In this brochure the suitability of a paper for various processes is put to the text – by the use of selected photographs, illustrations, and various reproduction techniques. (USA)

■ 236-238 Aus einer zu Weihnachten versandten Werbebroschüre der Druckerei Heritage Press. Verschiedene Designer, die zu den Kunden der Druckerei zählen, erzählen hier von Weihnachtswünschen aus ihrer Kindheit. (USA)

■ 239-242 Anhand von ausgesuchten Photos, Illustrationen und diversen Reproduktionstechniken soll in dieser Broschüre die Eignung einer Papierqualität für diverse Bereiche unter Beweis gestellt werden. (USA)

■ 236-238 Couverture et doubles pages d'une brochure publicitaire de l'imprimerie Heritage Press diffusée à Noël. Divers designers clients de l'entreprise y parlent de ce qu'ils attendaient de Noël quand ils étaient enfants. (USA)

■ 239-242 Un choix de photos et d'illustrations reproduites de différentes manières sert à démontrer dans cette brochure les qualités d'un nouveau papier aux multiples possibilités d'emploi. (USA)

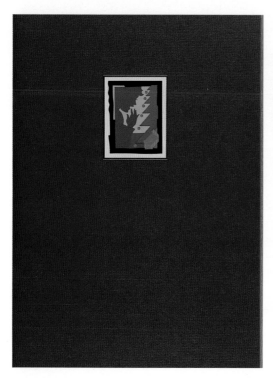

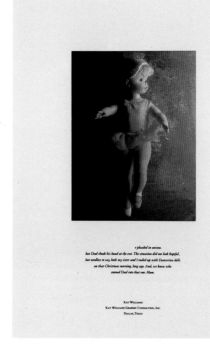

ART DIRECTOR:
KEVIN B. KUESTER
DESIGNER:
KEVIN B. KUESTER/
BOB GOEBEL
ILLUSTRATOR:
REX PETEET
PHOTOGRAPHER:
JOHN WONG/
GREG BOOTH & ASSOCIATES
COPYWRITER:
DICK CINQUINA
AGENCY:
MADSEN AND KUESTER, INC.
CLIENT:
HERITAGE PRESS
■ 236-238

ART DIRECTOR:
RON KOVACH/
KERRY GRADY
DESIGNER:
RON KOVACH/
KERRY GRADY
ILLUSTRATOR:
PAUL RAND (COVER)
VIVIENNE FLESHER 240
PHOTOGRAPHER:
TOM VACK/
CORINNE PFISTER 240
STEPHEN FELDMAN 241
TOM MADAY 242
COPYWRITER:
PHIL MURTAUGH
AGENCY:
MOBIUM
CLIENT:
CONSOLIDATED PAPERS
■ 239-242

ART DIRECTOR:
RON SULLIVAN

DESIGNER:
JON FLAMING

PHOTOGRAPHER:
GERRY KANO

COPYWRITER:
JON FLAMING/
MARK PERKINS

AGENCY:
SULLIVAN PERKINS

CLIENT:
DAN & STEPHANIE PRESCOTT
■ 244, 245

ART DIRECTOR:
SCOTT PARAMSKI

DESIGNER:
SCOTT PARAMSKI

COPYWRITER:
MELINDA MARCUS

STUDIO:
PETERSON & COMPANY

CLIENT:
MARK & KAREN SCHWANDT
▼■ 246, 247

■ 244, 245 Cover in form of a wallet and leporello type of birth announcement. (USA)

■ 246, 247 This announcement of birth can be read from top to bottom and vice versa. (USA)

■ 248-251 Front of a folder and examples of the pages it contains which relate to youth voluntary activities, issued by the Socialist Youth Union of Slovenia. (YUG)

■ 244, 245 Geburtsanzeige: «Das Baby hat einen ganz schönen Einfluss auf Dans und Stephanies Brieftasche.» (USA)

■ 246, 247 Diese Geburtsanzeige lässt sich von oben und unten lesen: «Wow» (Hui) und «Mom» (Mama). (USA)

■ 248-251 Vorderseite einer Mappe und Beispiele der darin enthaltenen Seiten über freiwillige Aktivitäten der Jugendlichen, herausgegeben von einem Jugendverband. (YUG)

■ 244, 245 Faire-part de naissance: «Ce bébé a déjà joliment puisé dans le porte-monnaie de Dan et de Stéphanie.» (USA)

■ 246, 247 Ce faire-part de naissance peut se lire d'en haut ou d'en bas «wow» (oh là là) ou «mom» (maman). (USA)

■ 248-251 Recto d'un dossier et exemples des feuillets qu'il contient. Il y est question des activités bénévoles des jeunes qui font partie de l'association éditant ce dossier. (YUG)

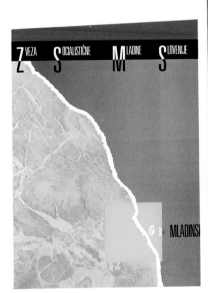
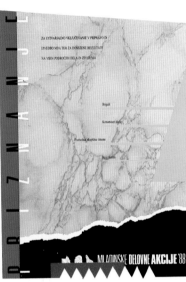

Art Director:
Edi Berk
Designer:
Edi Berk
Studio:
Krog
Client:
Socialist Youth Union of Slovenia
■ 248-251

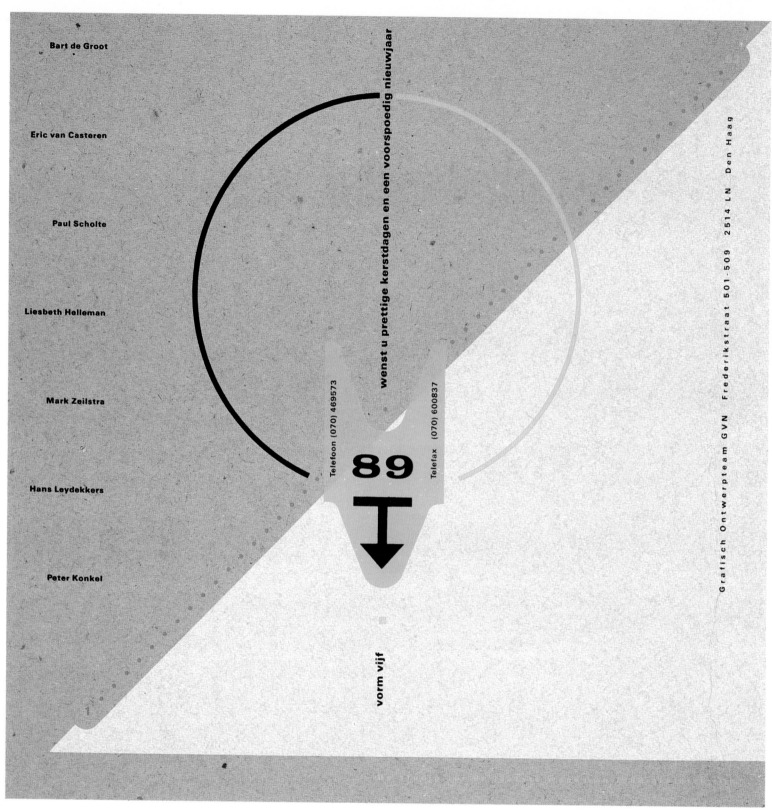

Bart de Groot

Eric van Casteren

Paul Scholte

Liesbeth Helleman

Mark Zeilstra

Hans Leydekkers

Peter Konkel

wenst u prettige kerstdagen en een voorspoedig nieuwjaar

Telefoon (070) 469573

Telefax (070) 600837

89

vorm vijf

Grafisch Ontwerpteam GVN   Frederikstraat 501-509   2514 LN   Den Haag

ART DIRECTOR:
BART DE GROOT
DESIGNER:
PETER KONKEL
AGENCY:
VORM VIJF ONTWERPTEAM BNO
CLIENT:
VORM VIJF ONTWERPTEAM BNO
■ 252

■ 252 Christmas and New Year's greetings from the design studio Vorm Vijf, in the form of a cardboard card. (NLD)

■ 253-256 Front and picture combinations (by folding) of a square brochure to promote the services and supplies available to photographers when renting studio time. (USA)

■ 252 Weihnachts- und Neujahrsgrüsse des Design-Studios Vorm Vijf, in Form einer grossen Kartonkarte. (NLD)

■ 253-256 Vorderseite und die durch die Falttechnik entstehenden Bildkombinationen eines quadratischen Faltprospektes, mit dem ein Photo-Studio wirbt. (USA)

■ 252 Vœux de Noël et Nouvel An du studio de design Vorm Vijf sous forme d'un carton au grand format. (NLD)

■ 253-256 Recto et combinaisons d'images obtenues par le pliage de ce dépliant carré publié par une agence louant un studio photo. (USA)

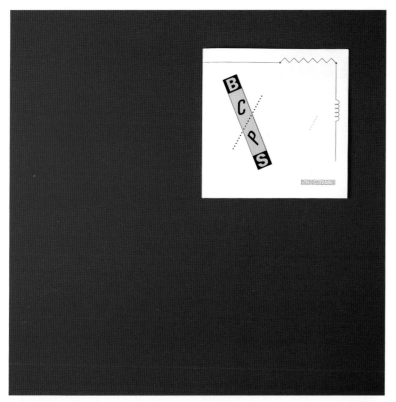

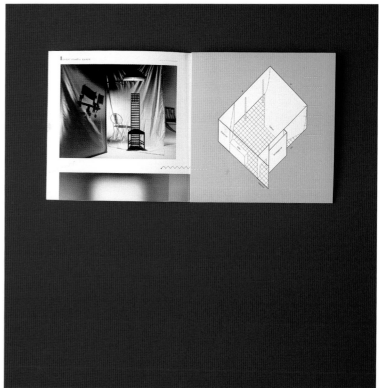

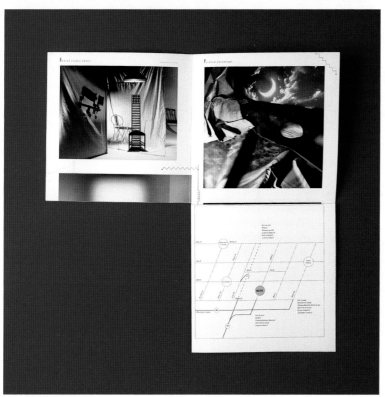

DESIGNER:
LAURA SILVERMAN
PHOTOGRAPHER:
THOMAS WEDELL
STYLIST:
THOMAS WEDELL/
LAURA SILVERMAN
AGENCY:
SKOLOS WEDELL +
RAYNOR, INC.
CLIENT:
BCPS
■ 253-256

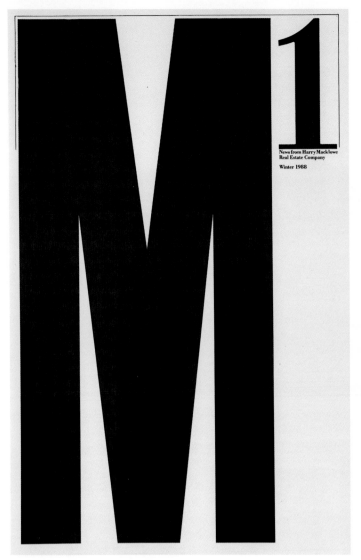

ART DIRECTOR:
MICHAEL BIERUT
DESIGNER:
MICHAEL BIERUT/
ALAN HOPFENSPERGER
AGENCY:
VIGNELLI ASSOCIATES
CLIENT:
MACKLOWE REAL ESTATE
■ 257

ART DIRECTOR:
NICOLAS SIDJAKOV/
JERRY BERMAN
DESIGNER:
NICOLAS SIDJAKOV/
JERRY BERMAN
COPYWRITER:
ALEX CICHY
AGENCY:
SIDJAKOV BERMAN
GOMEZ & PARTNERS
CLIENT:
SIDJAKOV BERMAN
GOMEZ & PARTNERS
■ 258

ART DIRECTOR:
PAT & GREG SAMATA
DESIGNER:
PAT & GREG SAMATA
ILLUSTRATOR:
PAUL THOMPSON
COPYWRITER:
STEVE HUGGINS
AGENCY:
SAMATA ASSOCIATES
CLIENT:
CHICAGO MUSEUM OF
SCIENCE & INDUSTRY
►■ 259-262

■ 257 Cover of the first issue of a quarterly published customer magazine issued by the Harry Macklowe real estate offices. (USA)

■ 258 Announcement in the form of a direct mail poster on the occasion of designer Barry Deutsch entering the firm of Sidjakov Berman Gomez & Partners. (USA)

■ 259-262 From a brochure issued by the Chicago Museum of Science and Industry, with various masks – and texts describing their fascination. (USA)

■ 257 Umschlag der ersten Ausgabe einer vierteljährlich erscheinenden Kundenzeitschrift des Immobilienbüros Harry Macklowe. (USA)

■ 258 Bekanntgabe der Aufnahme des Designers Barry Deutsch in die Firma Sidjakov Berman Gomez & Partners, in Form eines Direct-Mail-Plakates. (USA)

■ 259-262 Aus einer Broschüre des Chicago Museum of Science and Industry mit verschiedenen Masken und Texten über ihre Faszination. (USA)

■ 257 Couverture du premier numéro d'une publication trimestrielle destinée à la clientèle de l'agence immobilière Harry Macklowe. (USA)

■ 258 Annonce du recrutement du designer Barry Deutsch par la société Sidjakov Berman Gomez & Partners, publiée sous forme d'une affiche de publicité directe. (USA)

■ 259-262 Pour une brochure du Chicago Museum of Science and Industry: divers masques dont la fascination est exprimée par les textes accompagnants. (USA)

Show Girl

Lily, she came to Vegas
in the Sixties. Great legs
and a great smile. Now, 23
years later, she's tendin'
bar at a joint down
the Strip.

The legs, they're still
lookin' pretty good. And
that smile still curls up at
the end, y' know?

We get together sometimes
and talk about the old days.

Tammy Faye

Introducing the ultimate
mascara. It doesn't run. It
doesn't hide. It tells the
world—in no uncertain
terms—that you're
someone special.

You can sing in it. You can
cry in it. You can take up
the collection in it.

Tammy Faye Mascara.
Try it. And lash out at
wimpy eyes.

The Dating Game

"For those of you at home
who aren't familiar with
the rules, Bob here is
going to question each of
our three masked ladies
about their education,
morals, and goals in life.

No help from the
audience now.

Let's see if Bob can find
the best looking babe
in the bunch!

The Jetsons
His Daughter
Judy

How time flies. Just a few
short years ago, Judy
Jetson was a perky little
teen. Now she's Judy
Jetson Fleming, mother of
three and head of a Martian
missile project.

Her father George was
magical. In recent years
something seems to have
gone awry.

Enjoy a virgin Pluto.

ART DIRECTOR:
ANTHONY RUTKA
ILLUSTRATOR:
THEO RUDNAK 263
GARY OVERACRE 264
RAFAL OLBINSKI 265
GARY KELLEY 266
PHOTOGRAPHER:
BARRY HOLNIKER
COPYWRITER:
CINDY MORAN
AGENCY:
RUTKA WEADOCK DESIGN
CLIENT:
DREW UNIVERSITY, MADISON
■ 263-267

■ 263-267 Series of brochures for Drew University which give information about the individual study subjects. Shown are the covers and a double spread. (USA)

■ 268-272 Cover and double spreads of an informative brochure about the University of California in Santa Cruz. The illustrated topics are: buildings and equipment for science and research *(269, 272)*, the fine-art subjects *(270)* and the campus itself *(271)*. (USA)

■ 263-267 Prospektreihe der Drew-Universität, die über die einzelnen Studiengebiete informiert. Hier Umschläge und die Gestaltung einer Doppelseite. (USA)

■ 268-272 Umschlag und Doppelseiten einer Informationsbroschüre der University of California in Santa Cruz. Die illustrierten Themen: Gebäude und Einrichtung für Wissenschaft und Forschung *(269, 272)*, die musischen Fächer *(270)* und der Campus selbst *(271)*. (USA)

■ 263-267 Série de prospectus de l'Université Drew renseignant sur les diverses branches: couvertures, conception d'une double page. (USA)

■ 268-272 Couverture et doubles pages d'une brochure d'information de l'Université de Californie à Santa Cruz. Sujets illustrés: les bâtiments et installations pour la science et la recherche *(269,272)*, les branches artistiques *(270)*, le campus *(271)*. (USA)

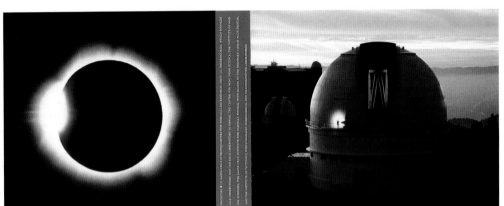

ART DIRECTOR:
LINDA HINRICHS
DESIGNER:
LINDA HINRICHS/
NATALIE KITAMURA
PHOTOGRAPHER:
WILL MOSGROVE (COVER)
ROGER RESSMEYER 269
BARRY ROBINSON 270
DON FUKUDA
(FACULTY PORTRAIT)
AGENCY:
PENTAGRAM DESIGN
CLIENT:
UNIVERSITY OF CALIFORNIA,
SANTA CRUZ
■ 268-272

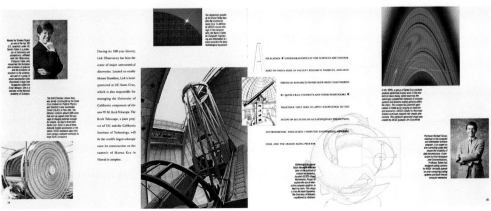

ART DIRECTOR:
WOODY PIRTLE
DESIGNER:
WOODY PIRTLE
ILLUSTRATOR:
WOODY PIRTLE
COPYWRITER:
LALLI ASSOCIATES
AGENCY:
PENTAGRAM DESIGN
CLIENT:
*INTERNATIONAL DESIGN
CONFERENCE IN ASPEN*
■ 273-276

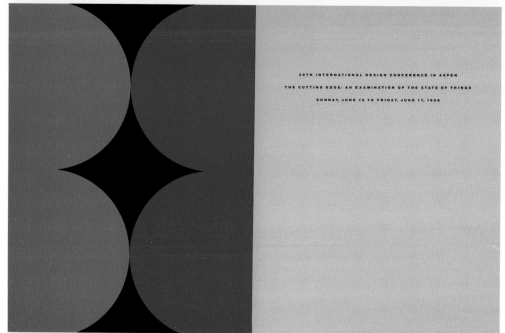

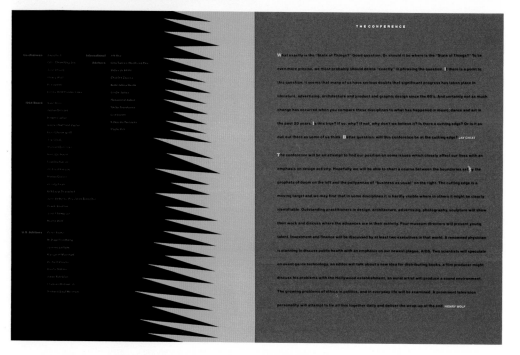

■ 273-276 "The cutting edge" was the subject of the International Design Conference in Aspen 1988. Shown are the cover and double spreads of an informative brochure about the conference. (USA)

■ 277 Invitation to an exhibition of paintings by Braldt Bralds at the Museum of American Illustration. (USA)

■ 273-276 «The cutting edge» (etwa Messers Schneide) war das Thema der International Design Conference in Aspen 1988, von der hier der Umschlag und Doppelseiten einer Informationsbroschüre gezeigt werden. (USA)

■ 277 Einladung zu einer Ausstellung der Bilder von Braldt Bralds im Museum of American Illustration. (USA)

■ 273-276 «Sur le fil du rasoir» (The cutting edge), c'est ainsi que s'intitulait l'International Design Conference d'Aspen 1988. On voit ici la couverture et diverses doubles pages de la brochure d'information. (USA)

■ 277 Invitation à une exposition de tableaux de Braldt Bralds au Museum of American Illustration. (USA)

ART DIRECTOR:
BRALDT BRALDS
DESIGNER:
BRALDT BRALDS
ILLUSTRATOR:
BRALDT BRALDS
AGENCY:
THE ATTIC, INC.
CLIENT:
BRALDT BRALDS
■ 277

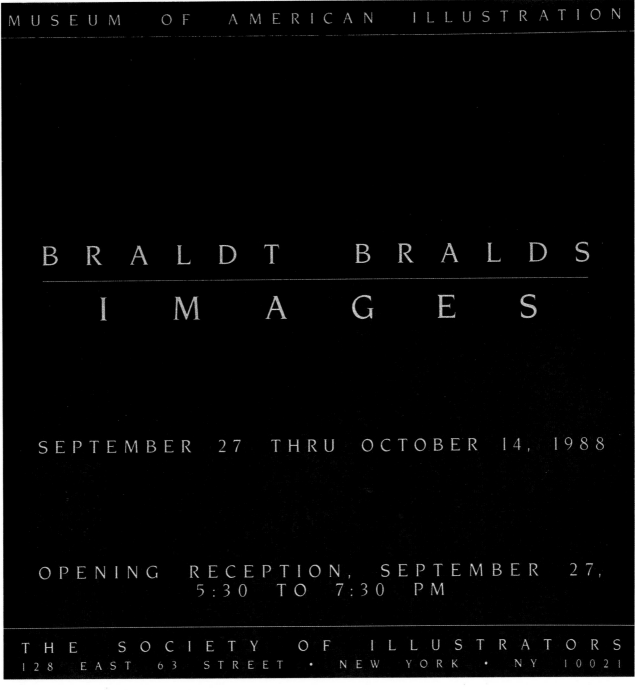

MUSEUM OF AMERICAN ILLUSTRATION

BRALDT BRALDS
IMAGES

SEPTEMBER 27 THRU OCTOBER 14, 1988

OPENING RECEPTION, SEPTEMBER 27, 5:30 TO 7:30 PM

THE SOCIETY OF ILLUSTRATORS
128 EAST 63 STREET · NEW YORK · NY 10021

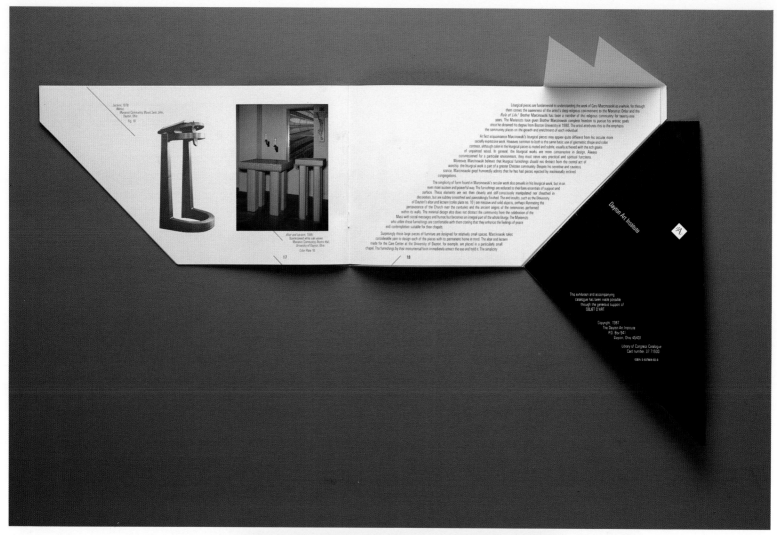

ART DIRECTOR:
JOHN F. EMERY
DESIGNER:
JOHN F. EMERY
PHOTOGRAPHER:
ROLLYN PUTERBAUGH
AGENCY:
VIE DESIGN STUDIOS
CLIENT:
DAYTON ART INSTITUTE
■ 278, 279

■ 278, 279 Open and closed catalog for an exhibition of contemporary furniture at the Dayton Art Institute. (USA)

■ 280 Concertina prospectus for the Paul Koeleman design studio located in Amsterdam. (NLD)

■ 281-283 Cover and double spreads from *Design Quarterly*, a catalog about the Minneapolis Sculpture Garden, issued by the Walker Art Center. Shown are Frank Gehry's "Standing Glass Fish" in the glasshouse and Claes Oldenburg's fountain "Spoonbridge and Cherry". (USA)

■ 278, 279 Auseinander- und zusammengefalteter Katalog für eine Möbelausstellung im Dayton Art Institute. (USA)

■ 280 Leporello-Prospekt des holländischen Design-Studios Paul Koeleman. (NLD)

■ 281-283 Umschlag und Doppelseiten aus *Design Quarterly*, ein vom Walker Art Center herausgegebener Katalog über den Skulptur-Garten in Minneapolis. Hier Frank Gehrys «Standing Glass Fish» im Glashaus und Claes Oldenburgs Brunnen «Spoonbridge and Cherry». (USA)

■ 278, 279 Catalogue plié et déplié pour une exposition de meubles contemporains au Dayton Art Institute. (USA)

■ 280 Dépliant en accordéon du studio de design néerlandais Paul Koeleman. (NLD)

■ 281-283 Couverture et doubles pages d'un catalogue que le Walker Art Center consacre au jardin de sculptures de Minneapolis. On voit ici le «Standing Glass Fish» de Frank Gehry dans la maison de verre et la fontaine de Claes Oldenburg, «Spoonbridge and Cherry». (USA)

A sample portfolio is available upon request. Call 20 - 24 67 33 or write to Studio Paul Koeleman, P.O. Box 16573, 1001 RB Amsterdam, The Netherlands.

ART DIRECTOR:
Paul Koeleman
DESIGNER:
Paul Koeleman
ILLUSTRATOR:
Paul Koeleman
STUDIO:
Paul Koeleman
CLIENT:
Paul Koeleman
■ 280

When the San Francisco landscape architect Barbara Stauffacher Solomon and Michael R. Van Valkenburgh, who teaches at Harvard and practices landscape architecture in Boston, began their collaboration on the Regis Gardens for the three glass houses, their charge was quite direct. Gehry's giant fish was already a "given" for the center house and their first task was to incorporate it into their scheme. Before this project, they had not worked together, but its slightly eccentric character—an interior landscape some 250 feet in length with a fish as its focal point—persuaded them to join forces. They treated Gehry's sculpture with all due reverence, siting it on a high pedestal over a lily pond whose four raised sides are faced with the same speckled red-orange brick used on the floor throughout the building. Around the fish, they planted rows of Washingtonia "feather duster" palms to create a somewhat unlikely Nilotic tableau. Only slightly more solemn in conception, but no less fanciful, was their treatment of the north house, for which they designed the permanent installation. They divided its long interior with four 14 foot high green arches, through which visitors can stroll. These shiny-leafed arches are grown on a steel framework that contains networks of plastic "veins" coursing with hydroponic growing solution; masses of ficus vines, nourished by the solution, intertwine, completely covering their underlying structures. Between these evergreen installations seasonal plantings bloom.

Unlike that of the formally defined north house, the south house space is open and flexible, with sections of its brick floor easily removed for special installations. The first temporary display in the south house was designed by Van Valkenburgh and Solomon and consists of a series of planes, wire screens that march across the floor like elements of a multi-part minimalist sculpture. Over these screens night-flowering jasmine, and sweet peas will climb in riotous profusion during the Conservatory's first year. Subsequent installations in this area will no doubt be less formal, especially those created by artists

who may move large mounds of earth about to form sculptured shapes, and utilize vegetation, rocks, and other natural materials as their media.

But, back to the Conservatory's center house: How did Frank Gehry's see-through leviathan win such a place of honor in the Cowles Conservatory? In 1984, while working with Mildred Friedman, Walker Art Center's curator of design, on a retrospective exhibition of his work, the architect frequently expressed the hope that an outsized glass fish might actually be constructed for the exhibition, particularly as this image was so recurrent throughout his work. A fluent draftsman, Gehry has long been in the habit of roughly sketching the outline of a fish on those areas of his architectural drawings that were not fully resolved, with the idea that he would return to them later. For this exhibition, he proposed to place his fish sculpture in the Walker's high-ceilinged outer lobby, where it would welcome visitors to the museum, but given the probable costs to the museum of fabricating such a creature, the idea was not ardently pursued at that time.

The origins of the piscine image itself, Gehry relates, are in cherished recollections of his Toronto childhood. Raised in an orthodox Jewish family, he recalls his devout grandmother bringing home a live carp from the market each week, before its magical transformation into gefilte fish; for the solemn Friday night dinner. He remembers watching these graceful, foredoomed creatures slosh about in the family bathtub, an ineradicable memory that has manifested itself in many ways throughout his work. His fascination with this theme was vividly evidenced when, in 1983, Gehry was sent a batch of plastic laminate by the Formica Corporation; at the time the firm was encouraging architects to use its product not only in their millwork designs, but to come up with new applications for it. After having the material around for a few months, with no particular idea of how he might use it, Gehry began, somewhat idly, exploring its properties. By breaking the Formica sheets into shards, he arrived at shapes that could

Frank Gehry's 22 foot high *Standing Glass Fish* (1986), which rises from a small pond filled with water lilies, is the focus of the central glass house. The glass "scales" echo the shape of the dried fronds of the palm tree trunks.

ART DIRECTOR:
Nancy Skolos
DESIGNER:
Nancy Skolos/
Craig Davidson
COPYWRITER:
Martin Friedman/
Marc Treib
AGENCY:
Skolos Wedell +
Raynor, Inc.
CLIENT:
Walker Art Center
■ 281-283

On a snowy day in 1987, Oldenburg arrived at the Barnes office, carrying a small model of the fountain. Those in attendance, Barnes, Peter Rothschild, Mildred Friedman, and I, had no notion of what it would look like. With an apprehensive glance around the room, Oldenburg slowly removed the layers of Kleenex, in which it had been swathed to protect it from the weather, to reveal a captivating object that was greeted with broad grins and applause. There it was—a spoon, whose

bowl rested on a small island in the center of a free-form pond and contained a rubicund cherry.

The spoon was not a new leitmotif in Oldenburg's art. A long-time connoisseur of popular culture objects, especially those whose idiosyncratic forms suggested points of departure for his own work, Oldenburg in 1962 had purchased a novelty spoon whose bowl rested on a glob of fake chocolate.

Minneapolis's skyline forms a backdrop for the *Spoonbridge and Cherry* fountain.

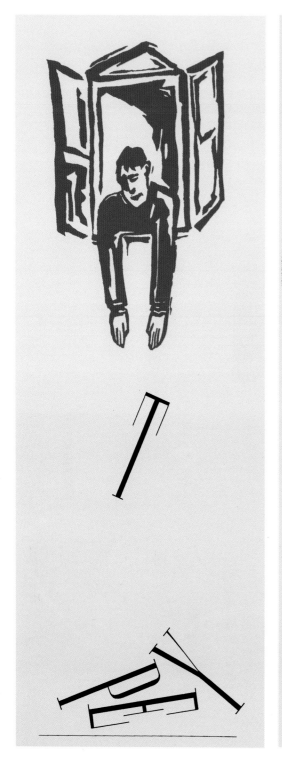

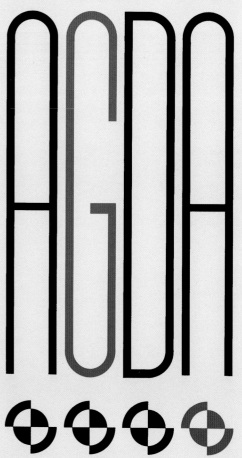

The recently formed Australian Graphic Design Association (AGDA) is calling for membership. Intended as a national association, the AGDA has set as its goal, the task of being the foundation for the graphic design industry. The AGDA will be for design as AWARD is for advertising. If you wish to join, or wish simply to find out more about it, please contact any of the people listed here.

ART DIRECTOR:
VANCE TRIMBLE

DESIGNER:
VANCE TRIMBLE

ILLUSTRATOR:
CHRISTINE HABERSTOCK

AGENCY:
BRÜCKE GROUP

CLIENT:
*AUSTRALIAN TYPE
DIRECTORS CLUB*

◄■ 284, 285

ART DIRECTOR:
VANESSA VARGO

DESIGNER:
VICKY WINTERINGHAM

ILLUSTRATOR:
*VANESSA VARGO/
VICKY WINTERINGHAM*

COPYWRITER:
CANDY VARGO

AGENCY:
V & A VARGO

CLIENT:
NORWICH SCHOOL OF ART

◄■ 286

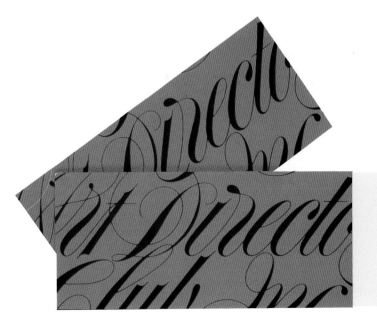

ART DIRECTOR:
FRÉDÉRIC METZ

DESIGNER:
TOM CARNASE (TYPEFACE)

AGENCY:
BRETELLE – UQAM

CLIENT:
*UNIVERSITÉ DU QUÉBEC
À MONTRÉAL/
CENTRE DE DESIGN*

◄■ 287

ART DIRECTOR:
Dan Olson
DESIGNER:
Dan Olson
PHOTOGRAPHER:
Joel Baldwin 289
Thomas Lea 290
Charles Thatcher 291
Greg Pease 292
Steve Brady 295
COPYWRITER:
Jon Anderson
AGENCY:
Dan Olson
CLIENT:
Goldsmith, Agio & Company
■ 289-292, 295

ART DIRECTOR:
David Prout
DESIGNER:
Kurt Ozficici
PHOTOGRAPHER:
David Prout
COPYWRITER:
Gerald Oliver/
Romy Stitt
AGENCY:
Creed Lane Studio
CLIENT:
Rank Xerox (UK) Ltd.
■ 293, 294

Rank Xerox want people to succeed

■ 289-292, 295 Cover and double spreads from a capabilities brochure that positioned Goldsmith, Agio & Company as a sophisticated, established, and successful investment banking firm. (USA)

■ 293, 294 With this graduate recruitment brochure Rank Xerox gives information about career potentialities in their company. Shown are the cover and a double spread. (USA)

■ 289-292, 295 Umschlag und Doppelseiten aus einer Broschüre, in der die Firma Goldsmith, Agio & Company als kultivierte, etablierte und erfolgreiche Bank dargestellt wird, die auf Anlageberatung spezialisiert ist. (USA)

■ 293, 294 Mit dieser Broschüre informiert Rank Xerox Universitätsabgänger über ihre beruflichen Möglichkeiten bei der Firma. Hier der Umschlag und eine Doppelseite. (USA)

■ 289-292, 295 Couverture et doubles pages d'une brochure où la société Goldsmith, Agio & Company apparaît comme une banque sophistiquée, bien implantée, spécialisée dans les placements à haut rendement. (USA)

■ 293, 294 Par cette brochure, Rank Xerox informe les futurs diplômés des universités des chances de carrière dans ce géant de la bureautique. (USA)

Order and simplification are vital first steps toward the completion of any successful financial deal. In practically every investment banking situation, order creates opportunities.

Noted German novelist Thomas Mann once wrote, "Order and simplification are the first steps toward the mastery of a subject." At Goldsmith, Agio & Company, order and simplification are vital first steps toward a successful deal. Over the years, we've built a solid reputation for planning every step in the transaction process carefully. And following through with laser-like precision. We start by helping our clients determine specific objectives. We then analyze our detailed, computerized records of potential acquirors worldwide. We screen prospective buyers according to criteria that meet our client's objectives. We negotiate firmly and consistently, advising our client at each decision point. In the end, this precise, methodical approach results in purchase price premiums that are well in excess of established norms.

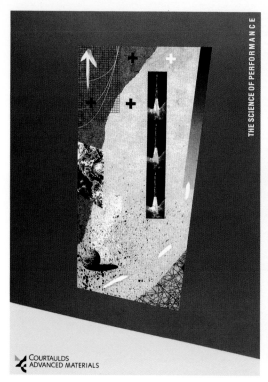

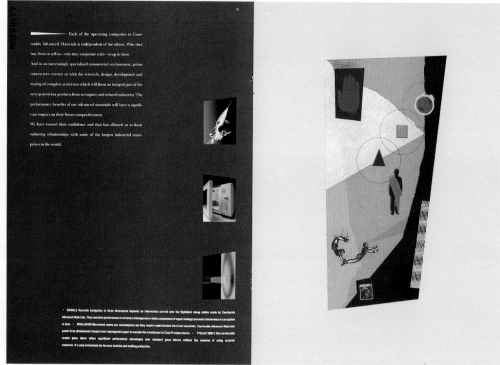

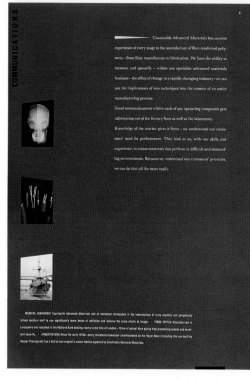

COURTAULDS
ADVANCED MATERIALS

ART DIRECTOR:
JIM NORTHOVER
DESIGNER:
NICK PUGH
ILLUSTRATOR:
NICK PUGH
COPYWRITER:
GREEN ROACH LIMITED
AGENCY:
LLOYD NORTHOVER LIMITED
CLIENT:
*COURTAULDS ADVANCED
MATERIALS*
■ 296-298

■ 296-298 From a corporate brochure for the high performance products sector of the chemical firm Courtaulds. The products are used in space travel, shipping, racing, etc. (GBR)

■ 299-301 The southwestern image of the new large-scale apartment complex Villa Terraza (Los Angeles) is reinforced in this leasing brochure, from which we show the cover and two double spreads. (USA)

■ 296-298 Aus einer Broschüre über Produkte der Chemiewerke Courtaulds, die in der Raumfahrt, der Schifffahrt, im Rennsport etc. Anwendung finden. (GBR)

■ 299-301 Das südwestliche Image des neuen Wohnkomplexes Villa Terraza in Los Angeles ist das zentrale Thema dieser Broschüre, von welcher der Umschlag und zwei Doppelseiten gezeigt sind. (USA)

■ 296-298 Couverture et doubles pages d'une brochure sur les produits du groupe chimique Courtaulds utilisés dans l'espace, dans la navigation, la course automobile, etc. (GBR)

■ 299-301 L'image typique du sud-ouest propre au nouvel ensemble résidentiel Villa Terraza de Los Angeles constitue le thème central de cette brochure dont nous reproduisons ici la couverture et deux doubles pages. (USA)

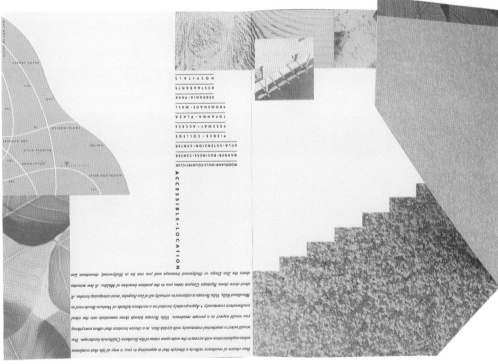

ART DIRECTOR:
B.J. KRIVANEK
DESIGNER:
TOM ROGERS/
BARBARA RIECHERS
ILLUSTRATOR:
NICK SPRINGETT
COPYWRITER:
BARBARA RIECHERS
AGENCY:
B.J. KRIVANEK ART & DESIGN
CLIENT:
GBW PROPERTIES, INC.
■ 299-301

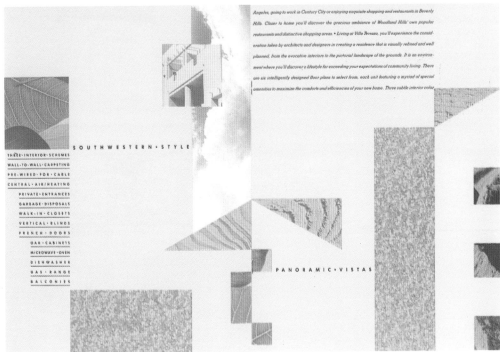

■ 302-305 Cover and double spreads from the menu of the Black Eyed Pea Restaurant in Dallas. (USA)

■ 306, 307 Cover with visible chapter index, and a double spread from a catalog presenting cruises with the Royal Viking Line. (USA)

■ 308 Two-part invitation to an event organized by the Children's Museum of Manhattan which also announces its new location. (USA)

■ 302-305 Umschlag und Doppelseiten aus der Speisekarte des Restaurants Black Eyed Pea in Dallas. (USA)

■ 306, 307 Umschlag mit sichtbarem Kapitelindex und eine Doppelseite aus einem Katalog für Kreuzfahrten mit der Royal Viking Line. (USA)

■ 308 Zweiteilige Einladung zu einer Veranstaltung des Kindermuseums in Manhattan, das seinen neuen Standort bekanntgeben möchte. (USA)

■ 302-305 Couverture et doubles pages du menu conçu pour le restaurant Black Eyed Pea de Dallas. (USA)

■ 306, 307 Couverture à l'index visible (division par chapitres) et page double d'un catalogue des croisières organisées par la Royal Viking Line. (USA)

■ 308 Invitation en deux parties à une manifestation organisée au Musée de l'enfance de Manhattan pour faire connaître le site où il vient de s'installer. (USA)

ART DIRECTOR:
DANNY KAMERATH
DESIGNER:
BRUCE WYNNE-JONES
COPYWRITER:
BRUCE WYNNE-JONES/
MARK SMITH
AGENCY:
EAST TEXAS STATE
UNIVERSITY
CLIENT:
BLACK EYED PEA RESTAURANT
■ 302-305

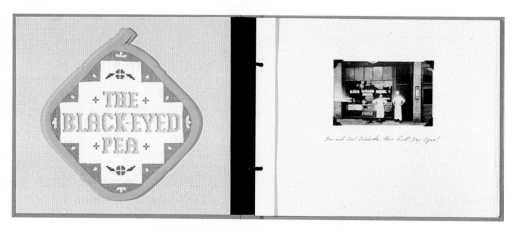

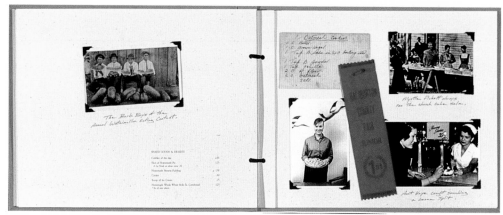

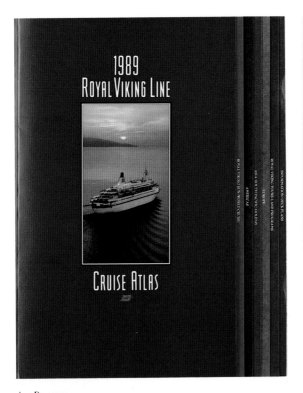

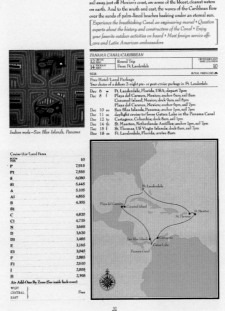

ART DIRECTOR:
KIT HINRICHS
DESIGNER:
KIT HINRICHS/
KAREN BERNDT/
GWYN SMITH
COPYWRITER:
GEORGE CRUYS
AGENCY:
PENTAGRAM DESIGN
CLIENT:
ROYAL VIKING LINE
■ 306, 307

ART DIRECTOR:
MICHAEL BIERUT
DESIGNER:
MICHAEL BIERUT/
ALAN HOPFENSPERGER
AGENCY:
VIGNELLI ASSOCIATES
CLIENT:
CHILDREN'S MUSEUM OF
MANHATTAN
▼■ 308

ART DIRECTOR:
CHARLES S. ANDERSON/
JOE DUFFY
DESIGNER:
CHARLES S. ANDERSON/
SARA LEDGARD
PHOTOGRAPHER:
GARY MCCOY
COPYWRITER:
CHUCK CARLSON
AGENCY:
THE DUFFY DESIGN GROUP
CLIENT:
DORSEY & WHITNEY
■ 309, 310

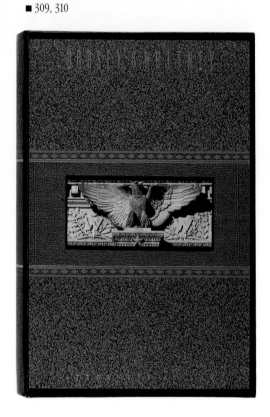

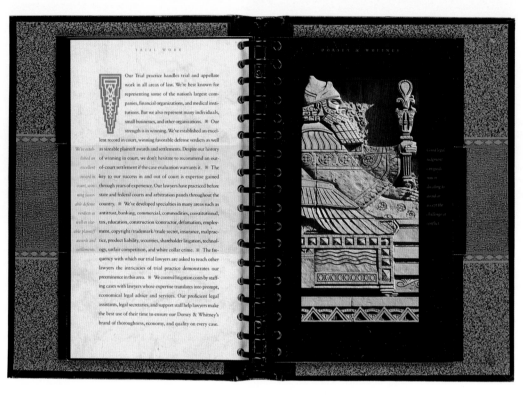

■ 309, 310 Cover and example of the double spreads from a hard-cover, ring-bound capability brochure for the attorneys Dorsey & Whitney. (USA)

■ 309, 310 Fester Einband und Doppelseite aus einem Ringordner, mit dem die Anwaltsfirma Dorsey & Whitney über ihre Fachbereiche und Dienste informiert. (USA)

■ 309, 310 Reliure rigide et page double type d'un classeur à anneaux où l'étude d'avocats Dorsey & Whitney renseigne sur sa spécialisation et ses services. (USA)

REDAKTIONELLES DESIGN

■ 311-314 Covers of the magazine *Almanac* on the following subjects: Hollywood, environmental sculptor Christo,
the American designer Raymond Loewy. *314* shows the
contents page of the Hollywood edition. (USA)

■ 311-314 Umschläge des Magazins *Almanac* zu folgenden
Themen: Hollywood, Verpackungskünstler Christo, der
amerikanische Designer Raymond Loewy. *314* zeigt die
Inhaltsseite der Hollywood-Ausgabe. (USA)

■ 311-314 Couvertures du magazine *Almanac* vouées aux
sujets suivants: Hollywood, l'as de l'emballage de sites
Christo, le designer américain Raymond Loewy. *314* est la
page de sommaire de l'édition de Hollywood. (USA)

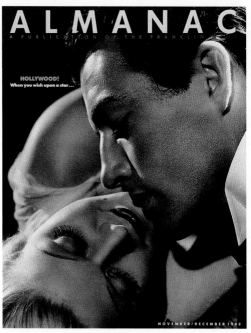

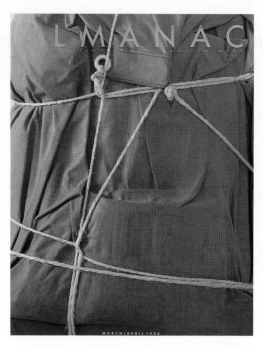

ART DIRECTOR:
BRIDGET DESOCIO
DESIGNER:
BRIDGET DESOCIO
PHOTOGRAPHER:
TED ALLEN 311
MARK LYON 312
RAYMOND LOEWY 313
GEORGE HURRELL 314
PUBLISHER:
THE FRANKLIN MINT ALMANAC
■ 311-314

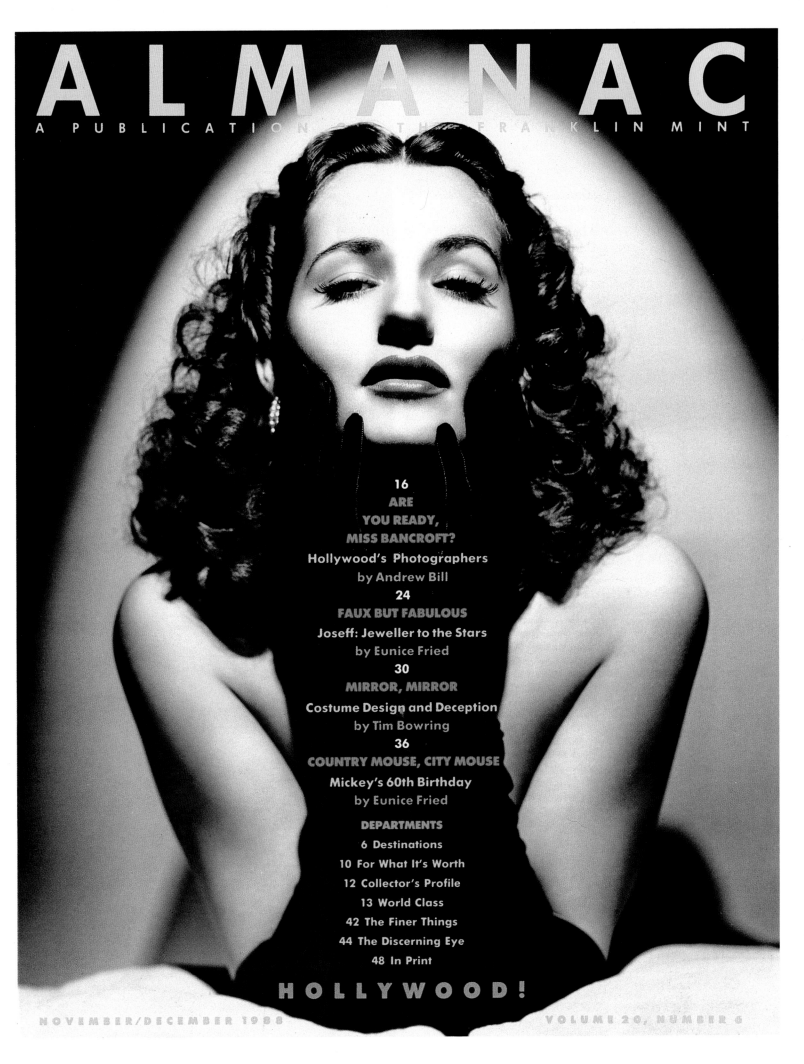

ALMANAC

A PUBLICATION OF THE FRANKLIN MINT

HOLLYWOOD!

NOVEMBER/DECEMBER 1988 · VOLUME 20, NUMBER 6

ACCESS

ACCESS

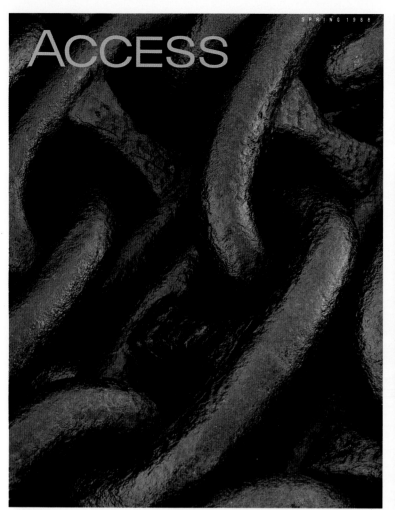

SOUL OF A SUBARU

A JAPANESE CAR COMPANY SHIFTS ITS VOICE

The building is a blocky, bold monolith of angles, edges and rectangles. If the soul of an automobile has colors, they're all here, on the exterior and throughout the carpets, walls and fixtures of the new office complex. Slate gray like cast aluminum. A charcoal hue befitting an engine block. Black as flat as anodized body trim. The gleaming mirror-metal of chrome. Glassy expanses like great windshields. ○ Inside, an atrium pierces the heart of the modern seven-story building—a huge, cylindrical elevator tower tying the levels together. As you peer up from the lobby, it makes the office complex look eerily as though it's a luxurious gantry for a rocket awaiting

AND DATA SYSTEM INTO FOUR-WHEEL DRIVE.

countdown. ○ Actually it's the new headquarters of Subaru of America, in Cherry Hill, New Jersey. Subaru is the U.S. importer of some unusual Japanese cars—a company that has carved out a tidy niche for itself in a crowded automotive market by dealing in distinctive small cars that some still think "odd and somewhat quirky," in the words of Subaru Director of Public Relations Fred Heiler. ○ Others, however, increasingly regard Subaru as the progenitor of one of the hotter new automotive markets: on-road passenger cars with four-wheel drive (4WD). Off-road four-wheeling has been around for decades—Jeeps, fat-tired pickups and the like—but only in the last half-dozen years has everybody from Porsche to Ford begun offering the option of powering all four corners of pure highway machinery.

6

7

ART DIRECTOR:
BRYAN L. PETERSON
DESIGNER:
BRYAN L. PETERSON
PHOTOGRAPHER:
GARY MCCOY 315
TOM RYAN 316, 317
AGENCY:
PETERSON & COMPANY
PUBLISHER:
NORTHERN TELECOM
◀■ 315-317

DESIGNER:
JEAN CLAUDE SUARES
ILLUSTRATOR:
JEAN CLAUDE SUARES 318
PHOTOGRAPHER:
HERB RITTS 319
PUBLISHER:
7 DAYS
▼■ 318, 319

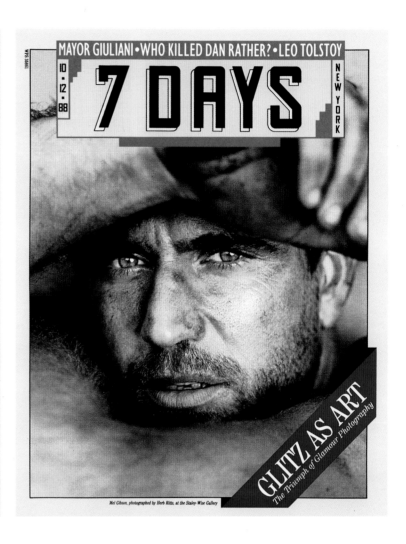

315-317 Covers and double spread from *Access*, the house organ of Northern Telecom. Topics of these pages are the firm's customers, i.e. the shipping industry *(315)* and *Mitsubishi* automobiles *(316, 317)*. (USA)

318, 319 Covers of the New York magazine *7 Days*. Shown is a portrait of actor Mel Gibson and a glance into the future of Manhattan. (USA)

315-317 Umschläge und eine Doppelseite aus *Access*, der Hauszeitschrift von Northern Telecom. Themen dieser Seiten sind Kunden der Firma: aus der Schiffahrt *(315)* und *Mitsubishi*-Automobile *(316, 317)*. (USA)

318, 319 Umschläge des New Yorker Magazins *7 Days*. Hier ein Porträt des Schauspielers Mel Gibson und ein Blick in die Zukunft Manhattans. (USA)

315-317 Couvertures et double page d'*Access*, le magazine d'entreprise de Northern Telecom. Les sujets ont trait aux clients du groupe: les armateurs *(315)*, les contructeurs automobiles, en l'occurence *Mitsubishi (316, 317)*. (USA)

318, 319 Couvertures du magazine new-yorkais *7 Days*, avec un portrait de l'acteur Mel Gibson et une vue futuriste de Manhattan. (USA)

■ 320-335 Covers and double spreads from various issues of the *Frankfurter Allgemeine Magazin*. The subjects of the cover illustrations are: navy fashion, the opera in Sydney, Swiss banks, and jazz. The subjects of the double spreads: the history of the Ku Klux Klan, problems with neighbors, a humorous story from old Egypt, the success series of heavyweight boxer Mike Tyson, thoughts on shaving and its history, and golf. (GER)

■ 320-335 Umschläge und Doppelseiten aus verschiedenen Ausgaben des *Frankfurter Allgemeine Magazins*. Die Themen der Umschlagillustrationen: Matrosenmode, die Oper in Sydney, die Schweizer Banken, Jazz. Die Themen der Doppelseiten: Die Geschichte des Ku-Klux-Klan; Probleme mit Nachbarn; eine humorvolle Geschichte aus dem alten Ägypten; Schwergewichtler Mike Tyson; Gedanken und Geschichtliches über das Rasieren; Golf. (GER)

■ 320-335 Couvertures et doubles page de divers numéros du *Frankfurter Allgemeine Magazin*. Les illustrations de couverture ont pour thème: la mode matelot, l'opéra à Sydney, les banques suisses, le jazz. Les doubles pages concernent: l'histoire du ku-klux-klan, les problèmes de voisinage, une histoire amusante empruntée à l'antiquité égyptienne, les succès du poids lourd Mike Tyson, des réflexions et rappels historiques sur l'art du rasage, le golf. (GER)

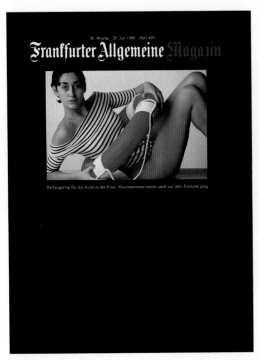

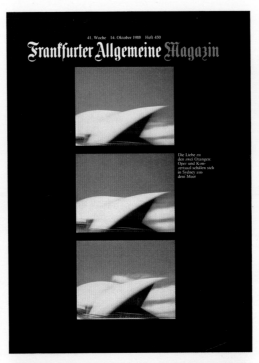

ART DIRECTOR:
HANS-GEORG POSPISCHIL
PHOTOGRAPHER:
FRANK HORVAT
STEPHEN ERFURT
ILLUSTRATOR:
SEYMOUR CHWAST
PUBLISHER:
FRANKFURTER ALLGEMEINE
ZEITUNG GMBH
■ 320-335

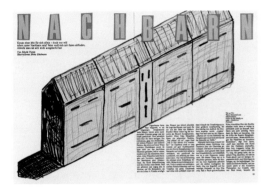

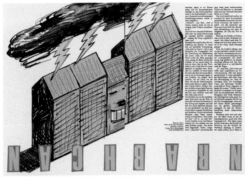

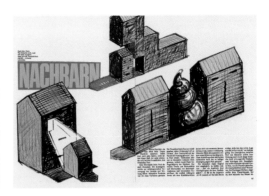

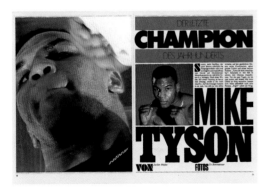

ILLUSTRATOR:
PAOLA PIGLIA

ILLUSTRATOR:
HEINZ EDELMANN

ILLUSTRATOR:
SEYMOUR CHWAST

PHOTOGRAPHER:
CO RENTMEESTER

ILLUSTRATOR:
PAOLA PIGLIA

ILLUSTRATOR:
HEINZ EDELMANN

ILLUSTRATOR:
SEYMOUR CHWAST

PHOTOGRAPHER:
LILIAN BIRNBAUM

ILLUSTRATOR:
PAOLA PIGLIA

ILLUSTRATOR:
HEINZ EDELMANN

ILLUSTRATOR:
SEYMOUR CHWAST

ILLUSTRATOR:
CHRISTOPH BLUMRICH

ILLUSTRATOR:
JEFF JACKSON
ILLUSTRATOR:
HEINZ EDELMANN
ILLUSTRATOR:
HEINZ EDELMANN

ILLUSTRATOR:
HEINZ EDELMANN
PHOTOGRAPHER:
ABE FRAJNDLICH
PHOTOGRAPHER:
WOLFGANG WESENER

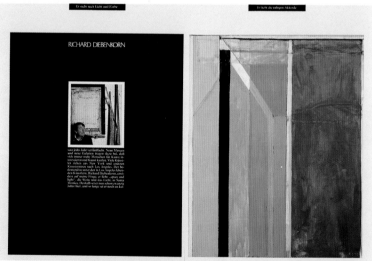

Konzentration auf ein Spiel mit geometrischer Klarheit: „Die vielleicht schwierigste Anwendung klassischer Mechanik in unserer Zeit", sagt der amerikanische Physiker Jearl Walker

Von Rolf Heggen
Illustrationen Brad Holland

BALL UND BANDE

Nach dem festlichen Diner bittet der Weltmeister feierlich zu Tisch: Billard um halb elf mit Raymond Ceulemans in der getäfelten Bibliothek des Kronberger Schloßhotels. Der flämische Magier arbeitet auf doppeltem Schieferboden, der mit einem sumpfgrünen Tuch überzogen ist. Den langen Zauberstab schwenkt er wie einen Taktstock bei rasch folgenden Einsätzen: Da, da, dort, dann hier – und Karambolage. Und, hastdunichtgesehen, rast die Kugel auch schon von Bande zu Bande, vor, zurück, kreuz und quer, scheinbar willkürlich und doch genau auf dem zuvor beschriebenen Zickzackkurs, erst sehr schnell

BILLARD

ART DIRECTOR:
HANS-GEORG POSPISCHIL
ILLUSTRATOR:
BRAD HOLLAND
PUBLISHER:
FRANKFURTER ALLGEMEINE
ZEITUNG GMBH
■ 336-342

■ 336-342 Introductory double spreads to features in the *Frankfurter Allgemeine Magazin* about the pleasures of bathing, the magic of the firmament, the students' revolt in 1968 in Germany, the American painter Richard Diebenkorn, monsters, the success of Julio Iglesias (who sings about love, luck, and the homeland), and billiards. (GER)

■ 336-342 Doppelseiten zu Beiträgen im *Frankfurter Allgemeine Magazin* über die Freuden des Badens; die Magie des Sternenhimmels; die Studentenunruhen von 1968; den amerikanischen Maler Richard Diebenkorn; Monster und Ungeheuer; den Erfolg des von Liebe, Glück und Heimat singenden Julio Iglesias; Billard. (GER)

■ 336-342 Doubles pages initiales d'articles parus dans le *Frankfurter Allgemeine Magazin:* les plaisirs du bain, la magie d'un ciel étoilé, les étudiants révoltés de 1968, le peintre américain Richard Diebenkorn, les monstres, le succès de Julio Iglesias, chanteur de l'amour, du bonheur et de la terre natale, les plaisirs du billard. (GER)

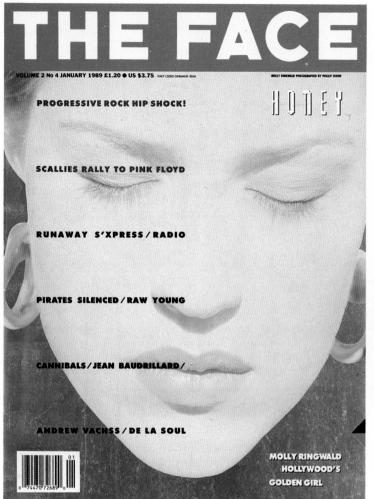

ART DIRECTOR:
Phil Bicker
PHOTOGRAPHER:
Phillip Dixon
PUBLISHER:
The Face
■ 343

ART DIRECTOR:
Hans Van Blommestein
PHOTOGRAPHER:
Thierry Mugler
PUBLISHER:
De Geillustreerde Pers B.V.
■ 344

ART DIRECTOR:
Sergio Sartori
DESIGNER:
Sergio Sartori
ILLUSTRATOR:
Giulia Orecchia
PHOTOGRAPHER:
Jeff Manzetti
STUDIO:
Sergio Sartori
PUBLISHER:
Nuova ERI Edizioni RAI
►■ 345

■ 343 Molly Ringwald, one of Hollywood's darling child stars, who grew up to be a serious actress, on the cover of *The Face* magazine. (GBR)

■ 344 Cover of an issue of the Dutch magazine *Avenue* with a special section on fashion. Shown is a designer outfit by Thierry Mugler up in New York's lofty heights. (NLD)

■ 345 Cover of *King,* a magazine published in Italy for the man of today. (ITA)

■ 343 Molly Ringwald, eines von Hollywoods Lieblingskindern, das sich zu einer ernsthaften Schauspielerin entwickelt hat, auf dem Umschlag von *The Face.* (GBR)

■ 344 Umschlag einer Ausgabe des holländischen Magazins *Avenue* mit einem Sonderteil über Mode. Hier ein Modell von Thierry Mugler in New Yorks luftigen Höhen. (NLD)

■ 345 Umschlag von *King,* einer Zeitschrift für den Mann von heute. (ITA)

■ 343 Molly Ringwald, l'une des enfants chéries de Hollywood devenue une actrice de talent, illustre cette couverture du magazine *The Face.* (GBR)

■ 344 Couverture d'un numéro du magazine hollandais *Avenue* comportant une section modes: modèle de Thierry Mugler en plein ciel de New York. (NLD)

■ 345 Couverture de *King,* un magazine pour l'homme d'aujourd'hui. (ITA)

KUG

FENOMENOLOGIA DELL'UOMO QUOTIDIANO

ESCLUSIVO

DALL'ALBUM SEGRETO
DI HITLER: «LASCIATE
CHE I BIMBI
VENGANO
A ME...»

NOSTALGIA CANAGLIA

RAPPORTO SU NEO-NAZISTI
E NUOVA DESTRA:
S'AVANZANO STRANI SOLDATI

SORPRENDENTE

BIONDE, BRUNE, GIOVANI E
VECCHIE; MAURIZIO
COSTANZO SI CONFESSA:
«AMORE E PETTING»

APPUNTAMENTI

Noi, due sconosciuti
PROBLEMA:
*dati 6 giubbotti,
18 pantaloni,
e gilet, polo,
camicie...*

DICONO CHE LUI
ABBIA IN TESTA SOLO
UNA «COSA».
NON È VERO: PIÙ «COSE».
LA DONNA
DESIDERIO,
QUELLA FAMIGLIA,
INNOCENZA,
FOLLIA... UN UOMO
quattro DONNE

NUOVA ERI EDIZIONI RAI • N. 3 • MAGGIO 1988 • L. 5000

THE
TAR
PIT
TEAHOUSE
LACMA

AND THE PAVILION OKLAHOMA CRUDE BUILT

BY AARON BETSKY

OPPOSITE PAGE: THE WEST WING OF LACMA'S NEW PAVILION FOR JAPANESE ART. THIS PAGE, FROM LEFT: 6TH-CENTURY "SEATED WARRIOR," SAMURAI KIMONO AND WOMAN'S KIMONO, BOTH EARLY 19TH CENTURY.

THE LOS ANGELES COUNTY MUSEUM OF ART, PERHAPS THE city's only populist metropolitan cultural center, seems to enjoy flirting with bad taste. Its collections are housed in what amounts to a grandiose stage set decorated with fragments of overdone architecture from three decades. It is the museum that almost became Armand Hammer's private mausoleum; the exhibition hall for the Norman Rockwell–like "Helga Pictures"; the only museum to have a room named after a comedian (Steve Martin, one of its greatest benefactors); and possibly the only institution to have grafted a postmodern mannerist addition onto a modern mannerist building. Now it has developed what may be the most appropriate form for the economics of the Pacific Rim: the Pavilion for Japanese Art.

The new building, also known as the Shin'enkan Pavilion after the collection it houses, is a wild excursion into cantilevered curves, plastic panels, fake shrines and hotel-lobby galleries. The last design initiated by "the Pied Piper from Norman" (Oklahoma, that is), the late Bruce Goff, the Pavilion is home for some 300 screens and scroll paintings from the Edo period (1615–1868), art long considered decadent, mannerist and populist itself. The building, the collection and the

GREY CRAWFORD

176

Still, Goff does have his defenders, especially among his clients (fortunately), who have been known to meet at churchlike socials with the shapes of their respective houses pinned to their lapels. Postmodern herald Charles Jencks calls Goff "the poet of the unredeemable," and the late champion of populist architecture, Reyner Banham, once described Goff as a "hundred-percent pure, good-to-the-last-drop, rolled-from-better-leaf American architect," which is as close as that distinguished historian ever came to outright adulation.

Unfortunately, the new Pavilion for Japanese Art as it now stands is a compromise. Goff originally designed the Shin'enkan Pavilion for a site in Bartlesville, Oklahoma, then adjusted it for LACMA prior to his death in 1982. One of his students, Bart Prince, flipped the plan around, adapting it to its new location, and finished the design. California earthquake and access codes, economics and the mysterious motives of major art museums then conspired to turn Goff's imaginative dragon into a mastodon that you only wish, to paraphrase another LACMA critic, would sink back into the primeval muck over which it stands.

Stands over and not on or in, because the building doesn't appear to sit on that ground. But neither does it soar as loftily above its site as Goff's first drawings implied it would. A series of elevated walkways connect the Pavilion to the rest of the museum at plaza level, so that you enter by a kind of freeway off-ramp, proceeding past a series of ersatz-Japanese gardens and walls beneath green stucco panels. There are two wings, in both senses of the word, held between two massive stone-clad elevator and stair towers. The roofs of the wings are suspended from wires tied into a network of crisscrossing concrete curves and posts. The exterior walls are largely covered with translucent panels called Kalwall. This is the same material used to cover the outdoor courtyard of the museum, but in the pavilion it is intended to look like translucent shoji screens.

179

ART DIRECTOR:
Marilyn Babcock
DESIGNER:
Michael Brock/
Marilyn Babcock
PHOTOGRAPHER:
Grey Crawford
AGENCY:
Michael Brock Design
PUBLISHER:
L.A. Style, Inc.
■ 346

ART DIRECTOR:
Norman Sunshine
PHOTOGRAPHER:
Gideon Lewin
PUBLISHER:
Lear Publishing, Inc.
▼■ 347, 348

GLUT
&
GLAMOUR

A block of ancient rusted cars, stacked one upon the other, would not likely catch our eye, case-hardened to glut as we are. Nor would a web of high-tension wires struck against a disinterested sky compel us to transfer the image to film. Yet the artist, blessed with a sight and sensibility other than yours or mine, sees graphic grist in masses, in too much of things. LEAR'S design director makes us notice by juxtaposing high-fashion glamour page for page with glut.

Photographs and Technique by
GIDEON LEWIN

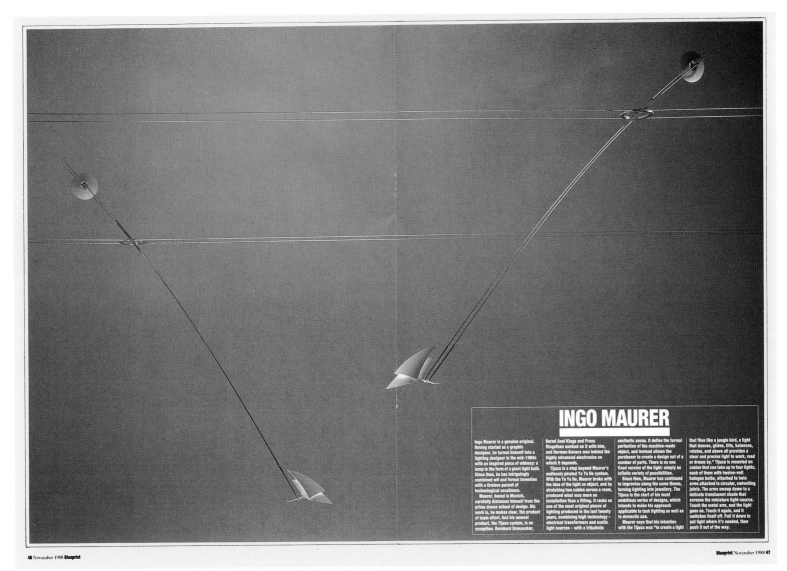

ART DIRECTOR:
*STEPHEN COATES/
SIMON ESTERSON*
DESIGNER:
STEPHEN COATES
PUBLISHER:
WORDSEARCH LTD.
■ 349

■ 346 Double spread from the magazine *L.A. Style* for an article about a new pavilion for Japanese art at the Los Angeles County Museum of Art. (USA)

■ 347, 348 "Glut Glamour", double spreads from the magazine *Lear's*. (USA)

■ 349 Designer Ingo Maurer's Ya Ya Ho light system is the subject on this double spread from *Blueprint*. (GBR)

■ 346 Doppelseite aus dem Magazin *L. A. Style* für einen Artikel über einen neuen Pavillon für Japanische Kunst des Los Angeles County Museum of Art. (USA)

■ 347, 348 «Überfluss und Glamour», Doppelseiten aus der Zeitschrift *Lear's*. (USA)

■ 349 Designer Ingo Maurers Ya-Ya-Ho-Lichtsystem ist Gegenstand dieser Doppelseite aus *Blueprint*. (GBR)

■ 346 Double page du magazine *L. A. Style* pour un article sur un nouveau pavilion d'art japonais dont vient de se doter le Los Angeles County Museum of Art. (USA)

■ 347, 348 «Abondance et glamour» – doubles pages du magazine *Lear's*. (USA)

■ 349 Cette double page de *Blueprint* a pour sujet le système lumineux Ya-Ya-Ho du designer Ingo Maurer. (GBR)

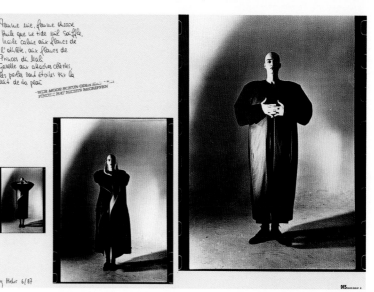

ART DIRECTOR:
Stephan Auer/
Norbert Herold/
Christian Kurz/
Achim Milkau/
Ralph Taubenberger
PHOTOGRAPHER:
Regine Schwarz/
Jan Michael 350
Jörg Hieber 351
PUBLISHER:
Verlag Design + Technik
■ 350-352

KULT UND COLA

GEFÜHL UND EINFÜHLUNGSVERMÖGEN AUF DER SUCHE NACH DEM EIGENEN WEG. SO VERKEHRT KANN DAS NICHT SEIN – WIE DIE FOLGENDEN SEITEN BEWEISEN ...

ASSI-BÖRSE: COME ON AND CALL
„ASSIS ZU HABEN – UND ZWAR GUTE": DAS IST, ETWAS SALOPP FORMULIERT, DIE IDEE EINER PFIFFIGEN INITIATIVE DER BAYERISCHEN STAATSLEHRANSTALT. DIE AUSGANGSSITUATION: JEDES JAHR IM JULI VERLASSEN RUND 30 ABSOLVENTEN DIE MÜNCHENER FOTOSCHULE. FÜR VIELE DER YOUNGSTER BEGINNT DANN DIE SUCHE NACH EINER GEEIGNETEN ASSISTENTEN-STELLE IN DEN BEREICHEN MODE, STILLIFE, WERBUNG, PEOPLE SOWIE JOURNALISMUS, PORTRAIT UND THEATERFOTOGRAFIE. WAS GAR NICHT SO EINFACH IST, DENN GUTE ASSIS SUCHEN GUTE BOSSE, KEINE DUMMEN SCHINDER.
UMGEKEHRT SIEHT'S ÄHNLICH AUS: GUTE FOTODESIGNER WOLLEN GUT GESCHULTE ASSISTENTEN, KEINE DILETTANTEN ODER GELANGWEILTEN KIDS. SIE BRAUCHEN LEUTE, DIE RECHTZEITIG MAGAZINE LADEN, SELBSTÄNDIG DAS RICHTIGE GRUNDLICHT BAUEN UND AUCH OHNE EXTRA-EINLADUNG FÜR FRISCHEN KAFFEE SORGEN. DESHALB DAS ANGEBOT DER SCHULE: RUFEN SIE AN UND BESCHREIBEN SIE IHREN „TRAUM-ASSISTENTEN". UM MISSVERSTÄNDNISSEN VORZUBEUGEN: DAS GANZE IST KEIN „SKLAVEN-HANDEL", SONDERN EHER EIN „HEIRATSMARKT FÜR EHEN AUF ZEIT", DIE BEIDEN SEITEN VIEL BRINGEN KÖNNEN. DEM ARRIVIERTEN FOTODESIGNER, WEIL IHM EIN HERVORRAGEND AUSGEBILDETER ASSI ZUR SEITE STEHT, DEN ER SICH NICHT MÜHSAM AUS DER FLUT (VIELFACH UNQUALIFIZIERTER) BEWERBER HERAUSSUCHEN MUSS, DIE IHM IMMER WIEDER DIE BUDE EINRENNEN. DEM ASSI SOWIESO, WEIL ER NOCH EINE MENGE PRAXIS BRAUCHT, BIS ER IM JOB AUF EIGENEN FÜSSEN STEHEN KANN.
WIE GESAGT: RUFEN SIE DIE SCHULE IN DER ZEIT VON ANFANG APRIL BIS ENDE MAI EINFACH 'MAL AN. ALS „EHEVERMITTLER" STEHEN DIE DOZENTEN KLAUS DEMUTH (WERBUNG), HADO PRÜTZMANN (MODE, PORTRAIT), DIETER HINRICHS (JOURNALISMUS) UND ROBERT BRAUNMÜLLER (ARCHITEKTUR/INDUSTRIE) GERNE ZU DIENSTEN. UND ZU GUTER LETZT NOCH SCHNELL DIE NUMMER: 0 89/34 76 73. COME ON AND CALL THEM! JT

„JUNGE WILDE", WO VIELE SIE NICHT UNBEDINGT VERMUTET HÄTTEN. AUSGERECHNET DIE KREATIV-KÜKEN DER ALTEHRWÜRDIGEN „BAYERISCHEN STAATSLEHRANSTALT FÜR PHOTOGRAPHIE" BEWEISEN MIT FRISCHEM WITZ UND DER RICHTIGEN PORTION FRECHHEIT, DASS DIE FOTOGRAFIE (DEM 150. GEBURTSTAG 1989 ZUM TROTZE) EIN LEBENDIGES, MODERNES MEDIUM GEBLIEBEN IST. WÄHREND ALLENTHALBEN DAS BEDÜRFNIS ZU VERSPÜREN IST, SICH IN DEN LEDERNEN OHRENSESSEL ZURÜCKZULEHNEN UND MIT VERKLÄRTEM BLICK GLANZTATEN VON FOTO-HEROEN VERGANGENER TAGE AUS DEN VERSTAUBTEN REGALEN DER GESCHICHTE ZU BEKLATSCHEN, SUCHEN SIE UNKOMPLIZIERT UND STRAIGHT NACH EIGENEN WEGEN.
DABEI IST ES DURCHAUS KEIN ZUFALL, DASS AUSGERECHNET SCHÜLER DER (ANNO DOMINI 1900 GEGRÜNDETEN) STAATSLEHRANSTALT ZU JENEN GEHÖREN, BEI DENEN MAN DEN SPASS AM UMGANG MIT DEM MEDIUM FOTOGRAFIE SO ERFRISCHEND BEMERKT. STAND DIE STAATSLEHRANSTALT NOCH VOR WENIGEN JAHREN IN DEM RUF EINER HANDWERKLICH ZWAR URSOLIDEN, ABER KREATIV EHER UNTERBELICHTETEN AUSBILDUNGSSTÄTTE, SO ZÄHLT SIE HEUTE ZWEIFELLOS ZU DEN INTERESSANTESTEN FOTO-SCHULEN DER REPUBLIK. „SCHULD" DARAN SIND ANSTALTSLEITER KOPPERMANN UND SEINE DOZENTEN, DARUNTER HADO PRÜTZMANN VOM BFF, DER SEIT 1986 DIE BEREICHE MODE UND PORTRAIT BETREUT. „FREIRAUM GEBEN, MACHEN LASSEN – NUR NICHT ZU SEHR IN IRGENDEINE RICHTUNG DRÄNGEN." PROFESSIONAL PRÜTZMANN, VOR DEM WECHSEL IN DIE STAATSLEHRANSTALT 17 JAHRE MIT EIGENEM STUDIO ERFOLGREICH IM JOB, UNTERSTÜTZT JEDEN SEINER SCHÜLER INDIVIDUELL MIT VIEL, VIEL FINGERSPITZEN-

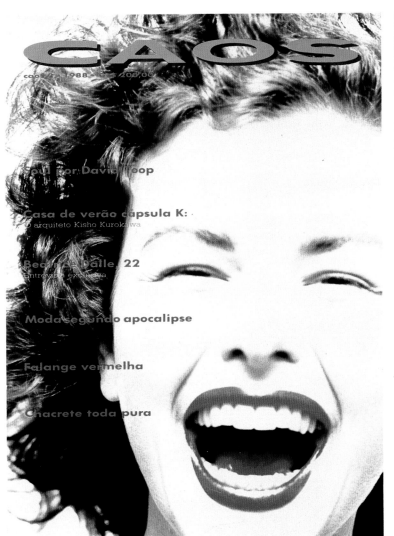

caos 3 ★ 1988 ★ Cz$ 300,00

Robert de Niro em Moscou
Entrevista exclusiva

MACONHA
Um banco de dados

Moda
20 páginas

Philip Glass

Os criadores da Tv Pirata

Nicolau Sevcenko e a moda futurista

Os Parques Nacionais

ART DIRECTOR:
ELIANE STEPHAN
DESIGNER:
ELIANE STEPHAN
AGENCY:
ELIANE STEPHAN LTDA.
PUBLISHER:
A.N. EDITORA LTDA.
■ 353, 354

■ 350-352 Double spreads from the magazine *Designers Digest* on the subject of Munich as a media center, fashion, and the Bavarian State College of Photography. (GER)

■ 353, 354 Covers of the magazine *Caos.* (BRA)

■ 350-352 Doppelseiten aus der Zeitschrift *Designers Digest* über München als Medienstadt, Mode und die Bayerische Staatslehranstalt für Photographie. (GER)

■ 353, 354 Umschläge der Zeitschrift *Caos.* (BRA)

■ 350-352 Doubles pages du magazine *Designers Digest:* Munich capitale des médias, la mode, l'Ecole de photographie de l'Etat de Bavière. (GER)

■ 353, 354 Couvertures du magazine *Caos.* (BRA)

■ 355-359 Covers and double spreads from the magazine *Rolling Stone*. 355 and 359 accompany an article about pop star Terence Trent D'Arby, 356 shows John Lennon, 357 Reggae King Bob Marley's son, and 358, pop singer Madonna. (USA)

■ 355-359 Umschläge und Doppelseiten der Zeitschrift *Rolling Stone*. 355 und 359 gehören zu einem Artikel über Pop Star Terence Trent D'Arby, 356 zeigt John Lennon, 357 den Sohn von Reggae-König Bob Marley und 358 Pop Star Madonna. (USA)

■ 355-359 Couvertures et doubles pages du magazine *Rolling Stone*. Les fig. 355 et 359 font partie d'un article consacré à la vedette pop Terence Trent d'Arby, la 356 représente John Lennon, la 357 le fils de Bob Marley, le roi du reggae, la 358 la vedette pop Madonna. (USA)

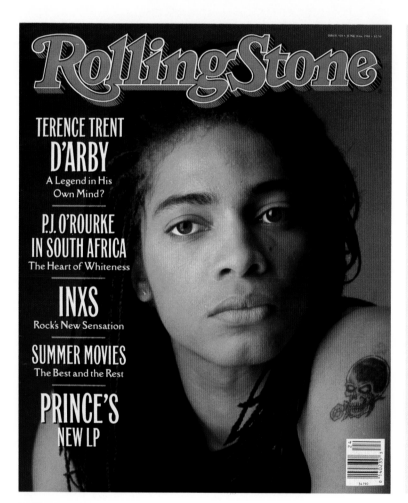
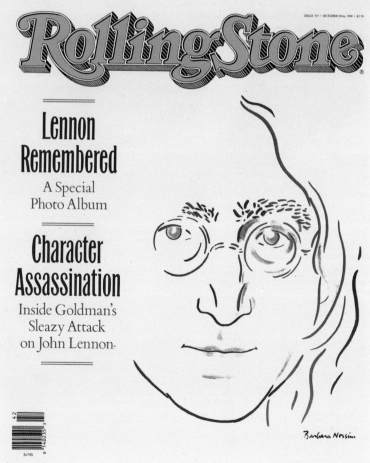

ART DIRECTOR:
FRED WOODWARD
ILLUSTRATOR:
BARBARA NESSIM 356
PHOTOGRAPHER:
MATTHEW ROLSTON 355
PUBLISHER:
ROLLING STONE
■ 355, 356

ART DIRECTOR:
FRED WOODWARD

DESIGNER:
GAIL ANDERSON

PHOTOGRAPHER:
TIMOTHY WHITE

PUBLISHER:
ROLLING STONE

■ 357

ZIGGY MARLEY
·REGGAE'S HEIR APPARENT·
Bob Marley's son claims his father's throne

YOU'RE IN HEAVEN here, mon," says Pi-kot, a member of the large, genial entourage that surrounds Jamaica's unofficial royal family, the Marleys. Indeed, the scene he's commenting on hardly seems earthly. The view from Jack's Hill – the location of the Marley estate, surrounded by the Blue Mountains – is staggering. The house overlooks growths of herb palm and pine trees and the gorgeous expanse of the Kingston harbor. But the view is the least of it. The weather is like something out of a fairy tale – or the Book of Revelation.

At 3:30 on a January afternoon the moon hangs in the sky, which is infinitely blue in some parts, menacingly cloudy in others. The sun is blazing, and it's raining so gently that you don't notice it until you realize you're wet. The wind is cold and blowing so hard that branches are flying off the trees. A brilliant rainbow arcs across the hills.

"See the rainbow?" says Rita Marley, the widow

of Bob Marley and the reigning presence at the Marley estate. "It's a good sign. I've never seen so much power at one time. I can feel it!"

The symbolism of the rainbow – a sign in the Old Testament of the covenant between God and mankind after the world was destroyed by the Flood – is not lost on Rita, a devout Rastafarian. To her, today's rainbow portends the success of Conscious Party, the new album about to be released by nineteen-year-old David "Ziggy" Marley, Rita and Bob's eldest son.

Since Bob Marley's death from cancer in 1981, the reggae world has awaited a new Messiah, someone who could restore the music to the prominence it enjoyed when Marley and the Wailers epitomized the third world's struggle for freedom and self-expression. While reggae has produced no shortage of talented performers, some – like Peter Tosh – have fallen victim to the violence that is as endemic to Jamaica as coconut trees, ganja and poverty. Others, like Sly Dunbar, Robbie Shakespeare, Judy Mowatt and Yellowman, have developed cult followings that mirror aspects of the music's fragmentation after Marley's death.

·BY ANTHONY DeCURTIS·

PHOTOGRAPHS *by Timothy White*

92 · ROLLING STONE, MARCH 24TH, 1988

ROLLING STONE, MARCH 24TH, 1988 · 93

ART DIRECTOR:
FRED WOODWARD

DESIGNER:
FRED WOODWARD

PHOTOGRAPHER:
HERB RITTS

PUBLISHER:
ROLLING STONE

■ 358

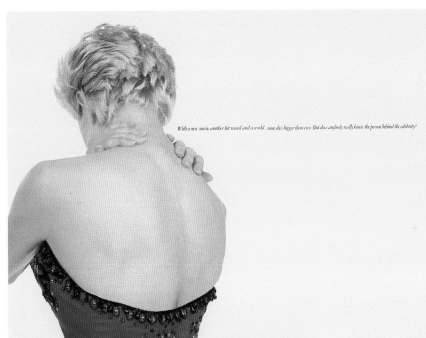

The Madonna Mystique

With a new movie, another hit record and a world tour, she's bigger than ever. But does anybody really know the person behind the celebrity?

IT IS A SEVERE, WIND-SWEPT SATURDAY NIGHT IN THE teeming city of Tokyo, and Madonna – the most notorious living blonde in the modern world – sits inclined into the corner of a crowded limousine, glaring at the rain that is lashing steadily against the windows. "We never had to cancel a show before," she says in a low, doleful voice. "Never, never, never." With her squeezed hairdo, her cardinal-red lips and her pearly skin, she looks picture perfect lovely – and also utterly glum.

Madonna has come to Japan to launch the biggest pop shebang of the summer, the worldwide Who's That Girl Tour, and since arriving at Narita Airport several days ago, she's been causing an enormous commotion. By all accounts, the twenty-eight-year-old singer, dancer, film star and hitleydom has been fawned over, feted, followed and photographed more than any visiting pop sensation since the Beatles way back in 1966. All this hubbub is nothing new in America, Madonna has attracted intense scrutiny throughout her career: from fans, inspired by her alluring manner; from critics, incensed by what they perceive as her vapid tawdriness; and from snoopers of all sorts, curious about the siren of her marriage to the gifted and often combative actor Sean Penn. But in Japan – where she enjoys a popularity that has lately eclipsed even that of Michael Jackson and Bruce Springsteen – Madonna is something a bit better than another hot or controversial celebrity: she is an icon of Western fixations.

Tonight, though, Madonna's popularity in the Far

BY MIKAL GILMORE

ART DIRECTOR:
FRED WOODWARD

DESIGNER:
*FRED WOODWARD/
KATHI ROTA*

PHOTOGRAPHER:
MATTHEW ROLSTON

PUBLISHER:
ROLLING STONE

■ 359

CAN TERENCE TRENT D'ARBY BE AS GOOD AS HE THINKS HE IS

BY MIKAL GILMORE

It is three in the morning, and Terence Trent D'Arby – the prettiest, most provocative pop star of the day – is seated in his dimly lighted hotel suite, high above New York City. He is busy studying the floor between his feet, pulling idly at a forearm-and-ankle bauble dangling from his left ear. "I just want to go on record," he says, measuring his tone for full effect, "that this is positively the last interview I will give anyone for at least another five years." He pauses for a moment, then looks up and flashes a roguish smile – and for good reason. "This is a fairly unexpected revelation for such an up-and-coming pop legend – especially considering that this is also the first lengthy interview

PHOTOGRAPHS BY MATTHEW ROLSTON

ROLLING STONE, JUNE 16TH, 1988 · 55

155

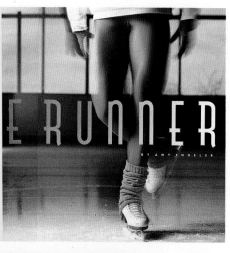

BLADE RUNNER

STRAIGHT TALK

RICHARDS

TRACY
CHAPMAN'S
BLACK
~AND~
WHITE
WORLD

A powerful new voice sings out about racism and poverty · By Anthony DeCurtis

DESIGNER:
FRED WOODWARD
PHOTOGRAPHER:
MARK SELIGER
▲■ 360

PHOTOGRAPHER:
ALBERT WATSON
▲■ 362

ILUSTRATOR:
BRAD HOLLAND
▲■ 361

PHOTOGRAPHER:
FRANK W. OCKENFELS
▲■ 363

■ 360-366 Double spreads from the magazine *Rolling Stone* on the following subjects: skating star Debi Thomas; the AIDS threat to heterosexuals; Keith Richards, member of the Rolling Stones; singer-songwriter Tracy Chapman; Robin Williams, TV's "Nanu, Nanu"; actor Tom Hanks; and David Byrne, member of the Talking Heads. (USA)

■ 360-366 Doppelseiten aus der Zeitschrift *Rolling Stone* zu folgenden Themen: Eislaufstar Debi Thomas; die AIDS-Bedrohung für Heterosexuelle; Keith Richards, Gitarrist der Rolling Stones; Sängerin und Texterin Tracy Chapman; Robin Williams, Komiker; Filmschauspieler Tom Hanks; David Byrne, Mitglied der Pop-Gruppe Talking Heads. (USA)

■ 360-366 Pages du magazine *Rolling Stone* sur les sujets suivants: la vedette du patinage artistique Debi Thomas; la menace du SIDA pour les hétérosexuels; Keith Richards, guitariste des Rolling Stones; Tracy Chapman, chanteuse-parolière; Robin Williams, comédien; acteur Tom Hanks; David Byrne, membre des Talking Heads. (USA)

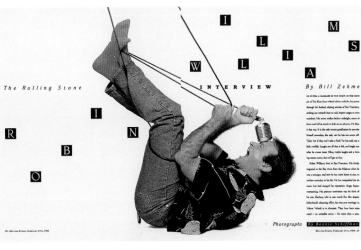

The Rolling Stone INTERVIEW *By Bill Zehme*

Mr.Big
BY BILL ZEHME

DESIGNER:
JOEL CUYLER
PHOTOGRAPHER:
BONNIE SCHIFFMAN
▲■ 364

PHOTOGRAPHER:
HERB RITTS
▲■ 365

PHOTOGRAPHER:
HIRO 366
ART DIRECTOR:
FRED WOODWARD
PUBLISHER:
ROLLING STONE
■ 360 – 366

DAVID

The Rolling Stone Interview
By Robert Farris Thompson

I N 1980 A REPORTER FOR A LOS ANGELES NEWS- paper called to tell me that Talking Heads had mentioned my book *African Art in Motion* in the press kit for their album *Remain in Light*. She wanted to know my reaction. Since I had already been tuned in to the Heads' innovative takes on rock music, I told her I was intrigued. And I was. I began to track the group's music more closely. I was especially impressed by the Afro-Atlantic excursions – *My Life in the Bush of Ghosts* (with Brian Eno) and *The Catherine Wheel* – by the band's singer and chief songwriter, David Byrne.

In the spring of 1987, I met Byrne for the first time. Jonathan Demme, who had directed *Stop Making Sense*, Talking Heads' concert film, invited us both to dinner at a café on Manhattan's Upper West Side. David came dressed im- maculately in white, appropriately evoking the image of an American initiate into the Yoruba religion. Through- out that first conversation, Demme and I did most of the talking: we were waxing poetic about Haitian *vodun* (vo- dun, not voodoo, is the respectful way to refer to this much-maligned African-rooted religion). But I could see that David genuinely dug Haiti and her arts.

Several weeks later, I invited him to accompany me to a Haitian *vodun* initiation ceremony. It was a *canzo*, a cere- mony in which two blacks and two whites (one was an adminis- trative assistant for a major magazine) would pass the fire test, holding their hands briefly in a scalding-hot mixture without feeling anything, as proof of self-control and one- ness with the spirit. The successful completion of the *canzo* would be celebrated with dancing and spirit possessions.

Photograph by
HIRO
BYRNE

ART DIRECTOR:
Lo Breier
DESIGNER:
Angela Dobrick/
Judith Grubinger/
Dirk Linke
PHOTOGRAPHER:
Jan Putfracken
PUBLISHER:
Jahreszeiten-Verlag GmbH
▼■ 367

ART DIRECTOR:
Terry Koppel
DESIGNER:
Terry Koppel
ILLUSTRATOR:
Dave Calver
AGENCY:
Koppel & Scher
PUBLISHER:
V Magazine
▼■ 369

ART DIRECTOR:
Lo Breier
DESIGNER:
Angela Dobrick/
Judith Grubinger/
Dirk Linke
PHOTOGRAPHER:
Rainer Leitzgen
PUBLISHER:
Jahreszeiten-Verlag GmbH
▼■ 368

ART DIRECTOR:
D.J. Stout
DESIGNER:
D.J. Stout
PHOTOGRAPHER:
Brian Smale
PUBLISHER:
Texas Monthly
▼■ 370

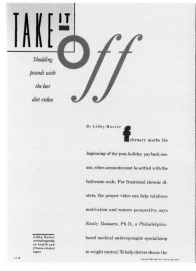

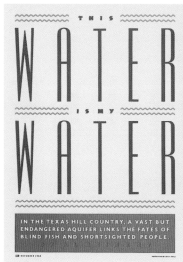

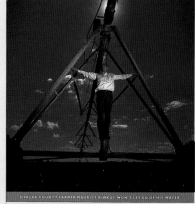

■ 367, 368 Introductory double spreads from the German magazine *Tempo:* "Masturbation – the Mass Movement" and "From St. Pauli with Love". (GER)

■ 369 Introductory double spread to an article about video diet plans in the *V Magazine.* (USA)

■ 370, 372 Double spreads from *Texas Monthly. 370* relates to a battle about water in the Texas hill country and *372* concerns grave doubts about a church minister. (USA)

■ 371 Double spreads from a feature in *Almanac* magazine about Frank Lloyd Wright's design. (USA)

■ 367, 368 Doppelseiten aus dem Magazin *Tempo* mit Beiträgen zu einem allgemein als Tabu behandelten Thema und einem aktuellen Hamburger Kriminalfall. (GER)

■ 369 «Nimm's weg» – einleitende Doppelseite zu einem Artikel über Video-Diätpläne in der Zeitschrift *V.* (USA)

■ 370, 372 Doppelseiten aus *Texas Monthly.* Die Themen: Ein Streit über Wasser in Texas und «Die Sünden des (Pastors) Walter Railey». (USA)

■ 371 Doppelseiten mit einem Beitrag über Design von Frank Lloyd Wright in der Zeitschrift *Almanac.* (USA)

■ 367, 368 Doubles pages du magazine *Tempo:* articles sur un sujet généralement considéré comme tabou, ainsi que sur une récente affaire criminelle à Hambourg. (GER)

■ 369 «Enlève ça!» – double page initiale d'un article du magazine *V* consacré aux régimes vidéo. (USA)

■ 370, 372 Doubles pages du mensuel *Texas Monthly.* Les thèmes abordés: une affaire d'eau au Texas et les soupçons d'assassinat pesant sur le pasteur Walter Railey. (USA)

■ 371 Doubles pages d'un article du magazine *Almanac* consacré au design de Frank Lloyd Wright. (USA)

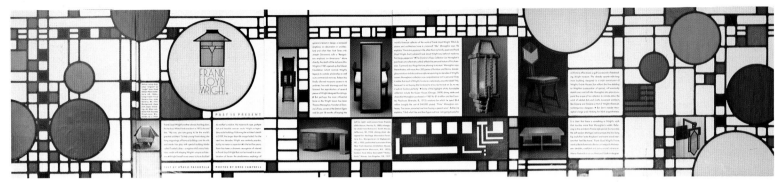

ART DIRECTOR:
Bridget DeSocio

DESIGNER:
Bridget DeSocio

PHOTOGRAPHER:
Greg Campbell

PUBLISHER:
*The Franklin
Mint Almanac*

▲■ 371

ART DIRECTOR:
D. J. Stout

DESIGNER:
D. J. Stout

PHOTOGRAPHER:
Geof Kern

PUBLISHER:
Texas Monthly

▼■ 372

THE SINS OF WALKER RAILEY

IFE OF ANTI-RACIST CLERIC IS ATTACKED, I read in the *New York Times* as I flew home from Los Angeles a few days after Easter. Margaret Railey, the 38-year-old wife of the Reverend Walker Railey of Dallas, was found beaten, choked, and unconscious on the floor of their garage when her husband returned from studying at the library shortly after midnight on April 22, 1987. The police had no leads in the case. "Dr. Railey, who is white, has been an outspoken critic of racial prejudice in this city," said the *Times.* According to the executive minister in Railey's church, Gordon D. Casad, Railey had received a series of threatening letters in the preceding weeks and had preached his Easter sermon wearing a bulletproof vest.

It took a moment for the realization to sink in that this bizarre episode had taken place in my very own church, the First United Methodist Church, on the corner of Ross and Harwood in downtown Dallas. This was the church I grew up in and angrily ran away from and retreated to on several guilty occasions. What I always had hated about my church was its instinctive fear of confronting society, but here was a minister who had spoken out against racial injustice and inequality in a city where such things are rarely said aloud. Here was a man threatened with death in that same sanctuary. And here was a man whose wife was strangled into what the doctors called a persistent vegetative state, for no other obvious reason than that someone wanted to punish Walker Railey for preaching the truth.

Was this Dallas? I asked myself. The open savagery of the Railey tragedy seemed oddly wrong in a city that is deeply preoccupied with appearances. From the beginning there was about the story a vague but haunting discordance.

And yet I was willing to believe that perhaps Dallas had returned to the racial violence of the fifties. Apparently Dallas worried about that too, for the next week the city was on its knees in prayer services and editorial self-reproach. It was a moment when people of various faiths and races stopped to pray for Walker and Peggy Railey and their two young children, Ryan and Megan. "Fight on, Railey family," cried the Reverend Daryll Coleman of the Kirkwood CME Temple Church in a rare gathering of the races at Thanks-Giving Square. "Fight on, soldiers of righteousness and truth. Thank God for today." The Baptists issued a statement that "the fact that a minister's clear stand against racial injustice and bigotry would jeopardize his life is an indicting commentary on our society." Rabbi Sheldon Zimmerman of Temple Emanu-El concluded that the Railey family had been "singled out because of his almost prophetic stance in regard to injustice in any form."

As Peggy lay in intensive care, hundreds of visitors came day after day to Presbyterian Hospital to pay homage to a woman few people knew well. The traffic was so great that volunteers from the church came to assist. Peggy's condition, at first critical, settled into an awful stasis. She was neither dead nor alive—it was as if she were waiting for some momentous resolution before she could either die or be released back into life. And as for her husband, his tragedy seemed unbearable. He had been the rising star of Methodism, as some called him, an electrifying preacher who had awakened the slumbering old church and infused it with his own extraordinary vigor. Now he was crushed by some unknown force too vast and heartless to be fended off by faith alone.

On the Sunday after the attack, the congregation of First Church returned to the sanctuary in a state of shock. There

*I had to know: did
the minister of the church I grew
up in try to murder
his wife? I told him I thought he
was guilty. "I hear
what you're saying," he said.*

✝

by Lawrence Wright

74·JANUARY 1988

Behind the public face of the gifted, caring preacher lay a volatile man hounded by demons and besieged every night by doubts.

PHOTO ILLUSTRATIONS BY GEOF KERN. MODEL COURTESY OF PEGGY TAYLOR, INC.
SMALL PHOTOGRAPHS COURTESY OF THE DALLAS MORNING NEWS.

ART DIRECTOR:
LESLIE SMOLAN
DESIGNER:
ALLISON MUENCH
PHOTOGRAPHER:
BRUCE PLOTKIN
AGENCY:
CARBONE SMOLAN ASSOCIATES
PUBLISHER:
POCKET BOOKS
■ 373

DESIGNER:
JÖRG WESNER
PUBLISHER:
FORUM TYPOGRAPHIE,
ARBEITSKREIS HANNOVER
■ 374

■ 373 Cover from *Vanity Fur* – a humorous parody on the fashion magazine *Vanity Fair*. (USA)

■ 374 An imitation of the *Prawda*, used as cover of *Grotesk*, a publication on typography. (GER)

■ 375-377 Double spreads from *Elegance* magazine with portraits of women by various artists, and imitated, amazingly similar photographs. (NLD)

■ 373 Umschlag von *Vanity Fur*, eine humorvolle Parodie auf die Modezeitschrift *Vanity Fair*. (USA)

■ 374 Eine Imitation der *Prawda* als Umschlag für *Grotesk*, eine Publikation über Typographie. (GER)

■ 375-377 Doppelseiten aus der Zeitschrift *Elegance* mit Frauenporträts verschiedener Künstler und nachgestellten, frappierend ähnlichen Photos. (NLD)

■ 373 Couverture de *Vanity Fur*, une parodie pleine d'humour du magazine de mode *Vanity Fair*. (USA)

■ 374 Une imitation du *Prawda*, utilisée comme couverture de *Grotesk*, une publication sur la typographie. (USA)

■ 375-377 Doubles pages zu magazine *Elegance* où les portraits féminins de divers artistes inspirent à des photographes des reconstitutions très proches des modèles. (NLD)

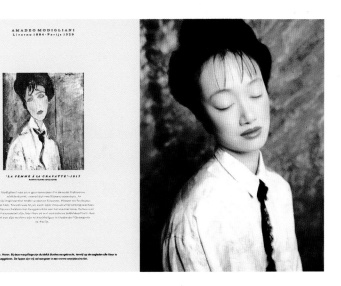

ROY LICHTENSTEIN
New York 1923

'HOPELESS'-1963

AMADEO MODIGLIANI
Livorno 1884 - Parijs 1920

'LA FEMME À LA CRAVATTE'-1917

ART DIRECTOR:
Dick Westerveld
PHOTOGRAPHER:
Marcel v/d Vlugt
PUBLISHER:
Elegance Magazine
■ 375-377

TAMARA DE LEMPICKA
Warschau ±1900-Mexico 1980

'L'HEURE BLEUE'-1935

Van de schilderes De Lempicka is vooral de periode tussen 1925 en
1935 een belangrijke geweest. In die tijd was zij woonachtig in Parijs
en schilderde zij de Art Deco-achtige portretten van vele
societyfiguren waartoe zij zelf ook behoorde. Uit haar schilderijen
spreekt de decadentie zelf: op een koele en tegelijk sensuele manier
worden de personen weergegeven. Haar dochter Kizette de Lempicka-
Foxhall heeft onlangs een boek over haar moeder geschreven dat is
uitgegeven bij Phaidon Press Limited.

Foto: Grijze zijde: Capsicum, Amsterdam; blauwe tafzijde; Stodel Decor, Amsterdam. Een dramatische, zware oogmake-up en
felrode lippen zijn voor deze make-up van essentieel belang. Het haar werd met ouderwetse golfklemmen ingezet en kreeg met gel het

105

...And Sometimes They're too Lovely for Words.

BY RICHARD CONNIFF

ere we are, amid the rising hems of the neo-miniskirt, and suddenly it's socially acceptable again to notice women's legs. While I personally am not the sort to ogle, I have to say I never actually stopped noticing them. What I've been noticing more, lately, is the effect women's legs can have on men. Why is it that a man will turn right when he has a pressing engagement two blocks to the left, simply because he is entranced by the way a woman's thighs flash in and out through the vent at the hem of her skirt? What are men thinking about when they think about women's legs? Let me explain.

The problem for a man talking about women's legs is that they are literally too lovely for words. To judge by our fascination with the subject, you might expect men to have a thoroughly articulated vocabulary of legs, like Eskimos with their 62 words for snow. We don't. Pins, gams, wheels–that's about the extent of it. The language of legs is unconscious, albeit universally understood. Where, for instance, is the word for that protuberance of bone at the base of the ankle, or for the vase-like swelling of the calf? What do we call the vertical dimpling at the back of a woman's knee? According to my dictionary, you could say, "May I kiss your popliteal space?" But

RICHARD CONNIFF *is the author of* The Devil's Book of Verse.

LEGS are BACK...

36 ▼ FEBRUARY 1988   PHOTOGRAPH BY CAROLINE GREYSHOCK   FEBRUARY 1988 ▼ 37

ART DIRECTOR:
Terry Koppel
DESIGNER:
Terry Koppel
PHOTOGRAPHER:
Caroline Greyshock
AGENCY:
Koppel & Scher
PUBLISHER:
V Magazine
▲■ 378

ART DIRECTOR:
*Stefano Baldassarre/
Mirta Lancellotti/
Maria Cristina Vitelli*
DESIGNER:
*Stefano Baldassarre/
Mirta Lancellotti/
Maria Cristina Vitelli*
AGENCY:
Nuovostudio snc
PUBLISHER:
Rivista Italian
▼■ 379, 380

Perché / Why ITALIAN

EDITORIALE

Viviamo da tempo in un unico villaggio dove l'intreccio dei linguaggi e delle idee costituisce il vero patrimonio della nuova cultura. In questa dimensione di universalità trova giustificazione il nostro impegno editoriale: raccontare l'Italia degli italiani e l'Italia del mondo.

A scrivere sono i protagonisti, i testimoni diretti degli eventi, gli autori dei modi di vita, gli animatori di iniziative che riconducono alla sinergia delle volontà e delle esperienze professionali.

Oggi non è più sufficiente mettere i lettori nella condizione di valutare le prospettive degli avvenimenti; né basta documentare che nel nostro Paese è concentrata poco meno della metà delle opere d'arte esistenti in tutto il mondo.

Ora è indispensabile aprirsi alla cultura planetaria del ventunesimo secolo e contribuire attivamente al suo progresso.

Lavoreremo in questo senso. Daremo conto di quanto gli italiani possono fare per un'intelligente interpretazione dei nostri tempi; annunceremo le disponibilità e gli apporti delle fantasie, anche le più lontane, volte alla competizione del progresso. Convinti, come siamo, che la storia accetta chi si impegna e non chi si cancella in tutto il mondo.

V For some time now we've been living in a planetary village where the intertwining of languages and ideas makes up the true heritage of a new culture. Our editorial commitment finds its raison d'être in this dimension of universality: we are committed to presenting the Italy of the Italians and the Italy of the world. The contributing writers are all protagonists, direct witnesses of events, innovators of life styles. It is they who, through the combined forces of professional experience and willpower, inspire creative initiatives.

Today, it is not enough to put the reader in a position to evaluate events. Nor is it sufficient to call attention to the fact that almost half of the works of art existing in the entire world are to be found in our country. Nowadays, it is indispensable that we be receptive to the planetary culture of the 21st century and contribute actively to it. We intend to work in that direction and to give an account of how Italians can intelligently interpret our times. We will note down their receptiveness and their imaginative contributions, even the most far-fetched, aimed at achieving progress.

Finally, convinced as we are that History accepts those who are committed, not those who leave no mark, we will bear witness to total engagement in everything that leads to the final design: Italy for the world and the world for Italy.

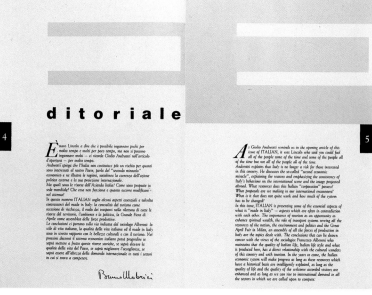

ditoriale   4   5

È stato Lincoln a dire che è possibile ingannare pochi per molto tempo e molti per poco tempo, ma non si possono ingannare molti — ci ricorda Giulio Andreotti nell'articolo d'apertura — per molto tempo.

Andreotti spiega che l'Italia non costituisce più un rischio per quanti sono interessati al nostro Paese, parla del "secondo miracolo" economico e ne illustra le ragioni, sottolinea la coerenza dell'azione politica estera e la sua proiezione internazionale.

Ma quali sono le risorse dell'Azienda Italia? Come sono proposte in sede mondiale? Che cosa non funziona e quanto occorre modificare – nel sistema?

In questo numero ITALIAN coglie alcuni aspetti essenziali e talvolta contrastanti del made in Italy: la centralità del turismo come occasione di ricchezza, il ruolo dei trasporti nella rilettura di tutte le risorse del territorio, l'ambiente e la politica, la Grande Fiera di Aprile come assemblea delle forze produttive.

Le conclusioni ci portano sulla via indicata dal sociologo Alberoni: lo stile di vita italiano, la qualità della vita italiana ed il made in Italy sono in stretto rapporto con le bellezze culturali e con il turismo. Nei prossimi decenni il sistema economico italiano potrà progredire se saprà mettere a frutto queste risorse storiche, se saprà elevare la qualità della vita del Paese, se saprà migliorare l'accoglienza, se saprà essere all'altezza della domanda internazionale in tutti i settori in cui si trova a competere.

As Giulio Andreotti reminds us in the opening article of this issue of ITALIAN, it was Lincoln who said you could fool all of the people some of the time and some of the people all of the time but not all of the people all of the time. Andreotti explains that Italy is no longer a risk for those interested in this country. He discusses the so-called "second economic miracle", explaining the reasons and emphasizing the consistency of Italy's behaviour on the international scene and the image projected abroad. What resources does this Italian "corporation" possess? What proposals are we making on an international encounters? What is it that does not quite work and how much of the system has to be changed?

In this issue, ITALIAN is presenting some of the essential aspects of what is "made in Italy" — aspects which are often in contradiction with each other. The importance of tourism as an opportunity to enhance spiritual wealth, the role of transport systems serving all the resources of the nation, the environment and politics and the Great April Fair in Milan, an assembly of all the forces of production in Italy are the topics dealt with. The conclusions that can be drawn concur with the views of the sociologist Francesco Alberoni who maintains that the quality of Italian life, Italian life style and what is produced here, have a direct relationship with the cultural wonders of this country and with tourism. In the years to come, the Italian economic system will make progress as long as these resources which "made in Italy" are intelligently exploited, as long as the quality of life and the quality of the welcome accorded visitors are enhanced and as long as we can rise to international demand in all the sectors in which we are called upon to compete.

SE NE PARLA

WILLIAM KENNEDY

Con «Ironweed», da cui è stato tratto il film con Meryl Streep e Jack Nicholson, ha vinto il premio Pulitzer. Come ha detto Saul Bellow: «Il suo linguaggio è vigoroso, pieno di energia. È uno scrittore molto dotato».

William Kennedy, che ha sessant'anni, è un uomo *tough* ma gentile e modesto che vive con sfarzo la sua fortuna in una grande casa munita degli immancabili word processor e teleschermo gigante e riceve gli amici la sera intrattenendoli fino all'alba con una conversazione brillante inframmezzata da esecuzioni al banjo e all'ukulele. Questo sfarzo è recente: per anni Kennedy ha condotto una vita economicamente durissima e psicologicamente frustrante finché la pubblicazione (dovuta all'intervento di Saul Bellow) di *Ironweed* nel 1983, ora pubblicato in Italia da Rizzoli, gli meritò il Pulitzer e il National Book Critics Circle Award del 1984.

Prima di questo successo Kennedy — figlio di un vice-sceriffo cattolico che lo portava con sé nelle sale da gioco e nei circoli politici dove il ragazzo assimilava la parlata irlandese-americana e osservava con attenzione i costumi di quella che ad Albany, capitale dello Stato di New York, era maggioranza etnica — campava dando lezioni saltuarie all'università o collaborando senza entusiasmo ai giornali locali.

Albany diventò il centro della sua attenzione e quando se ne allontanò per andare a fare l'inviato di un giornale a Miami e poi a San Juan in Portorico, si accorse che la sua immaginazione era fissata in questo unico luogo. Sposò però una portoricana, la dolce, paziente Dana che vive con lui da trentun anni. Portorico è una costante della sua fortuna. Fu a San Juan che Kennedy seguì nel 1960 i corsi di Saul Bellow e riuscì a fargli leggere un racconto che piacque al Premio Nobel 1976. Da allora pubblicò tre romanzi, *The Ink Truck* del 1969, *Legs* del 1976, ispirato alla biografia del gangster di Albany Jack Diamond (pubblicato in Italia col titolo *Il grande gangster* da Frassinelli nel 1985) e *Billy Phelan's Greatest Game* del 1978; gli ultimi due romanzi sono ambientati a Albany. Ma i romanzi non si vendevano. Quando Kennedy presentò il manoscritto di *Ironweed* se lo vide respingere da tredici editori preoccupati di vederlo finire in magazzino come i libri precedenti. Fu Saul Bellow a toglierlo dall'umiliazione di questi rifiuti scrivendo una lettera a Corlies Smith, editor della Viking che aveva pubblicato l'ultimo libro di Kennedy e ora aveva rifiutato *Ironweed*, dicendosi scandalizzato. «Questi romanzi di Albany diventeranno memorabili», disse Bellow. «Che l'autore di *Billy Phelan* possa avere un manoscritto respinto in cerca di un editore è disonorevole». L'editor disse in un'intervista: «Kennedy non cambiò nulla del libro ma ora il libro era stato baciato da un Premio Nobel... Nessuno trascura l'attenzione di Bellow». Da Bellow d'attenzione su Albany che secondo Bellow diventerà una capitale letteraria come Paterson nel New Jersey lo fu per William Carlos Williams e Jefferson, che raffigurava la città di Oxford nel Mississippi, lo fu nella trasfigurazione fantastica di William Faulkner creatore della Yoknapatawpha County.

L'idea fu di ristampare gli altri due libri di Kennedy ambientati a Albany e di presentarli con *Ironweed* come «Il ciclo di Albany»; e la trovata editoriale riuscì con enorme successo. Di *Ironweed* si vendettero subito centomila copie, venne richiesto da una quindicina di editori stranieri, fu acquistato con un altro dei romanzi di Kennedy dal produttore Gene Kirkwood, Kennedy ricevette la borsa di studio intestata a John e Catherine MacArthur che gli garantiva duecentosessantaquattromila dollari in cinque anni e si servì del denaro per fondare l'Istituto degli scrittori organizzando incontri e conferenze; il primo oratore naturalmente fu Saul Bellow e a lui seguirono John Updike e Toni Morrison. L'istituto ebbe un tale successo da indurre il governatore dello stato Mario Cuomo — che lavora e vive ad Albany — a assegnare i centomila dollari all'anno dell'Arts Award alla fondazione per incrementarne l'attività. Ora William Kennedy è direttore della sua fondazione, insegna a tempo pieno all'università e ha visto uscire all'inizio di quest'anno il suo quinto romanzo intitolato *Quinn's Book*. Francis Ford Coppola gli ha fatto scrivere la sceneggiatura per il suo *Cotton Club* di Harlem e di recente è uscita la riduzione cinematografica di *Ironweed* per la regia di Hector Babenco (il regista argentino che ha diretto *Il bacio della donna ragno*) e l'interpretazione di Meryl Streep e Jack Nicholson; nel frattempo ha scritto la sceneggiatura del suo terzo romanzo *Billy Phelan's Greatest Game*.

I cittadini di Albany sono rimasti così impressionati dalla fama colossale che ha improvvisamente circondato questo scrittore vissuto nell'ombra per tanti anni da organizzare per lui nel 1984 una celebrazione durata tre giorni e intitolata «La Albany di William Kennedy».

segue a pag. 171

Fernanda Pivano

130

ART DIRECTOR:
ALBERTO NODOLINO
PHOTOGRAPHER:
WILLIAM COUPON
CLIENT:
VOGUE ITALIA
PUBLISHER:
CONDÉ NAST S.P.A.

■ 381

ART DIRECTOR:
Franz Aumüller/
Thomas Feicht
DESIGNER:
Willi Demel
PHOTOGRAPHER:
Bernd Mayer 384
Reiner de Rooy 386
AGENCY:
Trust
PUBLISHER:
Instant
■ 383-386

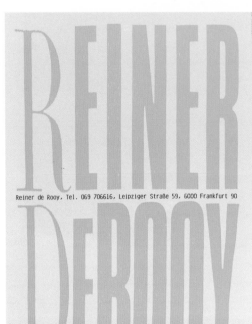

Jean Paul Gaultier

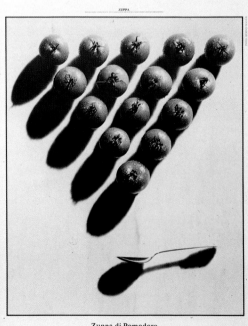

Zuppa di Pomodoro

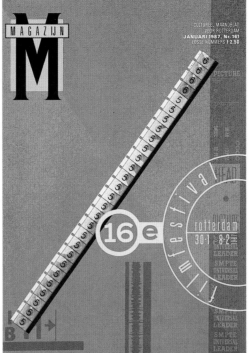

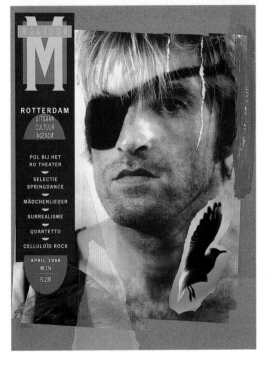

ART DIRECTOR:
ARNO BAUMAN/
IVO VAN LEEUWEN
DESIGNER:
ARNO BAUMAN/
IVO VAN LEEUWEN/
FEMKE MARIJNISSEN/
NORBERT VERMEER/
ANNETTE DE BRUEIJS/
EMMY VAN HARSKAMP
PHOTOGRAPHER:
ARNO BAUMAN
STUDIO:
BAUMAN
PUBLISHER:
ROTTERDAM ART COUNCIL
■ 387-392

■ 383-386 Covers and double spreads from two issues of the magazine *Instant* with unusual contrasts. (GER)

■ 387-392 Covers of the magazine *M.* (NLD)

■ 383-386 Umschläge und Doppelseite der Zeitschrift *Instant* mit ungewöhnlichen Gegenüberstellungen. (GER)

■ 387-392 Umschläge des Magazins *M.* (NLD)

■ 383-386 Couvertures et doubles page de deux numéros du magazine *Instant* avec des confrontations insolites. (GER)

■ 387-392 Couvertures du magazine *M.* (NLD)

SKALD

Vol. 5, Issue 1   THE PUBLICATION FOR ROYAL VIKING LINE'S SKALD CLUB MEMBERS   SPRING 1988

SKALD

VOL. 5, ISSUE 2   THE PUBLICATION FOR ROYAL VIKING LINE'S SKALD MEMBERS   FALL 1988

ART DIRECTOR:
KIT HINRICHS
DESIGNER:
*KIT HINRICHS/
SANDRA MCHENRY*
PHOTOGRAPHER:
*JOHNNY JOHNSON/
WILDLIFE PHOTOBANK 393
WILL MOSGROVE   394*
AGENCY:
PENTAGRAM DESIGN
PUBLISHER:
ROYAL VIKING LINE
■ 393, 394

Uma Thurman	Raoul Felder	Dan Dorfman	Alison Lurie
Transcendental Chic	*On Love and the Law*	*On Wall Street*	*The Politics of Fashion*

FAME

ART DIRECTOR:
PHILIP GIPS
DESIGNER:
RIKI SETHIADI
PHOTOGRAPHER:
DAVID SEIDNER
AGENCY:
FRANKFURT GIPS BALKIND
PUBLISHER:
FAME MAGAZINE GROUP, INC.
◀■ 395

■ 393, 394 Covers of the club magazine *Skald* issued by the shipping line Royal Viking Line, with an inhabitant of Alaska and the Captain of a cruiser. (USA)

■ 395 Cover of the magazine *Fame*. (USA)

■ 396-398 Cover and double spreads from a publication of the California College of Arts and Crafts with information about the study program in the arts, architecture, and design. (USA)

■ 393, 394 Umschläge der Zeitschrift *Skald*, herausgegeben von der Reederei Royal Viking Line, mit einem Bewohner Alaskas und dem Kapitän eines Kreuzschiffes. (USA)

■ 395 Umschlag der Zeitschrift *Fame* (Ruhm). (USA)

■ 396-398 Umschlag und Doppelseiten aus einer Publikation des California College of Arts and Crafts mit Informationen über das Studienprogramm im Bereich der Kunst, Architektur und des Designs. (USA)

■ 393, 394 Couvertures de *Skald* publié par les messageries maritimes Royal Viking Line. On y voit un habitant de l'Alaska et le capitaine d'un paquebot de croisière. (USA)

■ 395 Couverture du magazine *Fame* (Gloire). (USA)

■ 396-398 Couverture et doubles pages d'une publication du California College of Arts and Crafts où figurent des renseignements sur le programme d'études en art, architecture et design. (USA)

DESIGNER:
MICHAEL MABRY/
PIPER MURAKAMI
PHOTOGRAPHER:
LESLIE FLORES/
MONICA LEE/
JOHN DEGROOT
AGENCY:
MICHAEL MABRY DESIGN
PUBLISHER:
CALIFORNIA COLLEGE OF
ARTS & CRAFTS, OAKLAND
■ 396-398

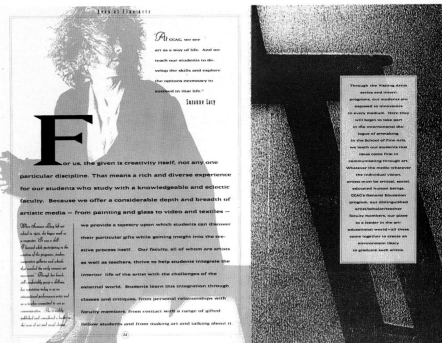

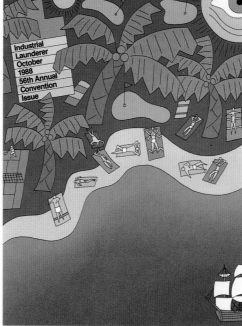

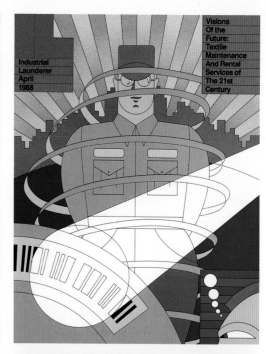

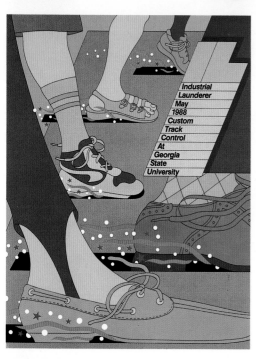

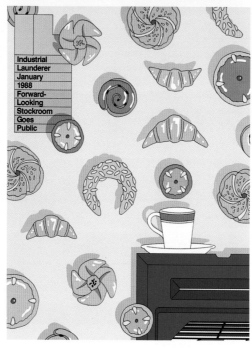

ART DIRECTOR:
JACK LEFKOWITZ
DESIGNER:
JACK LEFKOWITZ
ILLUSTRATOR:
M.V. STRNAD 399-403, 405
PATRICIA WINTERS 404
AGENCY:
JACK LEFKOWITZ INC.
PUBLISHER:
INDUSTRIAL LAUNDERER
■ 399-405

■ 399-405 These covers of the launderers' trade magazine *Industrial Launderer* relate to the following subjects: the right of every American to have a working uniform, the annual convention in Puerto Rico, new technologies coming to the laundry industry, treated floor mats, a breakfast reception to introduce a new stockroom to the community, how local market research helps the industrial launderer to a bigger market segment, and the sales people who have been extremely industrious. (USA)

■ 399-405 Diese Umschläge der Wäscherei-Fachzeitschrift *Industrial Launderer* beziehen sich auf folgende Themen: Das Recht auf Arbeitsuniformen für jeden Amerikaner; Puerto Rico, Ort der Jahreskonferenz; neue Technologien in der Wäscherei; in einer Universität erfolgreich eingesetzte, spezielle Fussmatten; ein Frühstücksempfang mit Gebäck und Kaffee; wie regional ausgerichtete Marktforschung Wäschereien zu grösseren Marktanteilen verhilft; der Fleiss der Aussendienstmitarbeiter. (USA)

■ 399-405 Ces couvertures de la revue professionnelle du blanchissage *Industrial Launderer* ont pour thème: le droit de tout Américain à un uniforme de travail; Porto Rico, site du congrès annuel de la profession; les nouvelles technologies appliquées au blanchissage; des essuie-pieds spéciaux qui ont prouvé leur utilité dans une université; un petit déjeuner officiel avec café et petits fours; l'utilité du marketing régional pour le développement du chiffre d'affaires des petites blanchisseries; le zèle des V.R.P. (USA)

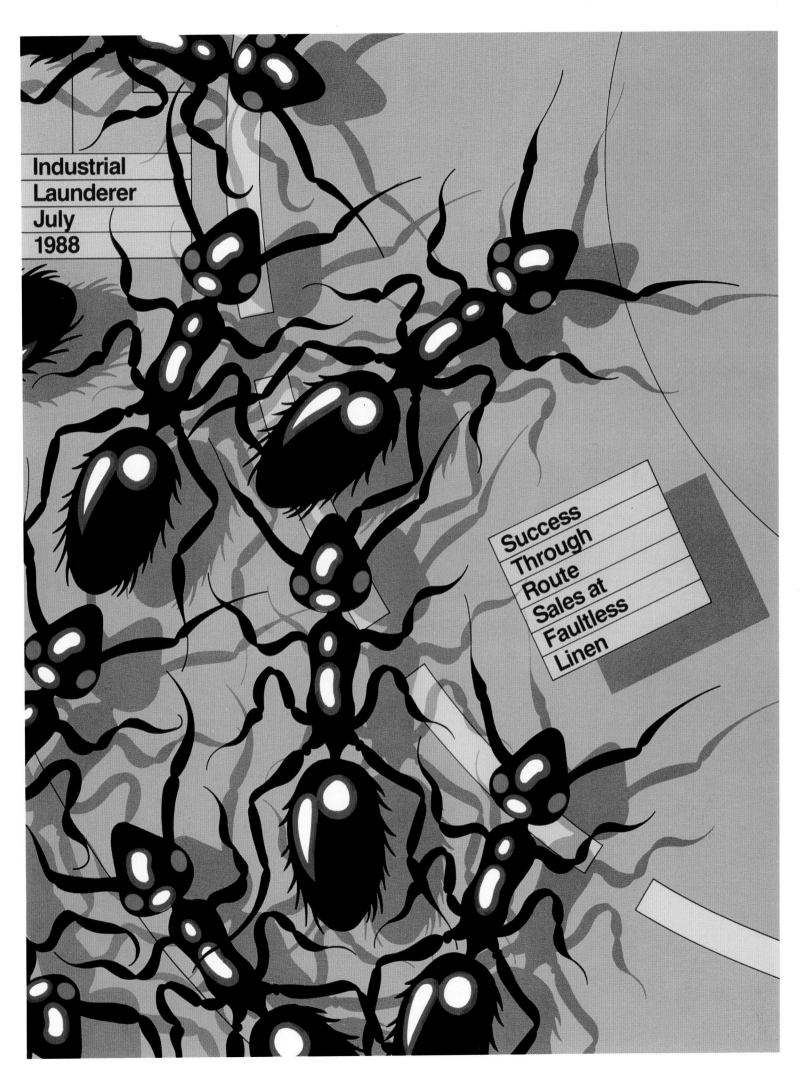

Industrial
Launderer
July
1988

Success
Through
Route
Sales at
Faultless
Linen

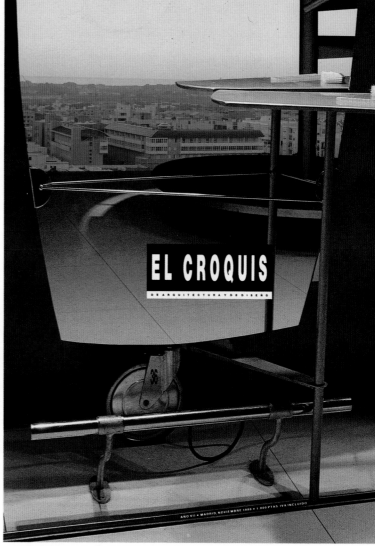

ART DIRECTOR:
RICHARD C. LEVENE
DESIGNER:
RICHARD C. LEVENE
PHOTOGRAPHER:
FERRAN FREIXA
PUBLISHER:
EL CROQUIS EDITORIAL
■ 406

ART DIRECTOR:
RICHARD C. LEVENE
DESIGNER:
RICHARD C. LEVENE
PHOTOGRAPHER:
JORDI SARRA/
HISAO SUZUKI
PUBLISHER:
EL CROQUIS EDITORIAL
■ 407

■ 406 Cover of an issue of the Spanish design magazine *De Diseno*. (SPA)

■ 407 For *El Croquis*, a Spanish magazine for architecture and design. (SPA)

■ 408-410 Covers of the magazine *HQ* issued by the Heidelberger Printing Machines AG. As mentioned on the covers each issue is devoted to a specific topic. *409* shows Jean-Paul Sartre in Lithuania. (GER)

■ 411, 412 From *Critical Issues*, a hospital's house magazine. The topics of this issue concern the debatable point of whether quality can still be upheld in a management health care system, and traumatic conditions. (USA)

■ 406 Umschlag einer Ausgabe der spanischen Design-Zeitschrift *De Diseno*. (SPA)

■ 407 Für *El Croquis*, eine spanische Zeitschrift für Architektur und Design. (SPA)

■ 408-410 Umschläge der von der Heidelberger Druckmaschinen AG herausgegebenen Zeitschrift *HQ*. Wie auf den Umschlägen vermerkt, ist jede Ausgabe einem Thema gewidmet. *409* zeigt Jean-Paul Sartre in Litauen. (GER)

■ 411, 412 Aus *Critical Issues*, Hauszeitschrift eines amerikanischen Spitals. Die Themen der Ausgaben: «Lässt die Verwaltung des Gesundheitswesens Qualität zu?» und «Behandlung traumatischer Zustände». (USA)

■ 406 Couverture d'un numéro du magazine de design espagnol *De Diseno*. (SPA)

■ 407 Pour *El Croquis*, un magazine espagnol voué à l'architecture et au design. (SPA)

■ 408-410 Couvertures du magazine *HQ* publié par la Heidelberger Druckmaschinen AG. Comme elles l'annoncent, chaque numéro est voué à une thématique particulière. Fig. *409*: Jean-Paul Sartre en Lituanie. (GER)

■ 411, 412 Extraits de *Critical Issues*, la revue maison d'un hôpital américain. Thèmes abordés: «La qualité est-elle compatible avec une gestion raisonnée?» et «Comment traiter les états traumatiques.» (USA)

ART DIRECTOR:
ROLF MÜLLER

DESIGNER:
*ROMAN LORENZ/
BARBARA MIEDANER/
PAUL SIMON*

AGENCY:
BÜRO ROLF MÜLLER

PUBLISHER:
*HEIDELBERGER DRUCK-
MASCHINEN AG*

▼■ 408-410

ART DIRECTOR:
KYM ABRAMS

DESIGNER:
*BARRY DECK/
SANDI WEINDLING*

ILLUSTRATOR:
*MARY FLOCK/
QUONG HO*

AGENCY:
KYM ABRAMS DESIGN

PUBLISHER:
LUTHERAN GENERAL HOSPITAL

▼■ 411, 412

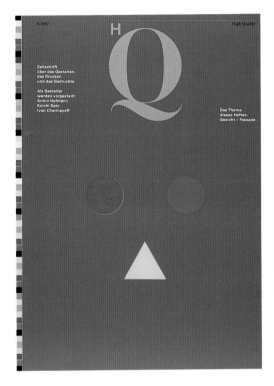

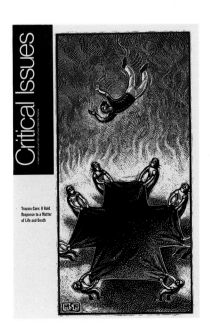

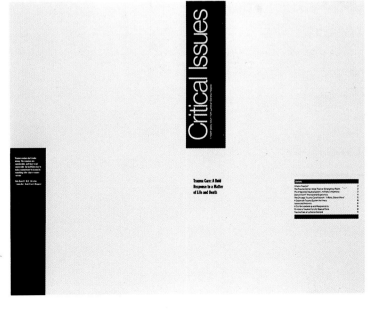

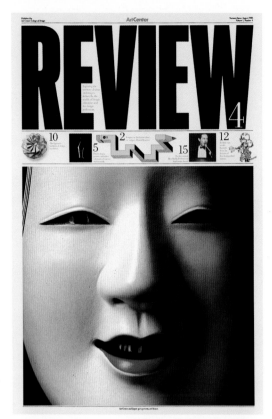

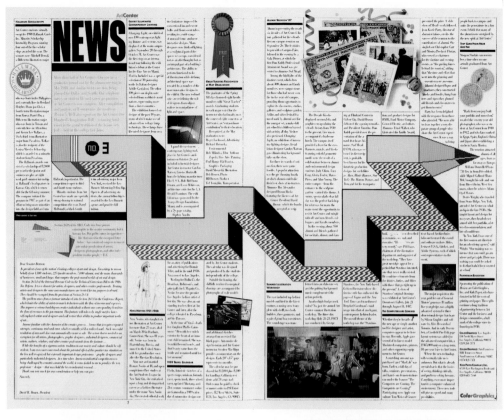

ART DIRECTOR:
KIT HINRICHS

DESIGNER:
KIT HINRICHS/
KAREN BOONE/
LENORE BARTZ/
TERRI DRISCOLL

ILLUSTRATOR:
JOHN HERSEY/
NINA NOVINS 414
DOUGLAS BOYD DESIGN 417

PHOTOGRAPHER:
STEVEN A. HELLER (COVERS)
BARRY ROBINSON 417

AGENCY:
PENTAGRAM DESIGN

PUBLISHER:
ART CENTER COLLEGE
OF DESIGN, PASADENA
■ 413-417

■ 413-417 The *Art Center Review* – house organ of the famous art school in Pasadena (and recently also located in Switzerland), gives details about the school's activities and the work of its present students and alumni. An element recurring in every issue is the pencil - interpreted in various ways by students and graduates of the school. Shown are two covers and double spreads on various topics. (USA)

■ 413-417 *Art Center Review*, die Hauszeitschrift dieser Kunstschule in Pasadena und neuerdings in der Schweiz, informiert über die Aktivitäten sowie über die Arbeiten gegenwärtiger und ehemaliger Studenten. Ein in jeder Ausgabe wiederkehrendes Element ist der Bleistift, von Studenten und Absolventen der Schule interpretiert. Hier zwei Umschläge und Seiten zu verschiedenen Themen. (USA)

■ 413-417 L'*Art Center Review*, la revue d'entreprise de la célèbre école d'art de Pasadena aujourd'hui dotée d'une branche en Suisse, informe ici sur les activités scolaires, ainsi que sur les travaux d'élèves et d'anciens élèves. Un élément qui revient dans chaque numéro, c'est l'interprétation du crayon par des élèves et d'anciens élèves. Ici deux couvertures et des doubles pages sur des sujets divers. (USA)

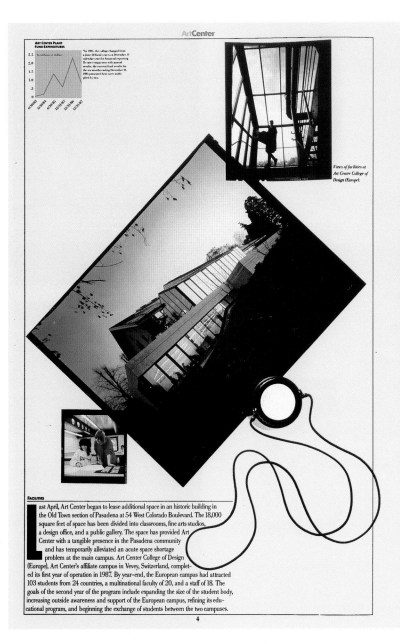

1987

First City Industries Inc.

Annual Report

ART DIRECTOR:
RON JEFFERIES
DESIGNER:
THOMAS DEVINE
ILLUSTRATOR:
TIM CLARK/
VICTOR HUGO ZAYAS
COPYWRITER:
NELSON FITCH
AGENCY:
THE JEFFERIES ASSOCIATION
CLIENT:
FIRST CITY INDUSTRIES, INC.
■ 418-421

■ 418-421 Cover and double spreads from the 1987 annual report for the First City Industries, a company dealing in the manufacture of industrial products, as well as in real estate and investments. (USA)

■ 418-421 Umschlag und Doppelseiten des Jahresberichtes 1987 für First City Industries, eine Firma, die sich mit der Herstellung industrieller Produkte und mit Immobilien und Investments befasst. (USA)

■ 418-421 Couverture et doubles pages du rapport annuel 1987 de First City Industries, spécialisé dans les produits industriels, mais aussi dans l'immobilier et les placements. (USA)

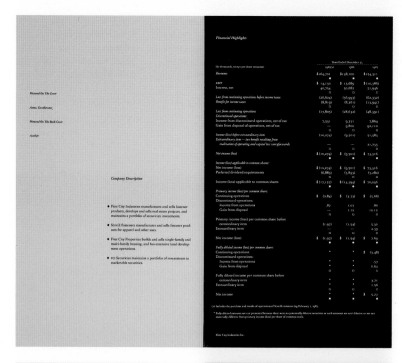

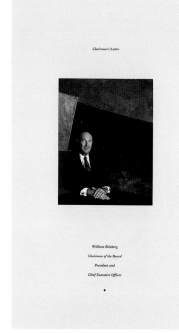

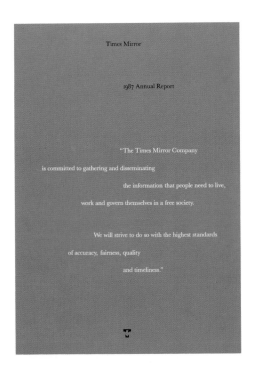

Times Mirror

1987 Annual Report

"The Times Mirror Company

is committed to gathering and disseminating

the information that people need to live,

work and govern themselves in a free society.

We will strive to do so with the highest standards

of accuracy, fairness, quality

and timeliness."

ART DIRECTOR:
JIM BERTÉ
DESIGNER:
JIM BERTÉ
ILLUSTRATOR:
PAUL BICE
COPYWRITER:
BONNIE CHAIKIND
AGENCY:
ROBERT MILES RUNYAN
& ASSOCIATES
CLIENT:
THE TIMES
MIRROR COMPANY
■ 422-425

■ 422-425 For the 1987
annual report for the newspaper publishers Times Mirror Company. The funda-
mental mission is formu-
lated as a quotation on the
cover. (USA)

■ 422-425 Für den Jahres-
bericht 1987 des Zeitungs-
verlags Times Mirror Com-
pany. Das grundsätzliche
Anliegen ist in einem Zitat
auf dem Umschlag formu-
liert. (USA)

■ 422-425 Pour le rapport
annuel 1987 de l'éditeur de
journaux Times Mirror
Company. La politique de
l'entreprise est définie par
une citation figurant en
couverture. (USA)

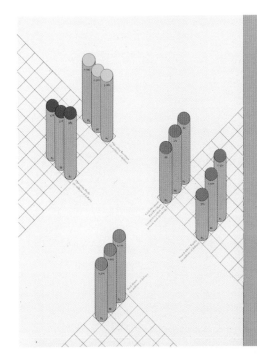

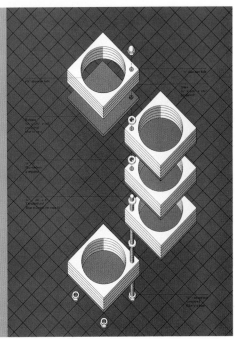

ART DIRECTOR:
Sharon Werner
DESIGNER:
Sharon Werner/
Haley Johnson
PHOTOGRAPHER:
D. Weaks/A. Meyerson/
T. Tracy/T. Berthiaume
AGENCY:
The Duffy Design Group
PUBLISHER:
US West
■ 426-428

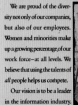

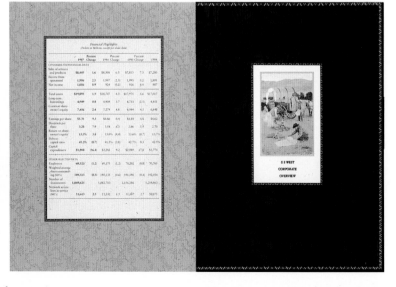

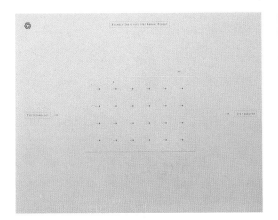

ART DIRECTOR:
JIM BERTÉ
DESIGNER:
JIM BERTÉ
PHOTOGRAPHER:
SCOTT MORGAN
COPYWRITER:
JULIE SUHR
AGENCY:
*ROBERT MILES RUNYAN
& ASSOCIATES*
PUBLISHER:
NICHOLS INSTITUTE
■ 429-432

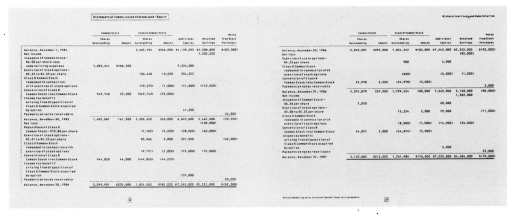

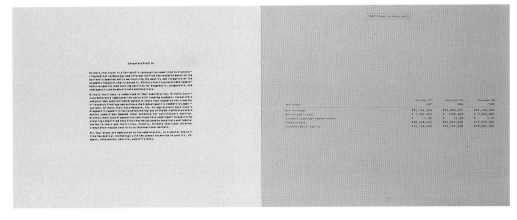

■ 426-428 Presentation of the annual report for U.S. West –
a company active in the telecommunications industry.
Nostalgic scenes from the Wild West illustrate the front of
the cardboard case and also both parts of the report contained inside, as well as various double spreads. (USA)

■ 429-432 Cover and double spreads from the 1987 annual
report for the Nichols Institute – a test laboratory to transfer
and utilize new medical technology and information. (USA)

■ 426-428 Jahresbericht für U.S. West, eine Firma aus der
Telekommunikationsindustrie. Nostalgische Szenen aus
dem Wilden Westen illustrieren den Kartonumschlag auf der
Vorderseite wie auch die beiden darin enthaltenen Teile des
Berichtes und verschiedene Doppelseiten. (USA)

■ 429-432 Umschlag und Doppelseiten aus dem Jahresbericht 1987 des Nichols Institute, eines medizinischen Testla-
bors für neue Technologien. (USA)

■ 426-428 Présentation d'un rapport annuel d'U.S. West,
société de télécommunications. Des scènes rétro évoquant
les charmes du far-Ouest illustrent la couverture cartonnée
(recto) aussi bien que les deux parties du rapport et diverses pages doubles. (USA)

■ 429-432 Couverture et doubles pages du rapport annuel
pour 1987 du Nichols Institute, un laboratoire médical spécialisé dans l'essai de technologies nouvelles. (USA)

■ 433, 434 Cover and double spread from *Zoo Views,* a publication of the zoological society of San Francisco. Shown is a 10-week-old bald eagle – already the size of an adult bird – and a snow leopard. (USA)

■ 433, 434 Aus *Zoo Views,* eine Publikation der zoologischen Gesellschaft von San Francisco. Hier ein 10-Wochen-altes Adlerkücken, das bereits die Grösse eines erwachsenen Vogels hat, und ein Schneeleopard. (USA)

■ 433, 434 Couverture et double page de *Zoo Views,* une publication de la Société de zoologie de San Francisco. On voit ici un aiglon de 10 semaines, de la taille d'un oiseau adulte, ainsi qu'un léopard des neiges. (USA)

ART DIRECTOR:
KEN COOK/
JAMES CROSS
DESIGNER:
KEN COOK
PHOTOGRAPHER:
STEVE UNDERWOOD
AGENCY:
CROSS ASSOCIATES
PUBLISHER:
SAN FRANCISCO
ZOOLOGICAL SOCIETY
■ 433, 434

ILLUSTRATION

ILLUSTRATION

ILLUSTRATION

ILLUSTRATION

ART DIRECTOR:
BILL WALLSGROVE/
NEIL HOGAN
DESIGNER:
BILL WALLSGROVE/
NEIL HOGAN
ILLUSTRATOR:
EDWARD BRIANT
AGENCY:
COLEY PORTER BELL
CLIENT:
AID OF SAVE THE CHILDREN
■ 435

ART DIRECTOR:
STEVE LISKA
DESIGNER:
BOB COSGROVE
ILLUSTRATOR:
JOHN KLEBER
AGENCY:
LISKA & ASSOCIATES
CLIENT:
CONSOLIDATED PAPERS INC.
►■ 436

■ 435 From a publication entitled "the inheritance - a better world for our children", issued by the design firm Coley Porter Bell & Partners. (GBR)

■ 436 From a brochure on behalf of Consolidated Papers in which the theme "Reflections" is interpreted by various artists. (USA)

■ 435 Aus einer Publikation mit dem Titel «Das Erbe, eine bessere Welt für unsere Kinder», herausgegeben von der Design-Firma Coley Porter Bell & Partners. (GBR)

■ 436 Aus einer Broschüre von Consolidated Papers, in der das Thema «Reflexionen» von verschiedenen Künstlern interpretiert wird. (USA)

■ 435 Extrait d'une publication de la société de design Coley Porter Bell & Partners, «L'Heritage, un meilleur monde pour nos enfants». (GBR)

■ 436 Illustration tirée d'une brochure de Consolidated Papers sur le thème des «Réflexions» qui est interprété par une série d'artistes. (USA)

ILLUSTRATOR:
DOLORES FAIRMAN
AGENCY:
TAYBURN
CLIENT:
EMI
■ 437

ART DIRECTOR:
MILTON GLASER
DESIGNER:
SUZANNE ZUMPANO
ILLUSTRATOR:
GUY BILLOUT
STUDIO:
MILTON GLASER, INC.
CLIENT:
SCHLUMBERGER LIMITED
■ 439

ART DIRECTOR:
MICHAEL RYAN
DESIGNER:
KASPER DESIGN
ILLUSTRATOR:
MARY ANNE LLOYD
POTOGRAPHER:
MICHAEL RYAN
CLIENT:
MICHAEL RYAN PHOTOGRAPHY
■ 438

■ 437 "Jealousy" is the title of this illustration from a portfolio of the illustrators' agency Sharp Practice. (GBR)

■ 438 "Top dog" – self-promotion for photographer Mike Ryan. (USA)

■ 439 Full-page illustration from a company brochure for the Schlumberger oil company. (USA)

■ 437 Aus einer Werbemappe der Illustratoren-Agentur Sharp Practice. Titel dieser Illustration «Eifersucht». (GBR)

■ 438 «Top dog» – Eigenwerbung des Photographen Mike Ryan. (USA)

■ 439 Ganzseitige Illustration aus einer Firmenbroschüre des Ölkonzerns Schlumberger. (USA)

■ 437 Illustration intitulée «Jalousie» tirée d'un portfolio publicitaire de l'agence d'illustrateurs Sharp Practice. (GBR)

■ 438 «Top dog» – autopromotion du photographe Mike Ryan. (USA)

■ 439 Illustration pleine page pour une brochure d'entreprise du groupe pétrolier Schlumberger. (USA)

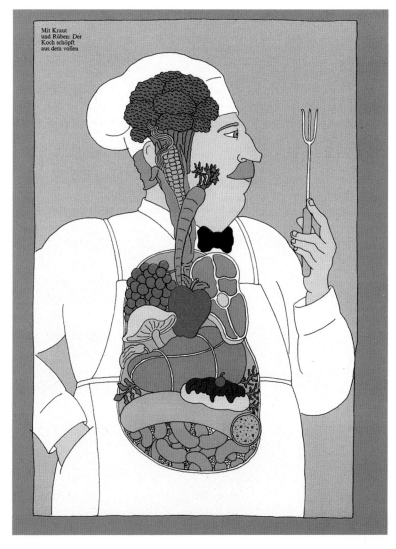

ART DIRECTOR:
HANS-GEORG POSPISCHIL
ILLUSTRATOR:
PAOLA PIGLIA
PUBLISHER:
FRANKFURTER ALLGEMEINE ZEITUNG GMBH
◀■ 440-442

ART DIRECTOR:
HANS-GEORG POSPISCHIL
ILLUSTRATOR:
SEYMOUR CHWAST
PUBLISHER:
FRANKFURTER ALLGEMEINE ZEITUNG GMBH
■ 443, 444

■ 440-442 Double-spread illustrations for an article about the unwritten laws of the coffee shop, in the *Frankfurter Allgemeine Magazin*. (GER)

■ 443, 444 The inner life of artists from various sectors – full-page illustrations from the *Frankfurter Allgemeine Magazin*. (GER)

■ 440-442 Doppelseitige Illustrationen aus einem Beitrag über ungeschriebene Gesetze des Coffee Shops, im *Frankfurter Allgemeine Magazin*. (GER)

■ 443, 444 Das Innenleben von Künstlern verschiedener Branchen – ganzseitige Illustrationen aus dem *Frankfurter Allgemeine Magazin*. (GER)

■ 440-442 Illustrations double page pour un article sur les lois non écrites du coffee shop, dans le *Frankfurter Allgemeine Magazin*. (GER)

■ 443, 444 La vie intérieure de divers artistes œuvrant chacun dans un domaine particulier – illustrations pleine page du *Frankfurter Allgemeine Magazin*. (GER)

ART DIRECTOR:
JERELLE KRAUS
DESIGNER:
JERELLE KRAUS
ILLUSTRATOR:
BRAD HOLLAND
PUBLISHER:
THE NEW YORK TIMES
■ 445

ART DIRECTOR:
MARTIN ZÜLLIG
DESIGNER:
LILIAN-ESTHER PERRIN
ILLUSTRATOR:
LILIAN-ESTHER PERRIN
AGENCY:
KIEFER, MOSIMANN & ZÜLLIG
CLIENT:
NIKON SCHWEIZ
■ 446

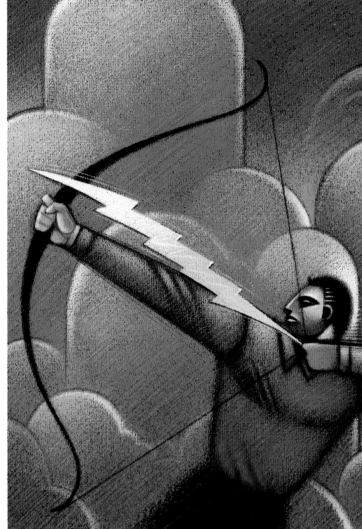

ART DIRECTOR:
TOM STAEBLER
DESIGNER:
LEN WILLIS
ILLUSTRATOR:
DAVE CALVER
PUBLISHER:
PLAYBOY
■ 447

ART DIRECTOR:
PETER CHAFFEY
DESIGNER:
PETER CHAFFEY
ILLUSTRATOR:
DAVID TILLINGHAST
PUBLISHER:
MONTAGE PUBLISHING, INC.
■ 448

■ 445 Illustration from the *New York Times* for an article which questions, "Why subsidize expensive private drug care?". (USA)

■ 446 For *Nikon* – image promotion in magazines. (SWI)

■ 447 Full-page illustration for a humorous contribution in *Playboy* magazine, which is entitled "The modern man's guide to life". (USA)

■ 448 From the magazine *AV Video*. The archer symbolizes the transmission of long-distance signals. (USA)

■ 445 Illustration aus der *New York Times* für einen Artikel, der sich mit der Frage staatlicher Hilfe für Drogenabhängige befasst. (USA)

■ 446 Für *Nikon*-Imagewerbung in Zeitschriften. (SWI)

■ 447 Ganzseitige Illustration für einen humorvollen Beitrag im *Playboy* mit dem Titel «Ein Lebensführer für den modernen Mann». (USA)

■ 448 Aus *AV Video*. Der Bogenschütze symbolisiert das Aussenden von Signalen über lange Distanzen. (USA)

■ 445 Illustration tirée du *New York Times* pour un article discutant du problème de l'aide que l'Etat apporte aux toxicomanes. (USA)

■ 446 Pour la publicité *Nikon* dans les magazines. (SWI)

■ 447 Illustration pleine page pour un article amusant dans le magazine *Playboy,* «Guide de vie pour l'homme moderne». (USA)

■ 448 Pour le magazine *AV Video*. Le tireur à l'arc symbolise l'émission de signaux sur de longues distances. (USA)

ART DIRECTOR:
JIM RUSSEK
DESIGNER:
JAMES MCMULLAN
ILLUSTRATOR:
JAMES MCMULLAN
AGENCY:
JAMES MCMULLAN, INC.
CLIENT:
LINCOLN CENTER THEATER
■ 449

ART DIRECTOR:
SEYMOUR CHWAST
DESIGNER:
SEYMOUR CHWAST
ILLUSTRATOR:
JOSÉ CRUZ
AGENCY:
THE PUSHPIN GROUP
CLIENT:
MOHAWK PAPER CO.
►■ 450

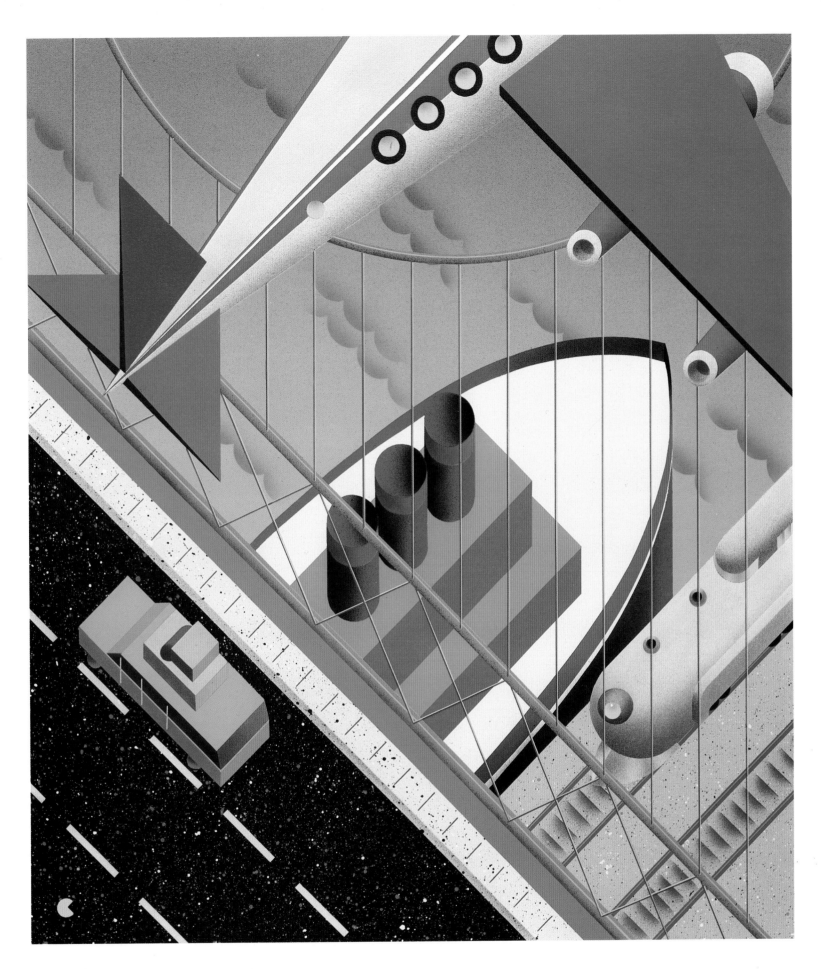

■ 449 "Anything goes" – illustration for the New York Lincoln Center Theater. (USA)

■ 450 José Cruz's post modern version of the French poster style of the twenties. From a feature about art deco in the semi-annual journal *Design & Style.* This illustration was originally used for the cover of *West* magazine. (USA)

■ 449 «Alles ist möglich.» Illustration für das New Yorker Lincoln Center Theater. (USA)

■ 450 José Cruz' postmoderne Version des Stils der französischen Plakate der 20er Jahre. Aus einem Beitrag über Art Deco in der Zeitschrift *Design & Style.* Ursprünglich wurde sie für den Umschlag des *West*-Magazins verwendet. (USA)

■ 449 «Tout est possible». Illustration pour le Lincoln Center Theater de New York. (USA)

■ 450 Version postmoderne du style des affiches françaises des années 20, par José Cruz, pour un article d'art déco dans le magazine *Design & Style.* Illustration employée à l'origine pour la couverture du magazine *West.* (USA)

ART DIRECTOR:
LESLIE SMOLAN
DESIGNER:
BETH BANGOR
ILLUSTRATOR:
MARK PENBERTHY
AGENCY:
CARBONE SMOLAN ASSOCIATES
CLIENT:
MERRILL LYNCH
■ 451, 452

ART DIRECTOR:
PHIL BICKER
ILLUSTRATOR:
JOHN HERSEY
PUBLISHER:
THE FACE
►■ 453

■ 451, 452 From a brochure for the insurance group of the Merrill Lynch company. The circus motif underscores the text in a particular way. (USA)

■ 453 Computer illustration from an article in *The Face* magazine about illustrator John Hersey, who works with an *Apple Mac.* (GBR)

■ 451, 452 Aus einer Broschüre der Versicherungsgruppe der Firma Merrill Lynch. Die Zirkusmotive unterstreichen den Text auf besondere Weise. (USA)

■ 453 Computer-Illustration aus einem Artikel in der Zeitschrift *The Face* über den Illustrator John Hersey, der mit einem *Apple Mac* arbeitet. (GBR)

■ 451, 452 Pour une brochure du groupe d'assurances de la société Merrill Lynch. Les motifs de cirque donnent un impact particulier au texte. (USA)

■ 453 Illustration d'ordinateur pour un article que le magazine *The Face* consacre à l'illustrateur John Hersey qui se sert d'un ordinateur *Apple Mac.* (GBR)

191

ART DIRECTOR:
RUDOLPH HOGLUND
ILLUSTRATOR:
RICHARD HESS
PUBLISHER:
TIME, INC.
■ 454

ART DIRECTOR:
FRED WOODWARD
DESIGNER:
FRED WOODWARD
ILLUSTRATOR:
RICHARD MANTEL
PUBLISHER:
ROLLING STONE
■ 455

■ 454 "We, the people". Cover illustration for a special issue of *Time* magazine. (USA)

■ 455 Portrait of Bob Dylan for a feature in *Rolling Stone* referring to his entry in the history of Rock 'n' Roll. (USA)

■ 454 «Wir, das Volk.» Umschlagillustration für eine Spezialausgabe der Zeitschrift *Time*. (USA)

■ 455 Porträt Bob Dylans für einen Artikel in *Rolling Stone* über seinen Eingang in die Geschichte des Rock'n'Roll. (USA)

■ 454 «Nous, le peuple.» Illustration de couverture pour un numéro spécial du magazine *Time*. (USA)

■ 455 Portrait de Bob Dylan pour un article de *Rolling Stone* retraçant les étapes de sa carrière. (USA)

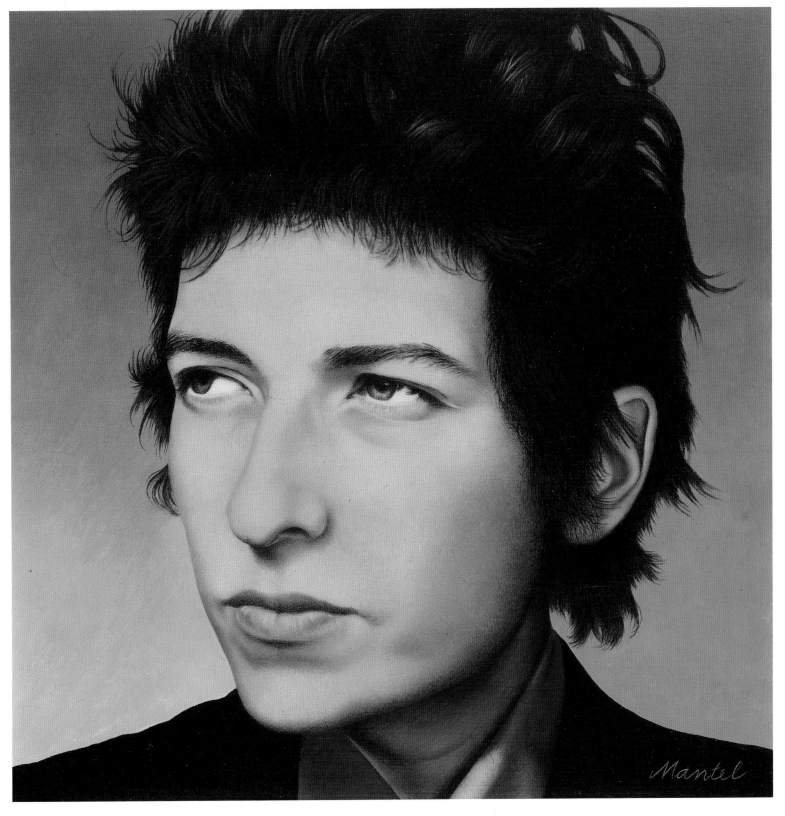

ART DIRECTOR:
Dan Carocca
ILLUSTRATOR:
Braldt Bralds
AGENCY:
O'Grady Advertising
CLIENT:
Donhecy Printers
■ 456

■ 456 Noah's Ark –
advertising for a printing
firm. (USA)

■ 456 Die Arche Noah –
Illustration für die Werbung
einer Druckerei. (USA)

■ 456 L'Arche de Noé –
publicité pour un impri-
meur. (USA)

ILLUSTRATOR:
PERE TORRENT (PERET)
CLIENT:
PRE-OLIMPICA BARCELONA '92
■ 457, 458

■ 457, 458 Illustrations for
the postage stamps that are
to be issued during the Barcelona Olympics. (SPA)

■ 457, 458 Illustrationen
für Briefmarken, die anlässlich der Olympiade in Barcelona herausgegeben wer-
den. (SPA)

■ 457, 458 Illustrations
pour des timbres-poste pour
les Jeux Olympiques de Barcelone. (SPA)

ART DIRECTOR:
HANS-GEORG POSPISCHIL

ILLUSTRATOR:
BRAD HOLLAND

PUBLISHER:
*FRANKFURTER ALLGEMEINE
ZEITUNG GMBH*

■ 459-463

■ 459-462 Illustrations for a feature on basketball, in the *Frankfurter Allgemeine Magazin.* (GER)

■ 463 Billiards is the subject of this illustration from the *Frankfurter Allgemeine Magazin.* (GER)

■ 459-462 Illustrationen für einen Beitrag über Basketball im *Frankfurter Allgemeine Magazin.* (GER)

■ 463 Billard ist das Thema dieser Illustration aus dem *Frankfurter Allgemeine Magazin.* (GER)

■ 459-462 Illustrations d'un article de base-ball publié dans le *Franfurter Allgemeine Magazin.* (GER)

■ 463 Cette illustration du *Frankfurter Allgemeine Magazin* a le billard pour sujet. (GER)

ILLUSTRATOR:
JOSEPH SZALAI
■ 464

■ 464 This illustration is entitled "Homage to Bayros" (oil on wood). (SWI)

■ 465 "It's a jungle out there. To find the right job you need all the help you can get." This is the title of the poster for a job agency. (USA)

■ 464 «Hommage à Bayros» ist der Titel dieses Bildes (Öl auf Holz). (SWI)

■ 465 Für das Plakat eines Stellenvermittlungsbüros: «Da draussen ist es wie im Dschungel. Um die richtige Stelle zu finden, können Sie Hilfe gebrauchen.» (USA)

■ 464 Illustration intitulée «Hommage à Bayros» (huile sur bois). (SWI)

■ 465 Pour l'affiche d'un bureau de placement: «Là dehors, c'est comme dans la jungle. Pour trouver la place qui vous convient, il vous faut toute l'aide imaginable.» (USA)

ART DIRECTOR:
MARV KUNZE
ILLUSTRATOR:
BILL MAYER
AGENCY:
BAUMWOLL & TANNEN ASSOC.
CLIENT:
DRAKE BEAM MORIN INC.,
CAREER NAVIGATOR
■ 465

ART DIRECTOR:
HAYDN MORRIS
ILLUSTRATOR:
WARREN MADILL
AGENCY:
SAATCHI & SAATCHI ADVERTISING
CLIENT:
BRITISH AIRWAYS
■ 466, 467

■ 466, 467 Illustrations for an advertising campaign for British Airways with bird's-eye-view paintings of the countryside at different seasons. (GBR)

■ 466, 467 Illustration für eine Werbekampagne der British Airways mit aus der Vogelperspektive gemalten Ansichten von Landschaften zu verschiedenen Jahreszeiten. (GBR)

■ 466, 467 Pour une campagne publicitaire de British Airways: paysages à vol d'oiseau interprétés par le peintre à différents moments de l'année. (GBR)

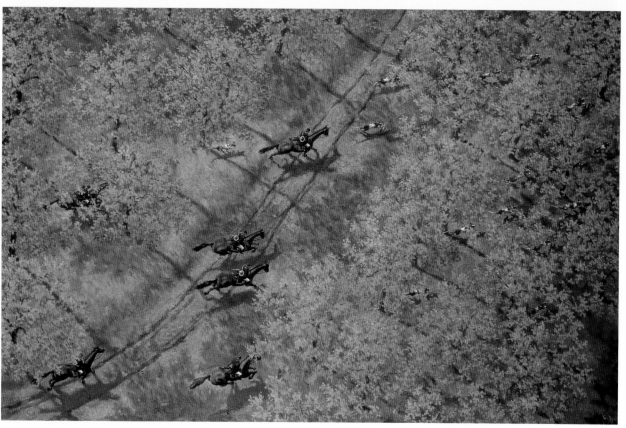

ART DIRECTOR:
MARTIN COTÉ
ILLUSTRATOR:
ALAIN LÉVESQUE
PUBLISHER:
ASSOCIATION DES ILLUSTRA-
TEURS DU QUÉBEC (A.I.I.Q.)
■ 468

■ 468 "Modern Times" -
airbrush illustration as self-
promotion for Alain Lévesque. (CAN)

■ 468 «Die modernen Zei-
ten.» Airbrush-Illustration
als Eigenwerbung von Alain
Lévesque. (CAN)

■ 468 «Les temps moder-
nes.» Illustration peinte au
pistolet pour l'autopromotion d'Alain Lévesque. (CAN)

ART DIRECTOR:
BOB UPTON
DESIGNER:
BOB UPTON
ILLUSTRATOR:
DAN CRAIG
AGENCY:
DESIGNED MARKETING
CLIENT:
THE MINNESOTA ZOO
■ 469

■ 469 Golden monkeys – a rare breed – from China. Illustration on a poster for the Minnesota Zoo. (USA)

■ 469 Seltende Affen aus China – Illustration eines Plakates für den Zoo von Minnesota. (USA)

■ 469 Singes chinois d'une espèce rare – illustration d'une affiche pour le zoo du Minnesota. (USA)

IDENTITE CORPORATE

CORPORATE IDENTITY

ART DIRECTOR:
BARRY TUCKER
DESIGNER:
BARRY TUCKER/
RAY CONDON/
NICOLA LLOYD
STUDIO:
BARRY TUCKER DESIGN
CLIENT:
WORLD EXPO '88
■ 470

ART DIRECTOR:
MARK ANDERSON
DESIGNER:
EARL GEE/
MARK ANDERSON
AGENCY:
MARK ANDERSON DESIGN
CLIENT:
Z TYPOGRAPHY
►■ 471

■ 470 Colorful environmental graphics designed for the main entrance of the Plaza Pavilion at the 1988 World Expo in South Brisbane, Australia. (AUS)

■ 471 Delivery vehicle for Z Typography. The zig-zag vertical design of black and white conveys the photographic positive/negative nature of the business. The various typestyles of Z are educational, each Z has its own typestyle identification and size beneath it. (USA)

■ 470 Farbenfrohe graphische Gestaltung des Eingangs des Plaza-Pavillons bei der Weltausstellung 88 in South Brisbane, Australien. (AUS)

■ 471 Lieferwagen für Z Typography, eine Interpretation der Art des Geschäftes. Der photographische Positiv/Negativ-Aspekt kommt durch das Schwarzweiss zum Ausdruck. Das Z erscheint in verschiedenen Schrifttypen und Grössen, die jeweils angegeben sind. (USA)

■ 470 Aménagement graphique haut en couleur de l'entrée du pavillon Plaza de l'Expo universelle 88 à South Brisbane en Australie. (AUS)

■ 471 Véhicule de livraison de Z Typography décoré d'une interprétation des activités de cette société. L'aspect photo négatif/positif est exprimé par le noir et blanc. Le Z apparaît en différentes types de caractères et corps, lesquels sont indiqués à chaque fois. (USA)

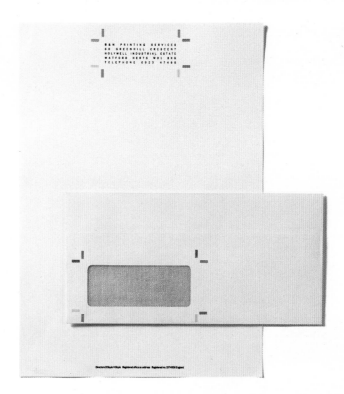

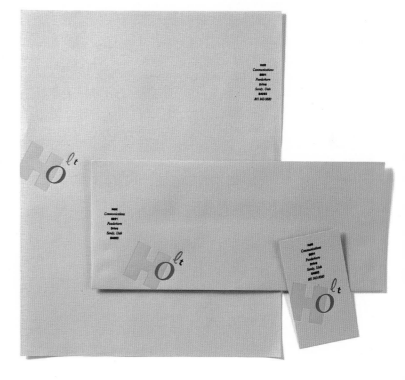

ART DIRECTOR:
JACK TOM
DESIGNER:
JACK TOM
ILLUSTRATOR:
JACK TOM
AGENCY:
JACK TOM DESIGN
CLIENT:
JACK TOM DESIGN
▲■ 478

ART DIRECTOR:
CHARLES S. ANDERSON
DESIGNER:
CHARLES S. ANDERSON
ILLUSTRATOR:
CHARLES S. ANDERSON
AGENCY:
THE DUFFY DESIGN GROUP
CLIENT:
MEDICAL INNOVATION CAPITAL
◀■ 477

ART DIRECTOR:
JENNIFER PHILLIPS
DESIGNER:
JENNIFER PHILLIPS
ILLUSTRATOR:
JENNIFER PHILLIPS
AGENCY:
DAVID ASHTON AND COMPANY
CLIENT:
G.J. PHILIPPS
▲■ 479

ART DIRECTOR:
DON WELLER
DESIGNER:
DON WELLER
ILLUSTRATOR:
DON WELLER
AGENCY:
THE WELLER INSTITUTE
FOR THE CURE OF DESIGN INC.
CLIENT:
BRAD BEAN
◀■ 480

■ 477 Letterhead with business card and sticker for the Medical Innovations Capital Inc. (USA)

■ 478 Stationery for Jack Tom Design. (USA)

■ 479 Letterhead with the blind embossing of a tooth bite – for a jaw orthopedist. (USA)

■ 480 Graphics for the letterhead of photographer Brad Bean. (USA)

■ 477 Briefpapier mit Geschäftskarte und Aufkleber für Medical Innovations Capital Inc. (USA)

■ 478 Geschäftspapier für Jack Tom Design. (USA)

■ 479 Briefpapier mit Blindprägung eines Gebissabdrucks für einen Kieferorthopäden. (USA)

■ 480 Graphik für den Briefkopf des Photographen Brad Bean (Bean = Bohne). (USA)

■ 477 Papier à lettres, carte de visite commerciale et autocollant pour Medical Innovations Capital Inc. (USA)

■ 478 Papier à lettres pour Jack Tom Design. (USA)

■ 479 Papier à lettres avec, gaufrée à sec, une empreinte dentaire, pour un spécialiste de chirurgie maxillaire. (USA)

■ 480 Composition graphique pour le papier à lettres du photographe Brad Bean («bean» veut dire «haricot»). (USA)

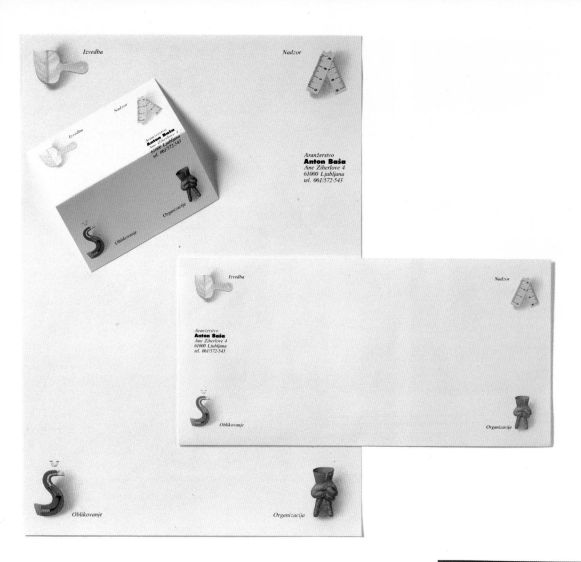

ART DIRECTOR:
EDI BERK
DESIGNER:
EDI BERK
ILLUSTRATOR:
EDI BERK/
ZVONE KOSOVELJ (AIR BRUSH)
STUDIO:
KROG
CLIENT:
ANTON BASA
◀■ 481

■ 481 Stationery for Anton Basa, stand constructor and store decorator. (YUG)

■ 481 Geschäftspapier für Anton Basa, Standbau und Ladendekoration. (YUG)

■ 481 Papier à lettres d'Anton Basa (stands d'exposition, décoration de magasins). (YUG)

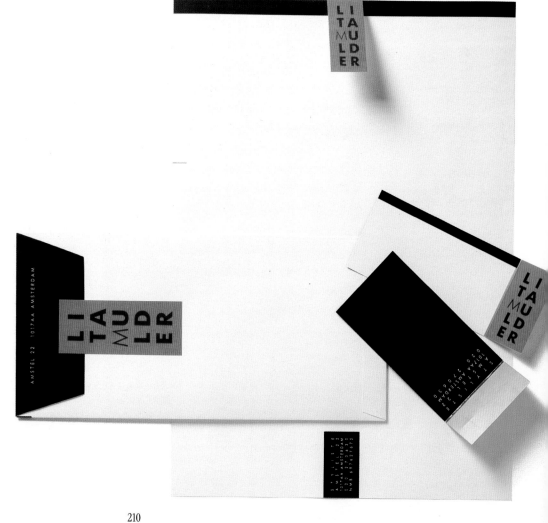

ART DIRECTOR:
RON V/D VLUGT
DESIGNER:
RON V/D VLUGT
CLIENT:
LITA MULDER
▶■ 482

■ 482 Stationery for fashion designer Lita Mulder. (NLD)

■ 482 Briefpapier für die Mode-Designerin Lita Mulder. (NLD)

■ 482 Papier à lettres pour la créatrice de mode Lita Mulder. (NLD)

ART DIRECTOR:
TIM HARTFORD
DESIGNER:
TIM HARTFORD
CLIENT:
TIM HARTFORD
GRAPHIC DESIGN
■ 483

■ 483 For Tim Hartford,
graphic designer. (USA)

■ 483 Für Tim Hartford,
Graphik-Design. (USA)

■ 483 Pour Tim Hardford
(design graphique). (USA)

ART DIRECTOR:
ROB VAN DEN BERG
DESIGNER:
ROB VAN DEN BERG
ILLUSTRATOR:
ROB VAN DEN BERG
AGENCY:
MILLFORD-VAN DEN BERG
DESIGN BV.
CLIENT:
MILLFORD-VAN DEN BERG
DESIGN BV.
■ 484

■ 484 Business card with
stuck on stamp for the
design firm Millford-van
den Berg. (NLD)

■ 484 Visitenkarte mit auf-
geklebter Briefmarke für die
Design-Firma Millford-van
den Berg. (NLD)

■ 484 Carte de visite ornée
d'un timbre collé, pour la
société de design Millford-
van den Berg. (NLD)

ART DIRECTOR:
MARK GEER/
RICHARD KILMER
DESIGNER:
MARK GEER/
RICHARD KILMER
AGENCY:
KILMER/GEER DESIGN, INC.
CLIENT:
SPECIALTY PRESS
■ 485

■ 485 Business card for a
printer. (USA)

■ 485 Visitenkarte für eine
Druckerei. (USA)

■ 485 Carte de visite pour
une imprimerie. (USA)

ART DIRECTOR:
PIERRE VERMEIR/
GEOFF HALPIN
DESIGNER:
DAVID JAMES
ILLUSTRATOR:
JOHN GEARY
AGENCY:
HALPIN GREY VERMEIR
CLIENT:
JOHN MITCHELL/
MITCHELL PHOENIX
■ 486

■ 486 Business cards for a
firm of consultants. (GBR)

■ 486 Visitenkarten für eine
Unternehmensberatungs-
firma. (GBR)

■ 486 Cartes de visite pour
une société de conseils d'entreprises. (GBR)

Bibs & Bubbles

Baby Accessories

2084 Hunt Cr.

Burlington, Ontario

Canada L7M 2N9

Telephone

(416) 332-4951

Bibs & Bubbles

Baby Accessories

2084 Hunt Cr.

Burlington, Ontario

Canada L7M 2N9

Elizabeth R. Sherrold

Bibs & Bubbles Baby Accessories

2084 Hunt Cr. Burlington, Ontario

Canada L7M 2N9 Tel (416) 332-4951

ART DIRECTOR:
PETER BAKER
DESIGNER:
PETER BAKER
AGENCY:
TAYLOR & BROWNING
CLIENT:
BIBS & BUBBLES
■ 487

■ 487 Letterhead and business card with a real safety
pin for a producer of baby
articles. (CAN)

■ 487 Briefpapier und Visitenkarte mit einer richtigen
Sicherheitsnadel für einen
Hersteller von Baby-Arti-
keln. (CAN)

■ 487 Papier à lettres et
carte de visite avec une
vraie épingle de nourrice,
pour un fabricant d'articles
pour bébés. (CAN)

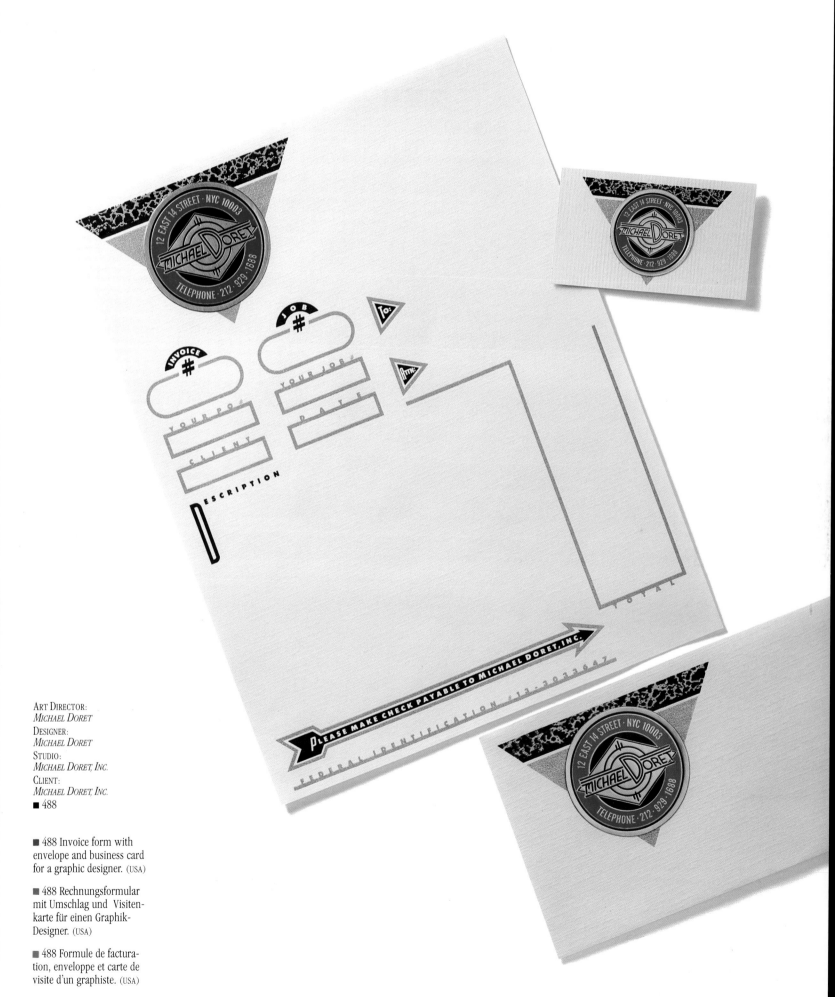

ART DIRECTOR:
MICHAEL DORET
DESIGNER:
MICHAEL DORET
STUDIO:
MICHAEL DORET, INC.
CLIENT:
MICHAEL DORET, INC.
■ 488

■ 488 Invoice form with
envelope and business card
for a graphic designer. (USA)

■ 488 Rechnungsformular
mit Umschlag und Visiten-
karte für einen Graphik-
Designer. (USA)

■ 488 Formule de factura-
tion, enveloppe et carte de
visite d'un graphiste. (USA)

■ 489 "Broken Rules" - for women's blue jeans. (USA)

■ 489 «Regelverstoss», Logo für Damen-Blue-Jeans. (USA)

■ 489 «Infraction aux règles», logo pour des jeans femmes. (USA)

■ 490 For Croydon Airport - marking the occasion of its 60th anniversary. (GBR)

■ 490 Für den Flughafen Croydon zum 60sten Geburtstag des Flughafengebäudes. (GBR)

■ 490 Pour l'aéroport de Croydon à l'occasion du 60e anniversaire du bâtiment central. (GBR)

■ 491 For Moda Hair Design, hairstylists in Ottawa. (CAN)

■ 491 Für das Haar-Studio Moda Hair Design in Ottawa. (CAN)

■ 491 Pour le salon de coiffure Moda Hair Design d'Ottawa. (CAN)

■ 492 For Union Station, a modern restaurant with shops, in Washington. (USA)

■ 492 Für Union Station, ein modernes Restaurant mit Ladenlokal in Washington. (USA)

■ 492 Pour l'Union Station, un restaurant moderne de Washington doté d'un magasin. (USA)

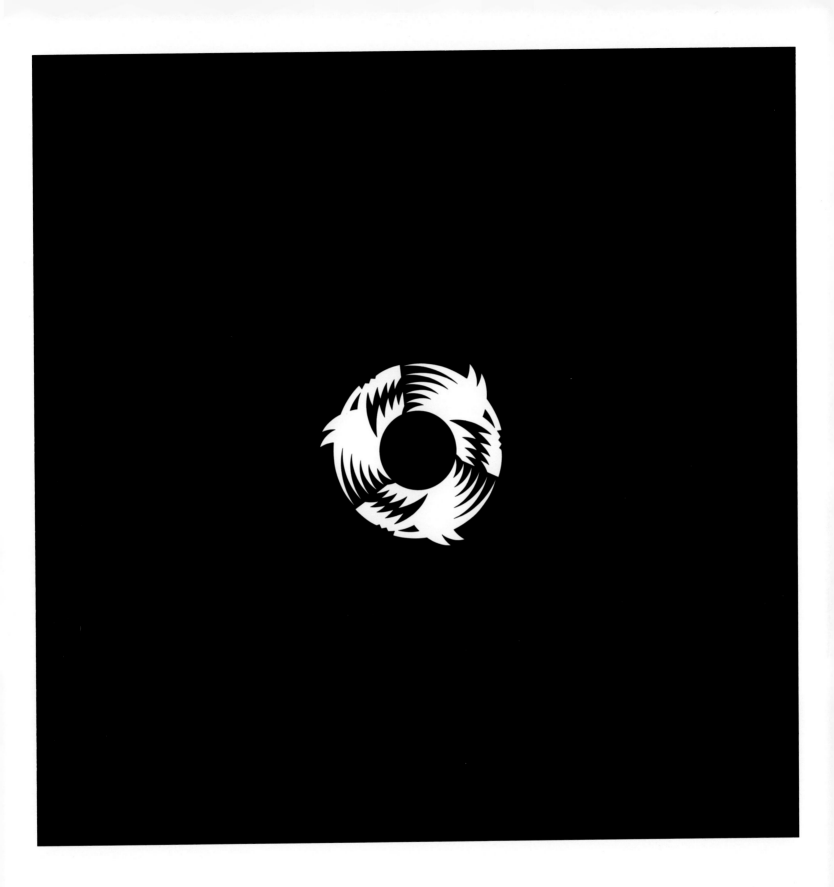

ART DIRECTOR:
KEN SHAFER
ILLUSTRATOR:
KEN SHAFER
AGENCY:
RICHARDS BROCK MILLER
MITCHELL & ASSOCIATES/
THE RICHARDS GROUP
CLIENT:
TEAM MAD DOG
■ 493

■ 493 Symbol for the
motorbike racing team
"Mad Dog". (USA)

■ 493 Symbol für das
Motorrad-Renn-Team «Mad
Dog». (USA)

■ 493 Emblème de l'équipe
de course motocycliste
«Mad Dog». (USA)

ART DIRECTOR:
REX PETEET
DESIGNER:
REX PETEET
AGENCY:
SIBLEY/PETEET DESIGN
CLIENT:
SHAVANO PARK
■
494

ART DIRECTOR:
DON WELLER
ILLUSTRATOR:
DON WELLER
AGENCY:
THE WELLER INSTITUTE
FOR THE CURE OF DESIGN, INC.
CLIENT:
MUSICUM LAUDE
■
495

ART DIRECTOR:
CHARLES S. ANDERSON
DESIGNER:
CHARLES S. ANDERSON/
HALEY JOHNSON
AGENCY:
THE DUFFY DESIGN GROUP
CLIENT:
GRAPHIQUE DE FRANCE
■
496

ART DIRECTOR:
WOODY PIRTLE
DESIGNER:
WOODY PIRTLE
AGENCY:
PENTAGRAM DESIGN
CLIENT:
DALLAS OPERA
■
497

ART DIRECTOR:
BÜLENT ERKMEN
DESIGNER:
BÜLENT ERKMEN
AGENCY:
REKLAMEVI
CLIENT:
CLUB ORA
■
498

ART DIRECTOR:
NEVILLE SMITH
DESIGNER:
NEVILLE SMITH
AGENCY:
NEVILLE SMITH
GRAPHIC DESIGN
CLIENT:
CANUS PLASTICS INC.
■
499

ART DIRECTOR:
NEVILLE SMITH
DESIGNER:
NEVILLE SMITH
AGENCY:
NEVILLE SMITH
GRAPHIC DESIGN
CLIENT:
PIANOCRAFT
■
500

DESIGNER:
JACK ANDERSON/
JULIE TANAGI
ILLUSTRATOR:
MARY HERMES
AGENCY:
HORNALL ANDERSON
CLIENT:
MISTY ISLE FARMS
■
501

ART DIRECTOR:
NEVILLE SMITH
DESIGNER:
NEVILLE SMITH
AGENCY:
NEVILLE SMITH
GRAPHIC DESIGN
CLIENT:
NOVARA HOLDINGS INC.
■
502

ART DIRECTOR:
KAZUMASA NAGAI
DESIGNER:
KAZUMASA NAGAI
AGENCY:
NIPPON DESIGN CENTER
CLIENT:
SEGIVIA GOLF CLUB
■
503

ART DIRECTOR:
STEPHEN FRANKS
DESIGNER:
STEPHEN FRANKS
AGENCY:
COLEY PORTER BELL
CLIENT:
GOOCH & WAGSTAFF
■
504

ART DIRECTOR:
WOODY PIRTLE
DESIGNER:
WOODY PIRTLE
AGENCY:
PENTAGRAM DESIGN
CLIENT:
TRAVIS CONSTRUCTION
■
505

GRAPHIQUE
DE FRANCE

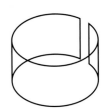

PIANOCRAFT

ART DIRECTOR:
FRANK ZEPPONI
ILLUSTRATOR:
MARK SUMMERS
AGENCY:
THE HIVELEY AGENCY
CLIENT:
FOR THE BIRDS

508

ART DIRECTOR:
TAKENOBU IGARASHI
DESIGNER:
NOREEN FUKUMORI
STUDIO:
IGARASHI
CLIENT:
FUJII & CO. LTD./
REIMEI DIVISION
■
506

ART DIRECTOR:
BOB PAGANUCCI
DESIGNER:
BOB PAGANUCCI
AGENCY:
SALPETER PAGANUCCI
CLIENT:
KIDDER, PEABODY + COMPANY,
INDUSTRIAL RELATIONS COUNCIL
■
507

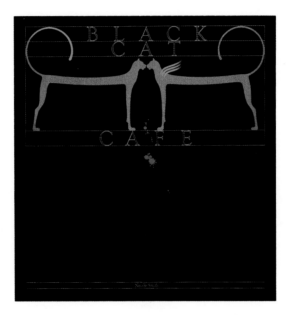

ART DIRECTOR:
NEVILLE SMITH
ILLUSTRATOR:
NEVILLE SMITH
AGENCY:
NEVILLE SMITH
GRAPHIC DESIGN
CLIENT:
BLACK CAT CAFE
■
511

ART DIRECTOR:
RICHARD HENDERSON
DESIGNER:
FLETT, HENDERSON & ARNOLD
AGENCY:
FLETT, HENDERSON & ARNOLD
CLIENT:
HYATT ON COLLINS HOTEL,
MONSOON'S NIGHTCLUB
■
509

DESIGNER:
KIT HINRICHS/
ALISA RUDLOFF
ILLUSTRATOR:
MARK SUMMERS
AGENCY:
PENTAGRAM DESIGN
CLIENT:
CLARKS OF ENGLAND
■
510

ART DIRECTOR:
Kenzo Nakagawa
DESIGNER:
Kenzo Nakagawa/
Satoh Morikami
ILLUSTRATOR:
Kumiko Nagasaki
AGENCY:
NDC Graphics
CLIENT:
Isetan Department Store
■ 512

■ 512 For the children's department of the Japanese stores Isetan. (JPN)

■ 512 Für die Kinderabteilung des japanischen Kaufhauses Isetan. (JPN)

■ 512 Pour le rayon enfants des grands magasins japonais Isetan. (JPN)

PACKUNGEN

EMBALLAGES

ART DIRECTOR:
DAVID LANCASHIRE
DESIGNER:
DAVID LANCASHIRE
ILLUSTRATOR:
DAVID LANCASHIRE
AGENCY:
DAVID LANCASHIRE DESIGN
CLIENT:
DAVID LANCASHIRE DESIGN
■ 514, 515

■ 514, 515 Red wine bottles with cardboard packaging as advertising gift from David Lancashire Design. (AUS)

■ 516 Square bottle with corresponding label for a cocktail blend. (GBR)

■ 517 Bottle for a chain of supermarkets' private label port wine, with the text applied directly on the bottle itself. The task was to create an image for their own product range that would underscore the new and innovative business policy of the stores. (GBR)

■ 514, 515 Als Werbegeschenke von David Lancashire Design gestaltete Rotweinflaschen mit Verpackung. (AUS)

■ 516 Rechteckige Flasche mit entsprechendem Etikett für ein Mix-Getränk. (GBR)

■ 517 Als Hausmarke einer Supermarktkette gestaltete Flasche für Portwein mit direkt auf die Flasche aufgetragenem Text. Aufgabe war es, für diese hauseigene Produktlinie ein Image zu schaffen, das der neuen, innovativen Geschäftspolitik des Unternehmens entspricht. (GBR)

■ 514, 515 Bouteilles de vin rouge étudiées par David Lancashire Design pour servir de cadeaux publicitaires. (AUS)

■ 516 Bouteille carrée avec l'étiquette correspondante, pour une boisson mélangée. (GBR)

■ 517 Bouteille de porto étudiée pour une chaîne de supermarchés. Le texte est imprimé à même le verre. Il s'agissait de créer pour cette marque maison couvrant toute une gamme de produits une image correspondant à la nouvelle politique novatrice de l'entreprise. (GBR)

ART DIRECTOR:
JOHN BLACKBURN
DESIGNER:
BELINDA CUGGAN/
GLYN HAWKINS
AGENCY:
BLACKBURN'S LTD.
CLIENT:
ALLIED LYONS
■ 516

ART DIRECTOR:
MARY LEWIS
DESIGNER:
MARY LEWIS
AGENCY:
LEWIS MOBERLY
CLIENT:
ASDA STORES LTD.
■ 517

ART DIRECTOR:
ERWIN SCHMÖLZER
DESIGNER:
KRISTIN KONIAREK
CLIENT:
SCHARTNER GETRÄNKE GMBH
■ 518-520

ART DIRECTOR:
LUIS D. ACEVEDO
DESIGNER:
LUIS D. ACEVEDO
ILLUSTRATOR:
LUIS D. ACEVEDO
AGENCY:
RICHARDS BROCK MILLER
MITCHELL & ASSOCIATES/
THE RICHARDS GROUP
CLIENT:
EL CHICO
◀■ 521

■ 518-520 Design of bottle livery for a series of refreshing drinks. (AUS)

■ 521 Label design for a Margarita cocktail. A solution had to be found that conformed to an economical four color flexographic printing process. (USA)

■ 522 This special gift packaging and the menu and place card were designed for a meal to mark the occasion of the 100th anniversary of *Foster's* beer. (AUS)

■ 523 Label design for "Mumba Wave Dip" – a fruity marinade. (USA)

■ 524 Package design for the introduction of *Masterchoice* – a new brand of pasta. (USA)

■ 518-520 Flaschenausstattung für eine Reihe von Erfrischungsgetränken. (AUS)

■ 521 Etikettgestaltung für ein Margarita-Mixgetränk. Es galt eine Lösung zu finden, die für den preisgünstigen 4-Farben-Flexodruck geeignet ist. (USA)

■ 522 Diese spezielle Geschenkverpackung sowie das Menu und die Platzkarte wurden für ein Essen anlässlich des 100jährigen Bestehens des *Foster's*-Biers entworfen. (AUS)

■ 523 Etikettgestaltung für «Mumba Wave Dip», eine fruchtige Marinade. (USA)

■ 524 Packungsgestaltung für die Einführung von *Masterchoice*, eine neue Teigwarenmarke. (USA)

■ 518-520 Etude de bouteilles pour une gamme de boissons rafraîchissantes. (AUS)

■ 521 Etiquette pour une boisson mélangée Margarita. La solution devait être appropriée au mode d'impression avantageux en flexographie quadrichrome. (USA)

■ 522 Cet emballage-cadeau spécial, le menu et le carton nominatif ont été réalisés en vue d'un banquet d'anniversaire pour le centenaire de la bière *Foster's*. (AUS)

■ 523 Etiquette pour la marinade fruitée «Mumba Wave Dip». (USA)

■ 524 Emballage de lancement pour la nouvelle variété de pâtes *Masterchoice*. (USA)

ART DIRECTOR:
BARRIE TUCKER
DESIGNER:
BARRIE TUCKER/
ELIZABETH SCHLOOZ/
LUCI GIANNATTILIO
AGENCY:
BARRIE TUCKER DESIGN
CLIENT:
CARLTON & UNITED BREWERIES
■ 522

ART DIRECTOR:
MICHAEL BROCK
DESIGNER:
GAYLEN BRAUN
AGENCY:
MICHAEL BROCK DESIGN
CLIENT:
DUGGAN'S INGREDIENTS
■ 523

ART DIRECTOR:
COLIN PORTER
DESIGNER:
COLIN PORTER/
MARK LLOYD
ILLUSTRATOR:
ANN SHARP
AGENCY:
COLEY PORTER BELL
CLIENT:
A & P
▼■ 524

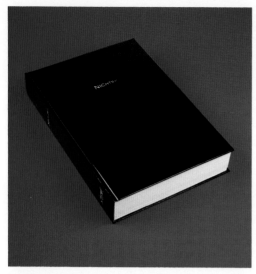

ART DIRECTOR:
Jürgen Dewet Schmidt
DESIGNER:
Sibylle Haase
AGENCY:
Haase & Knels
CLIENT:
Grashoff Delikatessen
■ 525-528

■ 525-528 "Nothing" is the title of an advertising gift from the Grashoff Delikatessen. It was produced in an edition of 2000. Shown is the cover, the title page, an "Introduction to nothing", and the contents in the form of a bottle with schnapps. (GER)

■ 529 The country of origin of this coffee, which is offered as private label by Safeware Stores, is the focal point of this packaging illustrated with a photographic collage. (GBR)

■ 530 Unpublished study for a pack for cigarettes without nicotine. (USA)

■ 525-528 «Nichts» ist der Titel eines Werbegeschenks von Grashoff Delikatessen, das in einer Auflage von 2000 Stück hergestellt wurde. Hier der Umschlag, die Titelseite, eine «Einführung in das Nichts» und der Inhalt in Gestalt einer Flasche mit einem Klaren. (GER)

■ 529 Das Herkunftsland dieses Kaffees, der als Eigenmarke der Safeware Stores angeboten wird, steht im Mittelpunkt dieser mit einer Collage illustrierten Verpackung. (GBR)

■ 530 Unveröffentlichte Studie einer Packung für Zigaretten ohne Nikotin. (USA)

■ 525-528 «Rien», voilà le titre d'un cadeau publicitaire de la maison de commerce Grashoff Delikatessen. Ce "livre" était produit à 2000 exemplaires. On en voit ici la couverture, la page de titre, l'«introduction à rien» et le contenu, une bouteille d'eau-de-vie. (GER)

■ 529 Le pays d'origine de ce café distribué sous la marque des Safeware Stores tient la vedette de cet emballage illustré d'un photocollage. (GBR)

■ 530 Etude du conditionnement d'une marque de cigarette dénicotinisée. (USA)

ART DIRECTOR:
MARY LEWIS
DESIGNER:
LUCY DREW
IPHOTOGRAPHER:
CARL WARNER
AGENCY:
LEWIS MOBERLY DESIGN CONSULTANTS
CLIENT:
SAFEWAY STORES LTD.
■ 529

ART DIRECTOR:
CHARLES S. ANDERSON
DESIGNER:
CHARLES S. ANDERSON
ILLUSTRATOR:
CHARLES S. ANDERSON/ LYNN SCHULTE
AGENCY:
THE DUFFY DESIGN GROUP
CLIENT:
LEO BURNETT/PHILLIP MORRIS
■ 530

ART DIRECTOR:
SHIGERU AKIZUKI
DESIGNER:
SHIGERU AKIZUKI
ILLUSTRATOR:
SHIGERU AKIZUKI
◄■ 531-534

ART DIRECTOR:
ADELAIDE ACERBI
DESIGNER:
GIORGIO GALLI
AGENCY:
ADELAIDE ACERBI
CLIENT:
DRIADE S.P.A.
■ 535, 536

■ 531-534 Paulownia wood cases with sliding lids, shown opened and closed, for Japanese decorative plates. (JPN)

■ 535, 536 Transparent carrier bag for a producer of multi-purpose bars, shelves, and coat hanging bars. (ITA)

■ 531-534 Holzschachteln mit Schiebeverschluss, hier geöffnet und geschlossen gezeigt, für japanische Zierteller. (JPN)

■ 535, 536 Transparente Plastiktragtasche für einen Hersteller von Gestellen, Aufhängevorrichtungen etc. (ITA)

■ 531-534 Coffrets de bois à coulisseau montrés ouverts et fermés, pour des assiettes décoratives japonaises. (JPN)

■ 535, 536 Sac plastique transparent illustré pour un fabricant de barres multi-usages. (ITA)

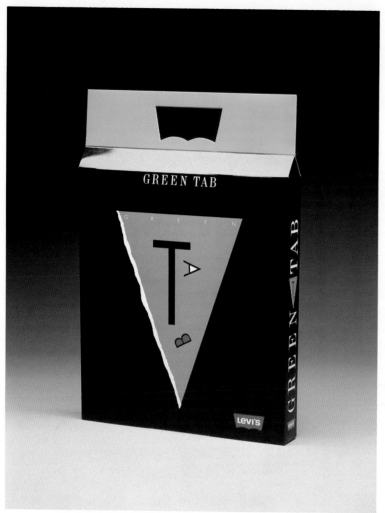

ART DIRECTOR:
MARIO ESKENAZI
DESIGNER:
MARIO ESKENAZI/
PABLO MARTIN
AGENCY:
MCCANN ERICKSON
CLIENT:
LEVI STRAUSS ESPAGNA
■ 537

ART DIRECTOR:
ROBERT VALENTINE
DESIGNER:
ROBERT VALENTINE
PHOTOGRAPHER:
MATTHEW ROLSTON
CLIENT:
BLOOMINGDALE'S
■ 538

■ 537 Carrier carton with integrated handle for *Green Tap*, a line by *Levi's*. (SPA)

■ 538 Hollywood is the subject of this photo collage as illustration on a carrier bag made out of layered paper for Bloomingdale's. (USA)

■ 539 An unusual flacon with box for a fragrance by Romeo Gigli. (ITA)

■ 540 Container for a tautening perfumed cream in the fragrance range of the perfume "Bleu de Chine". (FRA)

■ 537 Tragkarton mit integriertem Tragegriff für *Green Tap*, eine Linie von *Levi's*. (SPA)

■ 538 Hollywood ist das Thema dieser mit Photo-Collagen illustrierten Tragtasche aus beschichtetem Papier für das Kaufhaus Bloomingdale's. (USA)

■ 539 Ein ungewöhnlicher Flakon mit Karton für ein Parfum von Romeo Gigli. (ITA)

■ 540 Behälter für eine straffende Parfum-Creme in der Duftnote des Parfums «Bleu de Chine». (FRA)

■ 537 Carton de transport à poignée intégrée pour *Green Tap*, une ligne de produits *Levi's*. (SPA)

■ 538 Hollywood est le sujet de ce sac en papier couché aux matières plastiques, illustré de photocollages, pour les grands magasins Blommingdale's. (USA)

■ 539 Flacon aux formes insolites et carton pour un parfum de Romeo Gigli. (ITA)

■ 540 Conditionnement d'une crème raffermissante parfumée aux senteurs du parfum «Bleu de Chine». (FRA)

DESIGNER:
Serge Mansau
PHOTOGRAPHER:
Estelle Mansau
CLIENT:
Romeo Gigli
■ 539

ART DIRECTOR:
Marc de la Morandière
DESIGNER:
Serge Mansau
PHOTOGRAPHER:
Estelle Mansau
CLIENT:
MPM Productions
■ 540

ART DIRECTOR:
DAVID KESSLER/
HOCK WAH YEO
DESIGNER:
HOCK WAH YEO
ILLUSTRATOR:
CHRIS KIRBY
AGENCY:
WONG & YEO
CLIENT:
BRODERBUND SOFTWARE
■ 542

■ 542 Packaging for a high-spirited home computer game in the look of the technicolor, high adventure movies of the 40's and 50's era. (USA)

■ 542 Verpackung für ein Computer-Spiel für junge Leute, im Stil der in den 40er und 50er Jahren populären Abenteuerfilme. (USA)

■ 542 Emballage d'un jeu vidéo pour jeunes gens, dans le style des films d'aventures si populaires dans les années 40 et 50. (USA)

ART DIRECTOR:
ROBERT VALENTINE
DESIGNER:
MICHAEL BARTALOS
CLIENT:
BLOOMINGDALE'S
■ 543

■ 543 Packaging design for Bloomingdale's private label camera. (USA)

■ 543 Packungsgestaltung für eine Kamera, die vom Kaufhaus Bloomingdale's als Hausmarke angeboten wird. (USA)

■ 543 Emballage d'un appareil photo vendu sous la marque des grands magasins Bloomingdale's. (USA)

ART DIRECTOR:
BILLY COLE/
ROBERT VALENTINE
DESIGNER:
BILLY COLE
CLIENT:
BLOOMINGDALE'S
■ 544

■ 544 Cardboard packaging
for Bloomingdale's private
label party glasses. (USA)

■ 544 Kartonverpackung
für unter der Hausmarke
von Bloomingdale's ange-
botene «Party»-Gläser. (USA)

■ 544 Emballage carton
pour des verres de fête
distribués sous la marque
de Bloomingdale's. (USA)

ART DIRECTOR:
JACK ANDERSON/
JANI DREWFS
DESIGNER:
JANI DREWFS/
JACK ANDERSON/
DAVID BATES
AGENCY:
HORNALL ANDERSON
DESIGN WORKS
CLIENT:
MICROSOFT UNIVERSITY
■ 545

■ 545 Part of a packaging
system for the Microsoft
University Video Course Kit.
(USA)

■ 545 Teil eines Verpak-
kungssystems für einen
Universitäts-Videokursus.
(USA)

■ 545 Partie d'un système
d'emballage conçu pour un
cours universitaire vidéo.
(USA)

ART DIRECTOR:
SCOTT TAYLOR
DESIGNER:
JOHN PYLYPCZAK
PHOTOGRAPHER:
ROBERT WATSON
STYLIST:
GORDON SAUVÉ
AGENCY:
TAYLOR & BROWNING
DESIGN ASSOCIATES
CLIENT:
CAMPEAU CORPORATION
■ 546

■ 546 Cardboard box, shown closed and opened, holding leasing brochures for an office complex called WaterPark Place located in Toronto's harbor area. (CAN)

■ 546 Kartonschachtel, hier geschlossen und geöffnet gezeigt, für Prospekte, die potentielle Mieter über ein Geschäftshochhaus informieren. (CAN)

■ 546 Boîte de carton montrée fermée et ouverte. Elle renferme des prospectus informant la clientèle potentielle des possibilités de location dans une tour de bureaux. (CAN)

BOOKS
CALENDARS

BÜCHER
KALENDER

LIVRES
CALENDRIERS

■ 547 For a book showing previously unpublished photos of James Dean, taken by Dennis Stock who had gotten to know the young star in Hollywood in 1954 and who accompanied him on a journey. (USA)

■ 548 Cover of a book about Jean Tinguely, Swiss artist, inventor of phantasy mobiles, and sculptor. (USA)

■ 549 Cover of the book "The Night of Fire" by Sam Jaun, published by the Ex Libris Book Club. (SWI)

■ 550 For a book with an unusual format, subtitled "The Glass Submarine", published on the occasion of the art exhibition "transart 1" at the Danube Festival. (AUT)

■ 547 Für ein Buch mit bisher unveröffentlichen Photos von James Dean, aufgenommen von Dennis Stock, der den jungen Star 1954 in Hollywood kennenlernte und auf einer Reise begleitete. (USA)

■ 548 «Ein Zauber, stärker als der Tod.» Umschlag für ein Buch über den Schweizer Künstler Jean Tinguely. (USA)

■ 549 Umschlag für ein im Buchclub Ex Libris erschienenes Buch von Sam Jaun. (SWI)

■ 550 Für ein Buch in ungewöhnlichem Format, das anlässlich der Kunstausstellung «transart 1» im Rahmen des Donaufestivals erschienen ist. (AUT)

■ 547 Jaquette d'un livre de photos inédites à ce jour de James Dean (1931 – 1955) prises par Dennis Stock, qui rencontra la jeune vedette à Hollywood en 1954 et l'accompagna en voyage. (USA)

■ 548 «Une magie plus puissante que la mort.» Couverture d'un ouvrage consacré à l'artiste suisse Jean Tinguely. (USA)

■ 549 Couverture de l'ouvrage «La Nuit de l'incendie» par Sam Jaun publié au Club du Livre Ex Libris. (SWI)

■ 550 Pour un ouvrage au format inhabituel, «Le Sous-marin de verre», publié à l'occasion de l'exposition «transart 1» organisée dans le cadre du Festival danubien. (AUT)

ART DIRECTOR:
PAUL WOODS
DESIGNER:
PAUL WOODS
AGENCY:
WOODS & WOODS
PUBLISHER:
CHRONICLE BOOKS
■ 547

ILLUSTRATOR:
JEAN TINGUELY
PUBLISHER:
ABBEVILLE PRESS
■ 548

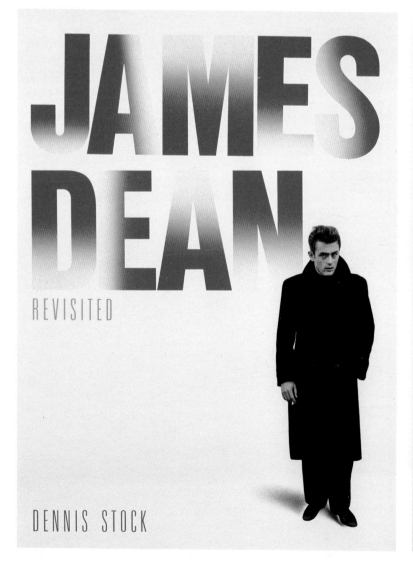

ART DIRECTOR:
Thomas Schaer
DESIGNER:
Thomas Schaer
ILLUSTRATOR
Thomas Schaer
AGENCY:
CAT Advertising
PUBLISHER:
Ex Libris Verlag
■ 549

ART DIRECTOR:
Walter Bohatsch
DESIGNER:
Walter Bohatsch/
Clemens Schedler
AGENCY:
Walter Bohatsch
Grafik Design
PUBLISHER:
NÖ/Landesregierung
Kulturabteilung
■ 550

ART DIRECTOR:
AMY NATHAN/
KATHRYN KLEINMAN
DESIGNER:
JACQUELINE JONES
PHOTOGRAPHER:
KATHRYN KLEINMAN
AGENCY:
JACQUELINE JONES DESIGN
PUBLISHER:
CHRONICLE BOOKS
■ 551

ART DIRECTOR:
ROBERT McKEE
DESIGNER:
ROBERT McKEE
PHOTOGRAPHER:
TOMIO OHASHI
PUBLISHER:
HARRY N. ABRAMS, INC.
■ 552

ART DIRECTOR:
LOUISE FILI
ILLUSTRATOR:
JAVIER ROMERO
PUBLISHER:
PANTHEON BOOKS
►■ 553

■ 551 Cover of a book giving recipes for entrées, illustrated with photographs by Kathryn Kleinman. (USA)

■ 552 Dustjacket of a book about current architecture. Shown is the entrance of the Saitama Museum of Modern Art by architect Kisho Kurokawa. (USA)

■ 553 For a book about the transformation of black music in a music industry dominated by whites. (USA)

■ 551 Umschlag für ein Buch mit Rezepten für Vorspeisen, illustriert mit Aufnahmen von Kathryn Kleinman. (USA)

■ 552 Schutzumschlag eines Buches über «Architektur heute». Hier der Eingang des Saitama Museum of Modern Art des Architekten Kisho Kurokawa. (USA)

■ 553 Für ein Buch über die Veränderung der schwarzen Musik in einer von Weissen dominierten Industrie. (USA)

■ 551 Couverture d'un livre de recettes de hors-d'œuvre illustré par la photographe Kathryn Kleinman. (USA)

■ 552 Jaquette d'un livre consacré à «l'architecture d'aujourd'hui». On voit ici l'entrée du Saitama Museum of Modern Art de l'architecte Kisho Kurokawa. (USA)

■ 553 Pour une étude sur la transformation de la musique noire entre les mains des éditeurs de musique blancs. (USA)

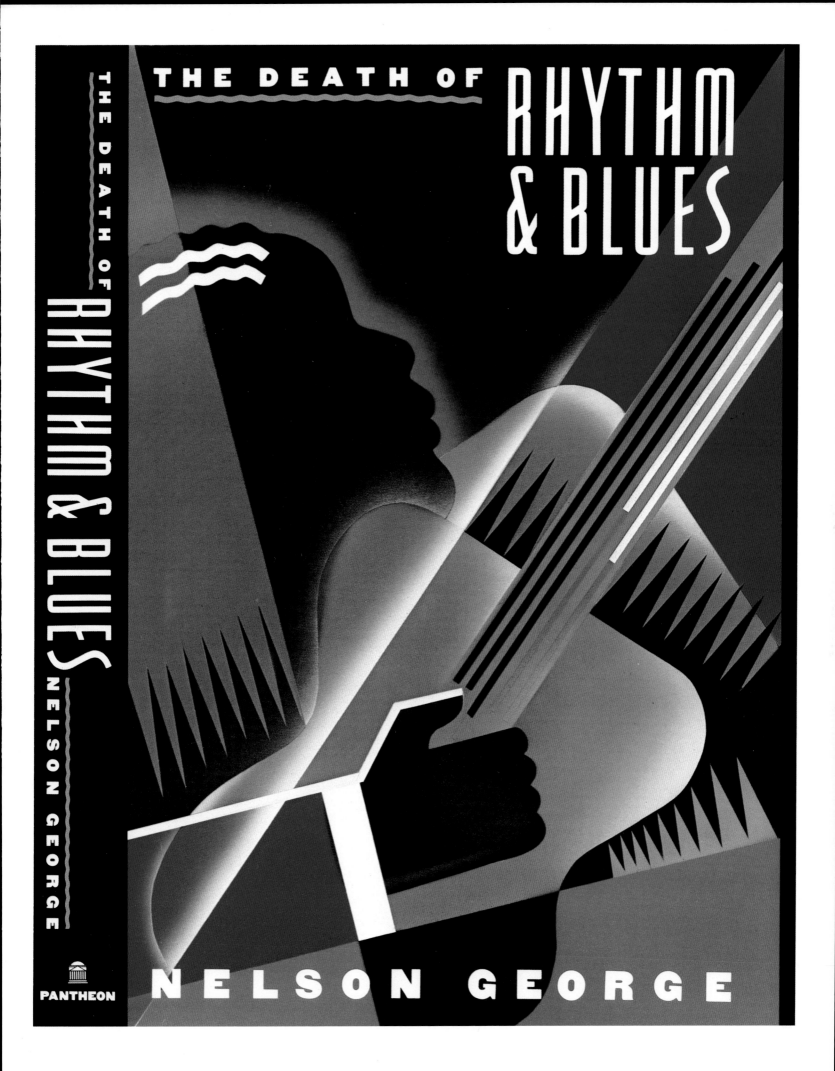

DESIGNER:
René Khatami
PUBLISHER:
Abbeville Press, Inc.
■ 554

ART DIRECTOR:
Jackie Merri Meyer/
Barbara Buck
DESIGNER:
George Corsello
PUBLISHER:
Warner Books
■ 555

■ 554 Dustjacket of an illustrated book with posters from the golden age of the cinema. (USA)

■ 555 Cover of a book about the Wild West and Theodore Roosevelt. (USA)

■ 556 For a book about the rise and fall of the film company 20th Century Fox. (USA)

■ 557 For a book published by Simon + Schuster. (USA)

■ 554 Schutzumschlag eines Bildbandes mit Plakaten aus der goldenen Zeit des Films. (USA)

■ 555 «Eindeutig Schicksal», Umschlag eines Buches über den Wilden Westen und Theodore Roosevelt. (USA)

■ 556 Für ein Buch über Aufstieg und Untergang der Filmgesellschaft 20th Century Fox. (USA)

■ 557 Für ein Buch mit dem Titel «Knabenwunder». (USA)

■ 554 Jaquette d'un album d'affiches datant de l'âge d'or du cinéma. (USA)

■ 555 «Destin manifeste», couverture d'un livre sur le Far-Ouest et le président Theodore Roosevelt. (USA)

■ 556 Pour un ouvrage relatant la grandeur et la décadence de la société cinématographique 20th Century Fox. (USA)

■ 557 Couverture d'un livre intitulé «Boy Wonder». (USA)

ART DIRECTOR:
STEVEN BROWER
DESIGNER:
STEVEN BROWER
ILLUSTRATOR:
DENNIS POTOKAR
PUBLISHER:
LYLE STUART INC.
■ 556

ART DIRECTOR:
FRANK METZ
DESIGNER:
PAULA SCHER
AGENCY:
KOPPEL & SCHER
PUBLISHER:
SIMON & SCHUSTER
■ 557

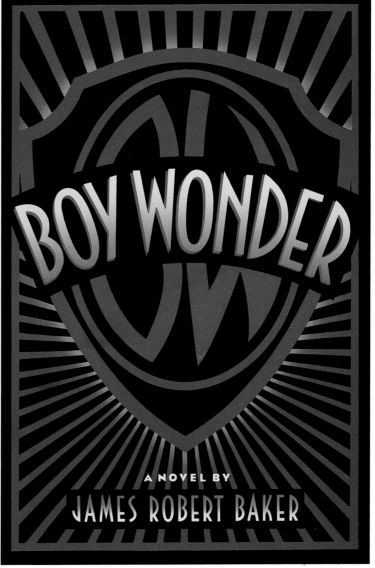

ART DIRECTOR:
THOMAS SCHAER
DESIGNER:
THOMAS SCHAER
ILLUSTRATOR:
THOMAS SCHAER
AGENCY:
CAT ADVERTISING
PUBLISHER:
EX LIBRIS VERLAG
■ 558

ART DIRECTOR:
KAREN KOLLMETZ
DESIGNER:
KAREN KOLLMETZ
■ 559

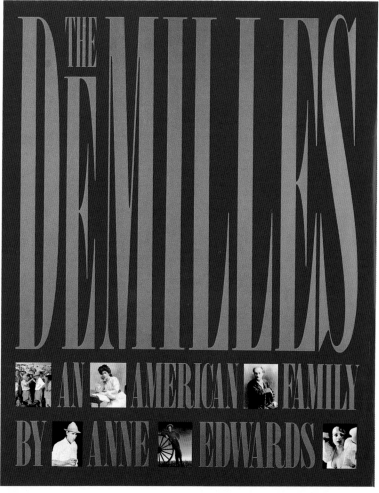

ART DIRECTOR:
SAM ANTUPIT
DESIGNER:
SEYMOUR CHWAST
ILLUSTRATOR:
SEYMOUR CHWAST
PUBLISHER:
HARRY N. ABRAMS, INC.
■ 560

ART DIRECTOR:
DIRK LUYKX
DESIGNER:
DIRK LUYKX
PUBLISHER:
HARRY N. ABRAMS, INC.
■ 561

■ 558 Cover of the book "The Puppets" published by the Swiss book club Ex Libris. (SWI)

■ 559 Project for a book cover. (GER)

■ 560 Dustjacket for a book about various styles of graphic design, from Victorian to post-modern. (USA)

■ 561 The subject of this book is the history of an American family. (USA)

■ 558 Umschlag für ein beim Buchclub Ex Libris erschienenes Buch. (SWI)

■ 559 Entwurf für einen Buchumschlag. (GER)

■ 560 Schutzumschlag für ein Buch über verschiedene Stilrichtungen des Graphik-Design. (USA)

■ 561 Eine amerikanische Familiengeschichte ist Gegenstand dieses Buches. (USA)

■ 558 Couverture d'un livre paru aux Editions du Club du Livre Ex Libris et intitulé «La Marionnette». (SWI)

■ 559 Projet d'une couverture de livre. (GER)

■ 560 Jaquette d'une étude des styles graphiques de l'époque victorienne aux temps postmodernes. (USA)

■ 561 Ce livre a pour sujet l'histoire d'une famille américaine. (USA)

PARROTS MACAWS AND COCKATOOS

THE ART OF ELIZABETH BUTTERWORTH

ART DIRECTOR:
Carol Robson
DESIGNER:
Carol Robson
ILLUSTRATOR:
Elizabeth Butterworth
PUBLISHER:
Harry N. Abrams, Inc.
◄■ 562

ART DIRECTOR:
Steven Brower
DESIGNER:
Peter A. Davis
PUBLISHER:
Lyle Stuart Inc.
▼■ 563-565

■ 562 A scarlet macaw in gouache, size 31 x 21" (from the collection of the artist Elizabeth Butterworth) is depicted on the cover of this book. Inside are more members of the parrot family by the artist, in various techniques. (USA)

■ 563-565 From a series of books about the films of famous Hollywood stars, published by Citadel Press. (USA)

■ 562 Papageien, Aras und Kakadus sind Gegenstand der Darstellungen der Künstlerin Elizabeth Butterworth in verschiedenen Techniken, die in diesem Buch gezeigt werden. Auf dem Umschlag ein Ara, Gouache. (USA)

■ 563-565 Aus einer Buchreihe über die Filme bekannter Hollywood-Stars, erschienen bei Citadel Press. (USA)

■ 562 Les perroquets, les aras et les cacatoès sont le sujet des interprétations qu'Elizabeth Butterworth nous livre ici dans différentes techniques. En couverture, gouache d'un ara. (USA)

■ 563-565 Livres publiés dans une collection des Ed. Citadel Press consacrée aux films des stars hollywoodiens. (USA)

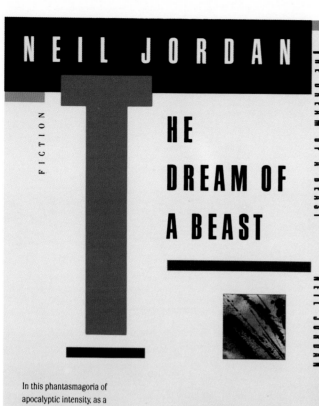

NEIL JORDAN

FICTION

THE
DREAM OF
A BEAST

In this phantasmagoria of
apocalyptic intensity, as a
storm breaks over a city—the
world—the beast achieves
an apotheosis both frightening
and heartrending.

$5.95

50595

9 780394 758145

ISBN 0-394-75814-5

AVENTURA

DESIGNER:
KEITH SHERIDAN/
CRAIG WARNER
ILLUSTRATOR:
KEITH SHERIDAN
AGENCY:
KEITH SHERIDAN
ASSOCIATES, INC.
PUBLISHER:
RANDOM HOUSE, INC.
■ 567, 568

DARCY RIBIERO

FICTION

MULE

"This document, penned
in my own hand, is my last
will and testament.
It is also my confession.
Here I will..."

$12.95

51295

9 780394 758152

ISBN 0-394-75815-3

AVENTURA

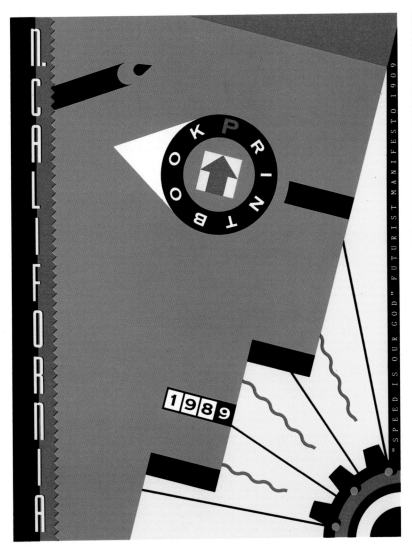

DESIGNER:
Mark Fox
ILLUSTRATOR:
Mark Fox
STUDIO:
Black Dog
PUBLISHER:
Matam Publishing
■ 569

DESIGNER:
René Khatami
PHOTOGRAPHER:
Douglas Kent Hall
PUBLISHER:
Abbeville Press, Inc.
■ 570

■ 567, 568 Complete covers of a paperback series for stories of adventure. (USA)

■ 569 For a book with a collection of advertisements for the printing industry of northern California. (USA)

■ 570 Life in the border area between the USA and Mexico forms the subject of this book. (USA)

■ 567, 568 Vollständige Umschläge einer Taschenbuchreihe mit Abenteuerromanen. (USA)

■ 569 Für ein Buch mit einer Sammlung von Anzeigen für die Druckindustrie in Nordkalifornien. (USA)

■ 570 Das Leben im Grenzgebiet zwischen den USA und Mexiko ist Gegenstand dieses Buches. (USA)

■ 567, 568 Couvertures complètes d'une collection de romans d'aventures parus en poche. (USA)

■ 569 Pour un recueil d'annonces publiées par les imprimeries du nord de la Californie. (USA)

■ 570 Ouvrage ayant pour thème la vie sur la frontière des Etats-Unis et du Mexique. (USA)

ON FLOWERS

VARIATIONS

DESIGNER:
MICHAEL MABRY
PHOTOGRAPHER:
KATHRYN KLEINMAN
STYLIST:
SARA SLAVIN
AGENCY:
MICHAEL MABRY DESIGN
PUBLISHER:
CHRONICLE BOOKS
■ 571-574

Hand-tied bouquets. Potpourri. Perfumes. Attars. Wreaths. Remedies. ¶ The true flower lover is never limited by so pedestrian a concept as the vase. ¶ Flowers are Nature's best and most extravagant ornaments. The opportunities to learn about ornamentation from Nature herself are endless. Consider the lilies of the field, those Biblical miracles that turned a field of grass, overnight, into a sweep of color. The lilies that "toiled not, neither did they spin," were in fact probably anemones that grew in Galilee. ¶ Sometimes the variations in which we see flowers are miracles, not of ornament, but of desperation. During the cold, bleak winters between 1940 and 1945, when Germany occupied Holland and food was scarce, many Dutch dug their tulip bulbs out of the garden. Scrubbed clean, the bulbs were baked or boiled, then eaten to ward off starvation. ¶ Then, there was the rebellious young doctor, Edward Bach. Though he had a prosperous practice on London's exclusive Harley Street in the 1930s, he gave it up to develop a branch of herbal medicine. He used nonpoisonous flowers to create remedies for mental and emotional distress. Homeopaths still respect the Bach Flower Remedies, named for the gentle man who attacked Loneliness and Despair with Nature's own prescriptions. Antibiotics can't relieve grief, but Bach believed the larch or the Star of Bethlehem could. ¶ He offered no complex scientific explanation to support his remedies. Instead, he traveled the countryside of England and Wales, gathering flowers and working on new remedies. He wrote, "And may we ever have joy and gratitude in our hearts that the Great Creator of all things, in His Love for us, has placed the herbs in the fields for His healing."

My HOMAGE TO COLETTE: YOU SAW A WOODEN SHOE, A BIRD, A SILVER PLANT.

■ 571-574 Dustjacket and examples of the double spreads from a book with photographs by Kathryn Kleinman. (USA)

■ 575, 576 Cover (shown here also upside down) of a photo book, showing photographs of Andy Warhol taken by one of his closest friends, Christopher Makos. (USA)

■ 571-574 Umschlag und Doppelseiten aus einem Buch mit Aufnahmen der Photographin Kathryn Kleinman. (USA)

■ 575, 576 Umschlag (hier auch umgekehrt gezeigt) eines Photobandes mit Aufnahmen, die einer der engsten Freunde des Künstlers, Christopher Makos, von ihm machte. (USA)

■ 571-574 Jaquette et doubles pages types d'un ouvrage illustré par la photographe Kathryn Kleinman. (USA)

■ 575, 576 Couverture (montrée aussi à l'envers) d'un album photo réalisé par l'un des proches de cet artiste, Christopher Makos. (USA)

ART DIRECTOR:
VINCENT McEVOY
DESIGNER:
VINCENT McEVOY/
CHRISTOPHER MAKOS
PHOTOGRAPHER:
CHRISTOPHER MAKOS
AGENCY:
OGILVY & MATHER
PUBLISHER:
VIRGIN/W.H. ALLEN
■ 575, 576

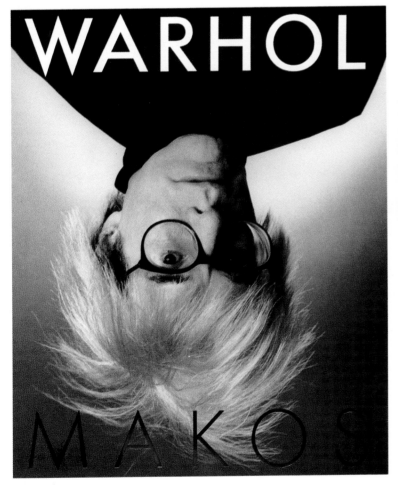

249

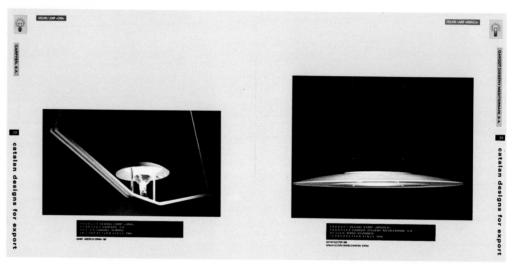

ART DIRECTOR:
MAI FELIP HÖSSELBARTH
DESIGNER:
ALFONS SOSTRES
PUBLISHER:
BARCELONA DESIGN CENTER
■ 577-580

■577-580 Cover and examples of the double spreads in a book with a catalog character about Catalonian design. (SPA)

■ 577-580 Umschlag und Beispiele der Doppelseiten aus einem Buch mit Katalogcharakter über katalanisches Design. (SPA)

■ 577-580 Couverture et doubles pages types d'un livre-catalogue consacré au design catalan. (SPA)

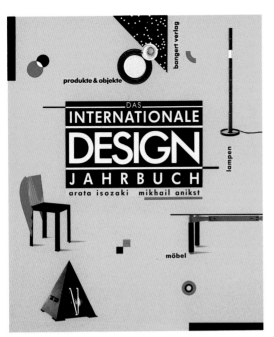

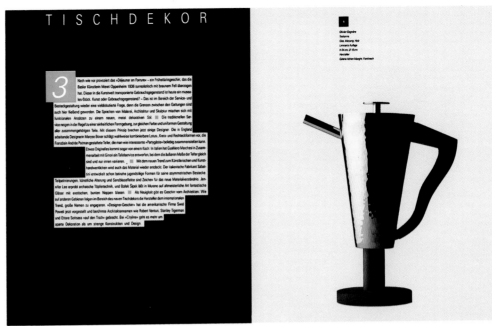

3 Nach wie vor provoziert das »Déjeuner en Fourrure« - ein Frühstücksgeschirr, das die Basler Künstlerin Meret Oppenheim 1936 surrealistisch mit braunem Fell überzogen hat. Dieser in die Kunstwelt transponierte Gebrauchsgegenstand ist heute ein museales Stück. Kunst oder Gebrauchsgegenstand? - Das ist im Bereich der Service- und Bestückgestaltung wieder eine vieldiskutierte Frage, denn die Grenzen zwischen den Gattungen sind auch hier fließend geworden. Die Sprachen von Malerei, Architektur und Skulptur mischen sich mit funktionalen Ansätzen zu einem neuen, meist dekorativen Stil. Die traditionellen Service neigen in der Regel zu einer einheitlichen Formgebung, zur gleichen Farbe und uniformen Gestaltung aller zusammengehörigen Teile. Mit diesem Prinzip brechen jetzt einige Designer. Die in England arbeitende Designerin Maryse Boxer schlägt wahlweise kombinierbare Lotus-, Kreis- und Rechteckformen vor, die Französin Andrée Putman gestaltete Teller, die man wie interessante »Partygäste« zusammenstellen kann. Etwas Originelles kommt sogar von einem Koch: In Italien hat Gualtiero Marchesi in Zusammenarbeit mit Ginori ein Tafelservice entworfen, bei dem die äußeren Maße der Teller gleich sind und nur innen variieren. Mit dem neuen Trend zum Künstlerischen und Kunsthandwerklichen wird auch das Material wieder entdeckt. Der italienische Fabrikant Sabattini entwickelt schon beinahe jugendstilige Formen für seine asymmetrische Art. Teilzinnierungen, künstliche Alterung und Sandblasereliefe sind Zeichen für das neue Materialverständnis. Jennifer Lee erprobt archaische Töpfertechnik, und Bořek Šipek läßt in Murano auf altmeisterliche Art fantastische Gläser mit exotischen, bunten Nippen blasen. Als Neuigkeit gibt es Geschirr vom Architekten: Wie auf anderen Gebieten folgen im Bereich des Tischdekors die Hersteller dem internationalen Trend, große Namen zu engagieren. »Designer-Geschirr« hat die amerikanische Firma Swed Powell jetzt vorgestellt und berühmte Architektennamen wie Robert Venturi, Stanley Tigerman und Ettore Sottsass »auf den Tisch« gebracht. Bei »Cryline« geht es mehr um aparte Dekoration als um strenge Konstruktion und Design.

ART DIRECTOR:
MIKHAIL ANIKST
DESIGNER:
MIKHAIL ANIKST
PUBLISHER:
BANGERT VERLAG
■ 581-584

■ 581-584 Dustjacket and double spreads from the 1988/89 annual on international design. *583* relates to re-editions of classical furniture designs. (GER)

■ 581-584 Schutzumschlag und Doppelseiten aus dem Jahrbuch 1988/89 über internationales Design. Bei *583* handelt es sich um Re-editionen klassischer Möbelentwürfe. (GER)

■ 581-584 Jaquette et doubles pages de l'annuel de design international 1988/89. Fig. *583:* rééditions de meubles classiques. (GER)

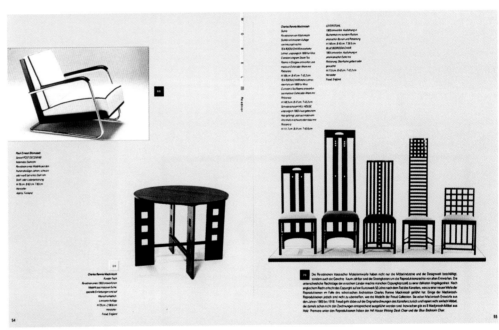

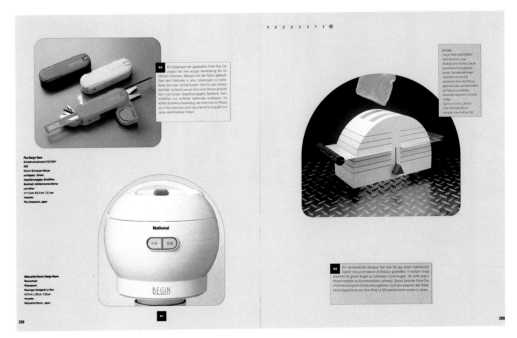

■ 585 For a book in the series written by this authoress about various countries. (USA)

■ 586 The Afro-American author Richard Wright and his work form the subject of this book. (USA)

■ 587 For a book about jewelry made from this thermoplastic resin – an unusual product for adornment. (USA)

■ 585 Für ein Buch aus einer Reihe der Autorin über verschiedene Länder. (USA)

■ 586 Der afro-amerikanische Schriftsteller Richard Wright und sein Werk sind Gegenstand dieses Buches. (USA)

■ 587 Umschlag für ein Buch über Schmuck aus Bakelit, einem nach seinem Erfinder benannten Kunststoff. (USA)

■ 585 Pour l'un des titres qu'une femme écrivain consacre à une série de pays. (USA)

■ 586 Ouvrage consacré à l'auteur afro-américain Richard Wright et à son œuvre. (USA)

■ 587 Couverture d'un livre sur «La Joaillerie en bakélite» (résine synthétique). (USA)

ART DIRECTOR:
JOY CHU
DESIGNER:
KAREN KATZ
PUBLISHER:
HBJ HARCOURT BRACE JOVANOVICH
■ 585

ART DIRECTOR:
JACKIE MERRI MEYER
DESIGNER:
MARIO PULICE
PUBLISHER:
WARNER BOOKS
■ 586

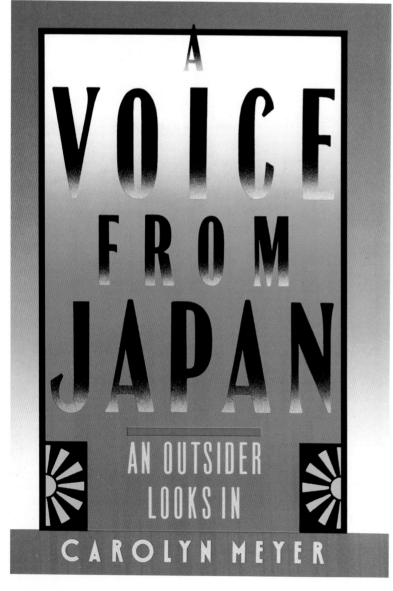

The Bakelite Jewelry Book

DESIGNER:
RENÉ KHATAMI
PHOTOGRAPHER:
STEVEN MARK NEEDHAM
AGENCY:
PUBLISHER:
ABBEVILLE PRESS, INC.
■ 587

DESK DIARY 1989

TAKEO CO., L

ART DIRECTOR:
Kazumasa Nagai
DESIGNER:
Yoshiteru Mamada
ILLUSTRATOR:
Kazumasa Nagai
AGENCY:
Nippon Design Center
CLIENT:
Takeo Co., Ltd.
■ 588-592

■ 588-592 Dustjacket, cover with gold-embossed illustration, and double spreads from a diary issued by the paper producers Takeo Company. (JPN)

■ 588-592 Schutzumschlag, Einband mit Illustration in Goldprägung und Doppelseiten aus einer Agenda, die von dem Papierhersteller Takeo Co. herausgegeben wurde. (JPN)

■ 588-592 Jaquette, couverture ornée d'une illustration gaufrée or et doubles pages d'un agenda publié par le papetier Takeo Co. (JPN)

水・水・水——あけっぴろげな虚無——　　　米倉　守

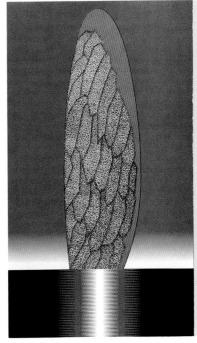

天皇御容体がしだいにかんぴ状態のなか、時間を盗むようにして奈良・東大寺と国立博物館に行ってきた。かねてから補陀落渡海に関する古絵図をみるため後期の開館申請をしてあったための独行だった。補陀落山浄土の説明はほぼ、開催中のシルクロード展をとも見て"あった"と思った。補陀落山浄土の彼方にあるぬの厨子絵はやはり海が描かれている。水井一正さんのグラフィックスをともみて、その底知れない澄かる機味と透みに満ちた水空間を多彩の色彩にえがいたものを——

（朝日新聞編集委員）

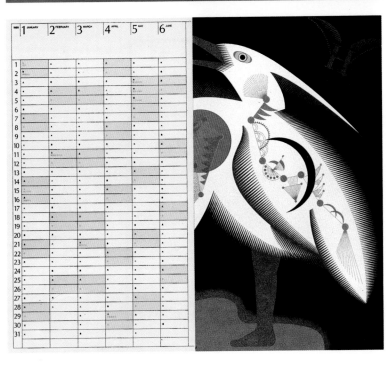

256

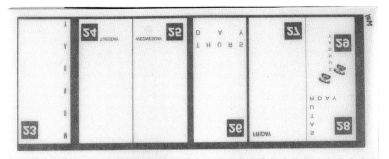

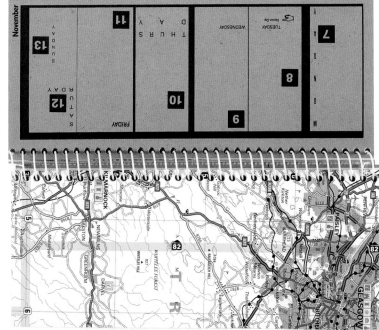

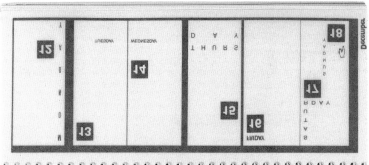

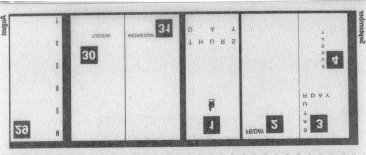

DESIGNER:
URSULA BENDIXEN/
SUZANNE REDDING
AGENCY:
BENDIXEN REDDING
CLIENT:
BENDIXEN REDDING
■ 593-598

■ 593-598 Front page and double spreads from a spiral-bound weekly calendar that serves as self-promotion for a design studio. The illustrations consist of a collection of misprints. (USA)

■ 593-598 Vorderseite und Doppelseiten aus dem Inhalt einer Agenda mit Spiralbindung, die als Eigenwerbung eines Design-Studios dient. Die Illustrationen bestehen aus gesammelten Fehldrucken. (USA)

■ 593-598 Recto et doubles pages d'un agenda à reliure spirale servant à l'autopromotion d'un studio de design. L'iconographie est constituée d'une collection d'impression manquée. (USA)

ART DIRECTOR:
Michael Brock
DESIGNER:
Michael Brock/
Gaylen Braun
PHOTOGRAPHER:
Herb Ritts 600
Kathryn Kleinman 601
Matthew Rollston 602
Tom Bonner 603
Frederic Ohringer 604
Phillip Dixon 605
AGENCY:
Michael Brock Design
CLIENT:
L.A. Style Magazine
■ 599-605

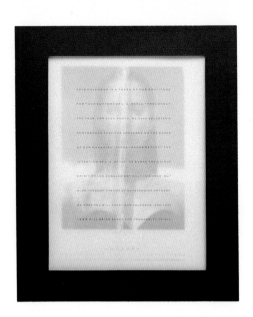

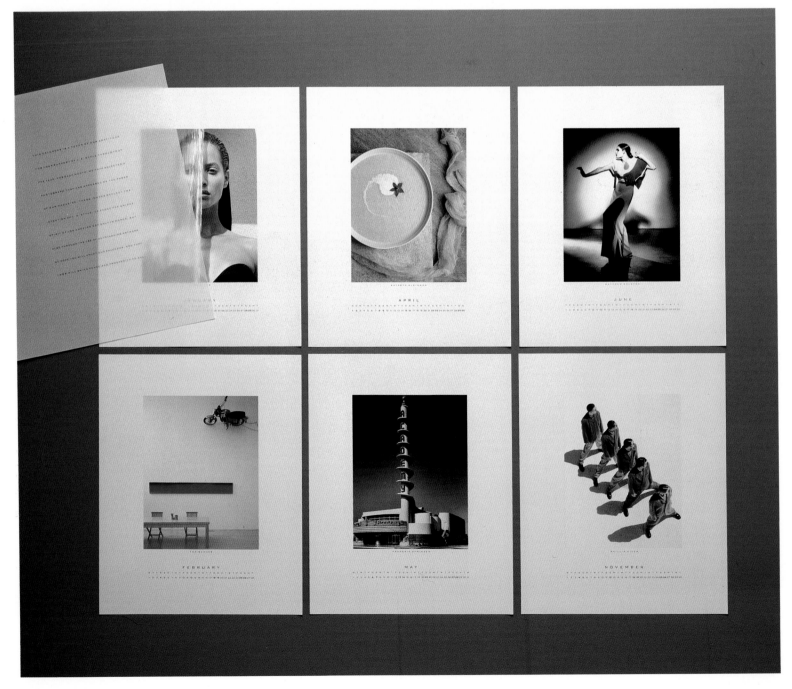

GEIGY

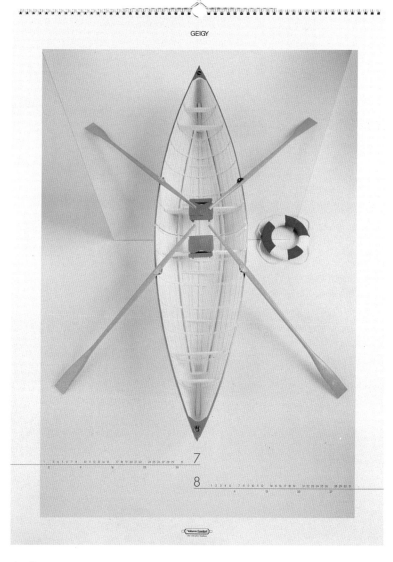

GEIGY

ART DIRECTOR:
JOSEPH PÖLZELBAUER
DESIGNER:
JOSEPH PÖLZELBAUER
PHOTOGRAPHER:
LOTHAR VOLLMER
AGENCY:
TARGET-MARKETING
CLIENT:
CIBA-GEIGY GMBH
■ 606, 607

■ 599-605 Transparent cover and monthly sheets from a calendar for the magazine *L.A. Style*. Shots taken by various photographers, and which had previously appeared in the magazine, were selected for the illustrations. (USA)

■ 606, 607 Monthly sheets from a calendar targeted at doctors, issued by Ciba-Geigy. The theme is: an ointment for the external treatment of pain, inflamations and swellings. All illustrations are an interpretation of the slogan, "The perfect synthesis". (GER)

■ 599-605 Transparentes Deckblatt und Monatsblätter aus einem Kalender der Zeitschrift *L.A. Style*. Ausgewählt wurden Aufnahmen von verschiedenen Photographen, die in der Zeitschrift erschienen sind. (USA)

■ 606, 607 Monatsblätter aus einem für Ärzte bestimmten Kalender von Ciba-Geigy, der einer Salbe zur äusserlichen Behandlung von Schmerzen, Entzündungen und Schwellungen gewidmet ist. Alle Illustration sind eine Interpretation des Slogans: «Die vollendete Synthese». (GER)

■ 599-605 Feuillet de couverture transparent et feuillets mensuels d'un calendrier publié par le magazine *L.A. Style*. L'illustration est fournie par des photos publiées auparavant dans le magazine. (USA)

■ 606, 607 Feuillets mensuels d'un calendrier Ciba-Geigy destiné au corps médical et consacré à une pommade efficace contre les douleurs, les inflammations et les enflures. Toutes les illustrations interprètent le slogan de «la synthèse parfaitement réussie». (GER)

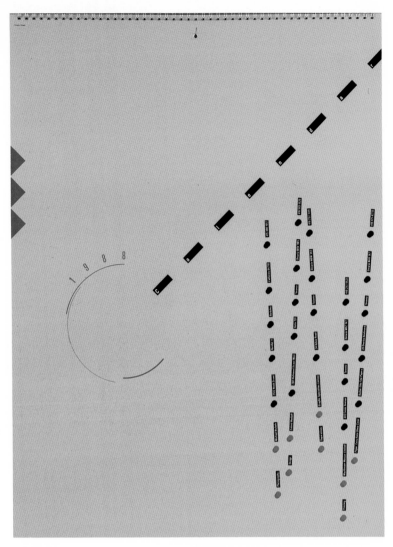

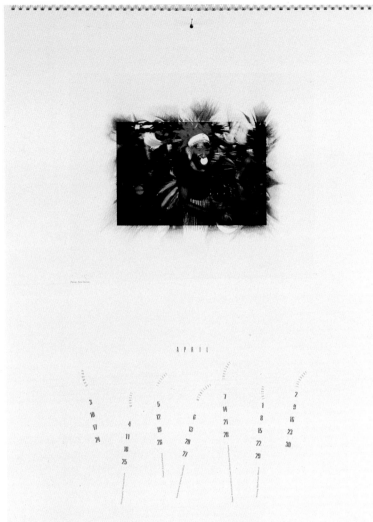

ART DIRECTOR:
MALCOLM WADDELL
DESIGNER:
ROSLYN ESKIND/
GLENDA RISSMAN/
MERCEDES ROTHWELL/
CHRISTOPHER CAMPBELL/
PETER SCOTT/
MALCOLM WADDELL
PHOTOGRAPHER:
MICHAEL NICHOLS
AGENCY:
ESKIND WADDELL
CLIENT:
MACKINNON-MONCUR LTD.
■ 608, 609

■ 608, 609 Cover and example of the monthly sheets (Papua, New Guinea) from a calendar serving as joint business promotion for a photographer, graphic artist, printer, lithographer, and paper manufacturer. (CAN)

■ 610-612 Cover and sheets from a tear-off calendar. (JPN)

■ 608, 609 Deckblatt und Beispiel der Monatsblätter (Papua, New Guinea) aus einem Kalender, der als Gemeinschaftswerbung für einen Photographen, Graphiker, Drucker, Lithographen und Papierhersteller dient. (CAN)

■ 610-612 Deckblatt und Seiten eines Abreisskalenders. (JPN)

■ 608, 609 Feuillet de couverture et feuillets mensuels types (Papouasie-Nouvelle Guinée) d'un calendrier servant de publicité collective à un photographe, un graphiste, un imprimeur, un lithographe et un papetier. (CAN)

■ 610-612 Couverture et pages d'une éphéméride. (JPN)

ART DIRECTOR:
SHIN MATSUNAGA
DESIGNER:
SHIN MATSUNAGA
CLIENT:
SHIN MATSUNAGA
■ 610-612

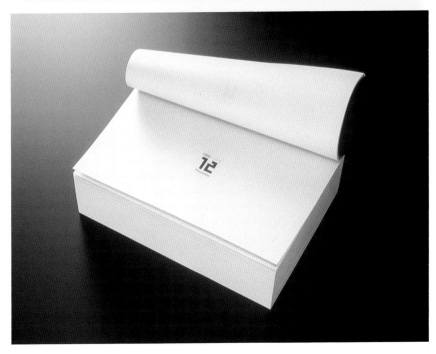

ART DIRECTOR:
Patrick Florville
DESIGNER:
Patrick Florville
AGENCY:
Florville Design & Analysis
CLIENT:
Florville Design & Analysis
■ 613

■ 613 A stand-up calendar that principally consists of two plastic discs, one of which can be moved. (USA)

■ 613 Aufstellbarer Jahreskalender, der aus zwei Kunststoffscheiben besteht, von denen sich eine bewegen lässt. (USA)

■ 613 Calendrier annuel de display composé de deux disques plastiques dont l'un est mobile. (USA)

INDEX

VERZEICHNIS

APICELLA, DAVID	USA 108, 109
AUGUSTIN, LUTZ	GER 161-164
BAGOT, ROB	USA 98
BARKER, STEVE	GBR 42
BARRETT, JAMIE	USA 80
BARTEL, JÖRG	GER 79
BEAMAN, LINDSAY	USA 182, 183
BELL, JOHN	USA 207-211
BERENDT, JOHN	USA 215-221
BLANK, JANET	USA 231-233
BRUCHMANN, FELIX	GER 40
CAIN, KATHY	USA 112
CARLSON, CHUCK	USA 147-149, 224, 225, 309, 310
CHAIKIND, BONNIE	USA 422-425
CICHY, ALEX	USA 258
CINQUINA, DICK	USA 236-238
COLLINS, ELLIOTT	CAN 226-250
CRUYS, GEORGE	USA 306, 307
CUNNINGHAM, FRANK	USA 145, 146
DEBECK, BESS	USA 186
DELANEY, TIM	GBR 8, 9
DEVITO, SAL	USA 81
DUBOSE, MARTHA	USA 117, 118
EDELSTEIN, DAVID	USA 12, 13
FARQUHAR, WILL	GBR 88
FEAGINS, CHRISSIE	GBR 101, 102
FITCH, NELSON	USA 418-421
FLAMING, JON	USA 244, 245
FLOOD, BRIAN	USA 212-214
FOSTER, RICHARD	GBR 47
FRENCH, LANNY	USA 12, 13
FRIEDMAN, MARTIN	USA 281-283
FURY, JERRY	USA 82
GEIGER, ELIZABETH	USA 89
GIBBS, MIKE	USA 56, 99, 100
GIOIA, DANA	USA 61
GOLDMAN, JOHN	USA 184, 185
GOODWIN, MARK	GBR 64
GREEN ROACH LIMITED	GBR 296-298
HACOHEN, DEAN	USA 52, 53, 62, 63, 157-160
HERRING, CHRIS	GBR 4-6
HJÄRTSJÖ, MIKAEL	SWE 94

HOLLANDER, ERIC	FRA 110
HOLMES, PETER	CAN 33
HOUK, GEORGE	USA 200-203
HUGGINS, STEVE	USA 259-262
ITO, DEE	USA 69
ITO, ICHIRO	JPN 58
JACKSON, CRAIG	GBR 74
JOHNSON, CAROLYN	USA 23
JOHNSON, KEVIN	USA 150-152
KELLY, KEVIN	USA 50, 51
KROUSE, AMY	USA 95, 96
LALLI ASSOCIATES	USA 273-276
MARCUS, MELINDA	USA 246, 247
MARSHALL, JO	USA 30-32
MATTER, DANIEL	SWI 55
MCCARLEY, LAURA	USA 34-36
MESSER, TOBY	GBR 87
MITCHELL, CORINNE	USA 10, 11
MONAGHAN, MONA	USA 49
MORAN, CINDY	USA 263-267
MURTAUGH, PHIL	USA 239-242
NAKANISHI, TOSHIHITO	JPN 26, 27
NASH, LEE	USA 137-139
NOLTE, RANDOLPH	GER 121
OLIVER, GERALD	GBR 293, 294
OZLBERGER, ISOLDE	AUT 155, 156
PEARCE, MICK	GBR 90
PEER, ANGELO	AUT 111
PERKINS, MARK	USA 244, 245
PETERSON, LINDA	USA 193-199
POWE, B.W.	CAN 200-203
READ, BARB	USA 3
RIECHERS, BARBARA	USA 299-301
RITTER, THOMAS	GER 79
ROSEN, MIKE	USA 70, 71
ROSSI, VICKY	USA 1, 2, 129
ROTHSCHILD, DIANE	USA 54
SCHEER, REINHOLD	GER 91-93
SCHNEIDER, GÜNTHER	GER 40

SCHWEIZER, HANSPETER	SWI 59
SHEVACK, BRETT	USA 49
SILVER, STEVE	USA 37-39
SIMON, GERD	GER 106, 107
SLOVER, SUSAN	USA 65
SMITH, MARK	USA 302-305
SOUTER, NICK	GBR 28, 29
STEIN, JOHN	USA 37-39
STITT, ROMY	GBR 293, 294
SUHR, JULIE	USA 429-432
SULLIVAN, PAMELA	USA 60
TREIB, MARC	USA 281-283
VARGO, CANDY	GBR 286
WONG, TRACY	USA 75-77
WRIGHT, MICHAEL	USA 66, 67
WYNNE—JONES, BRUCE	USA 302-305
YUNGER LINDER, RITA	CAN 226-230

STYLISTS

BELT, CHRISTY	USA 34-36
BERGTOLD, MARY	USA 1, 2
BLAME, JUDY	GBR 130-133
CASTELLANO, ERIC	USA 12, 13
D'APICE, MICHAEL	USA 16, 17
KOCH, STACY	USA 212-214
ROEMER, LIZ	USA 129
ROSS, LIZ	USA 182, 183
SAUVE, GORDON	CAN 546
SILVERMAN, LAURA	USA 253-256
SLAVIN, SARA	USA 571-574
STEWART, HOLLY	USA 207-211
TROVATI, ROBERTO	ITA 113-116
WEDELL, THOMAS	USA 253-256

CALL FOR ENTRIES

FOR GRAPHIS' INTERNATIONAL YEARBOOKS

GRAPHIS DESIGN

ALL ENTRIES MUST ARRIVE ON OR BEFORE NOVEMBER 30

Advertising: Newspaper and magazine
Design: Promotion brochures, catalogs, invitations, record covers, announcements, logotypes and/or entire corporate image campaigns, calendars, books, book covers, packages (single or series, labels and/or complete packages)
Editorial Design: company magazines, newspapers, consumer magazines, house organs
Illustration: All categories may be black and white or color

GRAPHIS ANNUAL REPORTS

ALL ENTRIES MUST ARRIVE ON OR BEFORE JANUARY 31/APRIL 30

All material printed and published in connection with the annual report of a company or other organization.
Design, illustration, photography, typography, as well as the overall conception of the annual report are the criteria to be judged.
In order to do justice to this complex medium, we will present double-page spreads from the annual reports selected which are exemplary in their design and/or illustration.

GRAPHIS PHOTO

ALL ENTRIES MUST ARRIVE ON OR BEFORE JUNE 30

Advertising Photography: Advertisements, promotional brochures, catalogs, invitations, announcements, record covers, calendars.
Editorial Photography for press media – journalism and features – for books, corporate publications, etc. on the following subjects: fashion, cosmetics, architecture, arts, nature, science, technology, daily life, sports, current affairs, portraits, still life, etc.
Fine Art Photography: Personal studies
Unpublished Photography: Experimental and student work

GRAPHIS POSTER

ALL ENTRIES MUST ARRIVE ON OR BEFORE APRIL 30

Culture: Posters announcing exhibitions and events of all kind, film, theater, and ballet performances, concerts etc.
Advertising: Posters for fashion, cosmetics, foods, beverages, industrial goods; image and self-promotional campaigns of companies and individuals
Society: Posters which serve primarily a social and/or political purpose; from the field of education; for conferences and meetings; as well as for political and charitable appeals.

GENERAL RULES

THESE ARE APPLICABLE TO ALL BOOKS MENTIONED.

By submitting work to GRAPHIS, the sender expressly grants permission for his publication in any GRAPHIS book, as well as in any article in GRAPHIS magazine, or any advertising brochure, etc. whose purpose is specifically to promote the sales of these publications.

Eligibility: All work produced in the 12 month period previous to the submission deadlines, as well as rejected or unpublished work from this period, by professionals and students.

A confirmation of receipt will be sent to each entrant, and all entrants will be notified at a later date whether or not their work has been accepted for publication. All the winning entries will be reproduced in a generous format and in four colors throughout.
By submitting work you qualify for a 25% discount on the purchase of the respective book.

What to send:
Please send the actual printed piece (unmounted but well protected). Do not send original art. For large, bulky or valuable pieces, please submit color photos or (duplicate) transparencies.
Please note that entries cannot be returned. Only in exceptional cases and by contacting us in advance will material be sent back.

Entry Fees:
For each single entry: North America: US$ 10.00 West Germany: DM 10,00 All other countries: SFr. 10.00
For each campaign entry of 3 or more pieces: North America: US$ 25.00 West Germany: DM 25,00 All other countries: SFr. 25.00
Please make checks payable to GRAPHIS PRESS CORP. Zurich, and include in parcel. These fees do not apply to students, if copy of student identification is included. (For entries from countries with exchange controls, please contact us.)

How and where to send:
Please tape (do not glue) the entry label provided (or photocopy) - with full information - on the back of each piece. Entries can be sent by airmail, air parcel post or surface mail. **Please do not send anything by air freight.** Declare "No Commercial Value" on packages, and label "Art for Contest". The number of transparencies and photos should be indicated on the parcel. (If sent by air courier, please mark "Documents, Commercial Value 00.00").

Thank you for your contribution. Please send all entries to the following address:
GRAPHIS PRESS CORP., DUFOURSTRASSE 107, CH-8008 ZURICH, SWITZERLAND

FÜR DIE GRAPHIS JAHRBÜCHER

GRAPHIS DESIGN

EINSENDESCHLUSS: 30. NOVEMBER

Werbung: In Zeitungen und Zeitschriften
Design: Werbeprospekte, Kataloge, Einladungen, Schallplattenhüllen, Anzeigen, Signete und/oder Imagekampagnen, Kalender, Bücher, Buchumschläge, Packungen (einzelne oder Serien, Etiketten und/oder vollständige Packungen)
Redaktionelles Design: Firmenpublikationen, Zeitungen, Zeitschriften, Jahresberichte
Illustration: Alle Kategorien, schwarzweiss oder farbig

GRAPHIS ANNUAL REPORTS

EINSENDESCHLUSS: 31. JANUAR/30. APRIL

Alle gedruckten und veröffentlichten Arbeiten, die im Zusammenhang mit dem Jahresbericht einer Firma oder Organisation stehen.
Design, Illustration, Photographie, Typographie und die Gesamtkonzeption eines Jahresberichtes sind die beurteilten Kriterien.
Um diesem komplexen Medium gerecht zu werden, werden aus den ausgewählten Jahresberichten verschiedene typische Doppelseiten gezeigt, die beispielhaft für die Gestaltung und/oder Illustration sind.

GRAPHIS PHOTO

EINSENDESCHLUSS: 30. JUNI

Werbephotographie: Anzeigen, Prospekte, Kataloge, Einladungen, Bekanntmachungen, Schallplattenhüllen, Kalender.
Redaktionelle Photographie für Presse (Reportagen und Artikel), Bücher, Firmenpublikationen usw. in den Bereichen Mode, Kosmetik, Architektur, Kunst, Natur, Wissenschaft und Technik, Alltag, Sport, Aktuelles, Porträts, Stilleben usw.
Künstlerische Photographie: Persönliche Studien
Unveröffentlichte Aufnahmen: Experimentelle Photographie und Arbeiten von Studenten und Schülern.

GRAPHIS POSTER

EINSENDESCHLUSS: 30. APRIL

Kultur: Plakate für die Ankündigung von Ausstellungen und Veranstaltungen aller Art, Film-, Theater- und Ballettaufführungen, Musikveranstaltungen.
Werbung: Plakate für Mode, Kosmetik, Lebensmittel, Genussmittel, Industriegüter; Image- und Eigenwerbung von Firmen und Einzelpersonen
Gesellschaft: Plakate, die in erster Linie einem sozialen oder politischen Zweck dienen, auf dem Gebiet der Ausbildung und Erziehung oder für die Ankündigung von Konferenzen und Tagungen sowie für politische und soziale Appelle

TEILNAHMEBEDINGUNGEN

DIESE GELTEN FÜR ALLE AUFGEFÜHRTEN BÜCHER.

Durch Ihre Einsendung geben Sie GRAPHIS ausdrücklich die Erlaubnis zur Veröffentlichung der eingesandten Arbeiten sowohl im entsprechenden Jahrbuch als auch in der Zeitschrift GRAPHIS oder für die Wiedergabe im Zusammenhang mit Besprechungen und Werbematerial für die GRAPHIS-Publikationen.

In Frage kommen alle Arbeiten von Fachleuten und Studenten – auch nicht publizierte Arbeiten – welche in den zwölf Monaten vor Einsendeschluss entstanden sind.

Jeder Einsender erhält eine Empfangsbestätigung und wird über Erscheinen oder Nichterscheinen seiner Arbeiten zu einem späteren Zeitpunkt informiert.
Alle im Buch aufgenommenen Arbeiten werden vierfarbig, in grosszügigem Format reproduziert.
Durch Ihre Einsendung erhalten Sie 25% Rabatt auf das jeweilige Jahrbuch.

Was einsenden:
Bitte senden Sie uns das gedruckte Beispiel (unmontiert, aber gut geschützt).
Senden Sie keine Originale. Bei unhandlichen, umfangreichen oder wertvollen Sendungen bitten wir um Farbphotos oder Duplikat-Dias.
Bitte beachten Sie, dass Einsendungen nicht zurückgeschickt werden können. Ausnahmen sind nur nach vorheriger Absprache mit GRAPHIS möglich.

Gebühren:
SFr. 10.00/DM 10,00 für einzelne Arbeiten
SFr. 25.00/DM 25,00 für Kampagnen oder Serien von mehr als drei Stück
Bitte senden Sie uns einen Scheck (SFr.-Schecks bitte auf eine Schweizer Bank ziehen) oder überweisen Sie den Betrag auf PC Zürich 80-23071-9 oder PSchK Frankfurt 3000 57-602.
Diese Gebühren gelten nicht für Studenten. Bitte schicken Sie uns eine Kopie des Studentenausweises.
(Für Einsendungen aus Ländern mit Devisenbeschränkungen bitten wir Sie, uns zu kontaktieren.)

Wie und wohin schicken:
Bitte befestigen Sie das vorgesehene Etikett (oder eine Kopie) – vollständig ausgefüllt – mit Klebstreifen (nicht mit Klebstoff) auf der Rückseite jeder Arbeit. Bitte per Luftpost oder auf normalem Postweg einsenden. **Keine Luftfrachtsendungen.** Deklarieren Sie «Ohne jeden Handelswert» und «Arbeitsproben für Wettbewerb». Die Anzahl der Dias und Photos sollte auf dem Paket angegeben werden. (Bei Air Courier Sendungen vermerken Sie «Dokumente, ohne jeden Handelswert»).

Herzlichen Dank für Ihre Mitarbeit. Bitte senden Sie Ihre Arbeiten an folgende Adresse:

GRAPHIS VERLAG AG, DUFOURSTRASSE 107, CH-8008 ZURICH, SCHWEIZ

APPEL D'ENVOIS

GRAPHIS DESIGN

DATE LIMITE D'ENVOI: 30 NOVEMBRE

Publicité: journaux et magazines
Design: brochures de promotion, catalogues, invitations, pochettes de disques, annonces, emblèmes, en-têtes, campagnes de prestige, calendriers, livres, jaquettes, emballages (spécimen ou série, étiquettes ou emballages complets)
Editorial Design: magazines de sociétés, journaux, revues, rapports annuels
Illustration: toutes catégories en noir et blanc ou en couleurs

GRAPHIS ANNUAL REPORTS

DATE LIMITE D'ENVOI: 31 JANVIER/30 AVRIL

Tous travaux imprimés et publiés en relation avec le rapport annuel d'une entreprise ou d'une organisation.
Les critères retenus pour l'appréciation sont le design, l'illustration, la photo, la typo et la conception d'ensemble des rapports annuels.
Afin de rendre justice à ce média complexe, nous présentons diverses doubles pages types des rapports annuels sélectionnés en veillant à ce qu'elles soient représentatives de la conception et/ou de l'illustration.

GRAPHIS PHOTO

DATE LIMITE D'ENVOI: 30 JUIN

Photographie publicitaire: annonces, brochures de promotion, catalogues, invitations, pochettes de disques, calendriers
Photographie rédactionnelle pour la presse (reportages et articles), livres, publications d'entreprises, etc. dans les domaines suivants: Mode, arts, architecture, nature, sciences et techniques, vie quotidienne, sports, l'actualité, portraits, nature morte, etc.
Photographie artistique: études personnelles
Photographie non publiée: travaux expérimentaux et projets d'étudiants

GRAPHIS POSTER

DATE LIMITE D'ENVOI: 30 AVRIL

Affiches culturelles: annonçant des expositions et manifestations de tout genre, des projections de films, des représentations de théâtre et de ballet, des concerts et festivals.
Affiches publicitaires: pour la mode, les cosmétiques, l'alimentation, les produits de consommation de luxe, les biens industriels; publicité institutionnelle et auto-promotion d'entreprises.
Affiches sociales: essentiellement au service d'une cause sociale ou politique dans les domaines de l'éducation et de la formation, ainsi que pour l'annonce de conférences et réunions et pour les appels à caractère social et politique.

MODALITÉS D'ENVOI

VALABLES POUR TOUS LES LIVRES CITÉS.

Par votre envoi, vous donnez expressément à GRAPHIS l'autorisation de reproduire les travaux reçus aussi bien dans le livre en question que dans le magazine GRAPHIS ou dans tout imprimé relatif aux comptes rendus et au matériel publicitaire concernant les publications GRAPHIS.

Sont acceptés tous les travaux de professionnels et d'étudiants – même inédits – réalisés pendant les douze mois précédant le délai limite d'envoi.

Pour tout envoi de travaux, nous vous faisons parvenir un accusé de réception. Vous serez informé par la suite de la parution ou non-parution de vos travaux. Tous les travaux figurant dans l'ouvrage en question sont reproduits en quadrichromie dans un format généreux.
Votre envoi vous vaut une réduction de 25% sur l'annuel en question.

Que nous envoyer:
Veuillez nous envoyer un exemplaire imprimé (non monté, mais bien protégé). N'envoyez pas d'originaux. Pour les travaux de grand format, volumineux ou de valeur, veuillez nous envoyer des photos ou des diapositives (duplicata). **Veuillez noter que les travaux ne peuvent pas être retournés,** sauf dans des cas exceptionnels et si vous nous en avisez à l'avance.

Droits d'admission:
SFr. 10.00 pour les envois concernant un seul travail
SFr. 25.00 pour chaque série de 3 travaux ou davantage
Veuillez joindre à votre envoi un chèque tiré sur une banque suisse ou en verser le montant au compte chèque postal Zürich 80-23071-9.
Les étudiants sont exemptés de cette taxe. Prière de joindre une photocopie de la carte d'étudiant.
(Si vous résidez dans un pays qui connaît le contrôle des changes, veuillez nous contacter préalablement.)

Comment et où envoyer:
Veuillez scotcher (ne pas coller) au dos de chaque spécimen les étiquettes ci-jointes (ou photocopies) – dûment remplies. Envoyez les travaux de préférence par avion, ou par voie de surface. **Ne nous envoyez rien en fret aérien.** Indiquez «Sans aucune valeur commerciale» et «Echantillons de spécimens pour concours». Le nombre de diapositives et de photos doit être indiqué sur le paquet. (Pour les envois par courrier, inscrire «Documents, sans aucune valeur commercial».)

Nous vous remercions chaleureusement de votre collaboration. Veuillez faire parvenir vos travaux à l'adresse suivante:

EDITIONS GRAPHIS SA, DUFOURSTRASSE 107, CH-8008 ZURICH, SUISSE

Please tape (do not glue) this label or a photocopy to the back of each entry.

SENDER:
Firm, Address, Telephone

ART DIRECTOR:
Name, City, State

DESIGNER:
Name, City, State

ILLUSTRATOR, PHOTOGRAPHER:
Name, City, State

STYLIST:
Name, City, State

COPYWRITER:
Name, City, State

AGENCY, STUDIO:
Name, City, State

CLIENT, PUBLISHER:
Complete address

DESCRIPTION OF ASSIGNMENT/OTHER INFORMATION:

■ I herewith grant GRAPHIS PRESS non-exclusive permission for use of the submitted material, for which I have full reproduction rights (copy, photography, illustration, and design).

SIGNATURE:

Bitte auf der Rückseite jeder Arbeit befestigen/veuillez scotcher au dos de chaque spécimen.

ABSENDER/ENVOYÉ PAR:
Firma(e), Adresse, Telephon(e)

ART DIRECTOR/DIRECTEUR ARTISTIQUE:
Name, Ort/Nom, Lieu

GESTALTER/DESIGNER:
Name, Ort/Nom, Lieu

KÜNSTLER/ARTISTE, PHOTOGRAPH(E):
Name, Ort/Nom, Lieu

STYLIST/STYLISTE:
Name, City, State

TEXTER/RÉDACTEUR:
Name, Ort/Nom, Lieu

AGENTUR/AGENCE:
Name, Ort/Nom, Lieu

KUNDE/CLIENT:
Adresse

ZWECK/UTILISATION:
INFORMATION:

■ Ich erteile hiermit dem GRAPHIS VERLAG die nicht-exklusive Erlaubnis zur Veröffentlichung der eingereichten Arbeiten, für die ich die Reproduktionsrechte besitze (Text, Photographie, Illustration und Design).

■ J'accorde par la présente aux EDITIONS GRAPHIS l'autorisation non exclusive d'utiliser le matériel soumis à leur appréciation, pour lequel je détiens les droits de reproduction (texte, photographie, illustration et design).

UNTERSCHRIFT/
SIGNATURE:

SUBSCRIBE TO GRAPHIS: FOR USA AND CANADA

MAGAZINE	USA	CANADA
☐ GRAPHIS (One year/6 issues)	US$ 59.00	CDN$ 82.00
☐ 1988 Portfolio (Case holds six issues)	US$ 11.00	CDN$ 15.00

☐ Check enclosed
☐ Please bill me (My subscription will begin upon payment)
☐ Students may request a 25% discount by sending student ID.
IMPORTANT! PLEASE CHECK THE LANGUAGE VERSION DESIRED:
☐ ENGLISH   ☐ GERMAN   ☐ FRENCH
Subscription fees include postage to any part of the world.
Surcharges: US$ 57.00 (CDN$ 75.00) for Airmail,
US$ 22.50 (CDN$ 30.00) for Registered Mail.

NAME

TITLE

COMPANY

ADDRESS

CITY

STATE/PROV.   POSTAL CODE

COUNTRY

PROFESSION

SIGNATURE   DATE

Please send coupon and make check payable to:
GRAPHIS US, INC., 141 LEXINGTON AVENUE, NEW YORK, NY 10016, USA.
Guarantee: You may cancel your subscription at any time and receive a full refund on all unmailed copies. Please allow 6-8 weeks for delivery of first issue.

REQUEST FOR CALL FOR ENTRIES
Please put me on your "Call for Entries" list for the following title(s).
Please check the appropriate box(es).
☐ GRAPHIS PHOTO   ☐ GRAPHIS POSTER   ☐ GRAPHIS DESIGN
☐ GRAPHIS PACKAGING   ☐ GRAPHIS DIAGRAM   ☐ GRAPHIS ANNUAL REPORTS
By submitting material to any of the titles listed above, I will automatically qualify for a
25% discount toward the purchase of the title.   GD 90

SUBSCRIBE TO GRAPHIS: FOR EUROPE AND THE WORLD

MAGAZINE	BRD	WORLD	U.K.
☐ GRAPHIS (One year/6 issues)	DM 156,-	SFr. 126.-	£ 48.00
☐ 1988 Portfolio (Case holds six issues)	DM 24.-	SFr. 19.-	£ 8.00

☐ Check enclosed (for Europe, please make SFr.-checks payable to a Swiss bank)
☐ Please bill me (My subscription will begin upon payment)
☐ Students may request a 25% discount by sending student ID.
IMPORTANT! PLEASE CHECK THE LANGUAGE VERSION DESIRED:
☐ ENGLISH   ☐ GERMAN   ☐ FRENCH
Subscription fees include postage to any part of the world.
Surcharges: SFr. 84.00/DM 102,00/£ 34.50 for Airmail,
SFr. 30.00/DM 36,00/£ 12.00 for Registered Mail.

NAME

TITLE

COMPANY

ADDRESS

CITY   POSTAL CODE

COUNTRY

PROFESSION

SIGNATURE   DATE

Please send coupon and make check payable to:
GRAPHIS PRESS CORP., DUFOURSTRASSE 107, CH-8008 ZÜRICH, SWITZERLAND
Guarantee: You may cancel your subscription at any time and receive a full refund on all unmailed copies. Please allow 6-8 weeks for delivery of first issue.

REQUEST FOR CALL FOR ENTRIES
Please put me on your "Call for Entries" list for the following title(s).
Please check the appropriate box(es).
☐ GRAPHIS PHOTO   ☐ GRAPHIS POSTER   ☐ GRAPHIS DESIGN
☐ GRAPHIS PACKAGING   ☐ GRAPHIS DIAGRAM   ☐ GRAPHIS ANNUAL REPORTS
By submitting material to any of the titles listed above, I will automatically qualify for a
25% discount toward the purchase of the title.   GD 90

BOOK ORDER FORM: FOR USA AND CANADA

ORDER YOUR GRAPHIS ANNUALS NOW!

BOOKS	USA	CANADA
☐ Graphis Design 90	US$ 65.00	CDN$ 98.00
☐ Graphis Corporate Identity 1	US$ 75.00	CDN$ 105.00
☐ Graphis Photo 89	US$ 65.00	CDN$ 98.00
☐ Graphis Poster 89	US$ 65.00	CDN$ 98.00
☐ Graphis Packaging 5	US$ 75.00	CDN$ 105.00
☐ Graphis Design 89	US$ 65.00	CDN$ 98.00
☐ Graphis Diagram 1	US$ 65.00	CDN$ 98.00
☐ Graphis Annual Reports 1	US$ 65.00	CDN$ 98.00
☐ 42 Years of Graphis Covers (1944-1986)	US$ 49.50	CDN$ 60.00

☐ Check enclosed
☐ Please bill me (Mailing costs in addition to above book price will be charged)

NAME

TITLE

COMPANY

ADDRESS

CITY/STATE/PROV.

POSTAL CODE   COUNTRY

PROFESSION

SIGNATURE   DATE

Please send coupon and make check payable to:
GRAPHIS US, INC., 141 LEXINGTON AVENUE, NEW YORK, NY 10016, USA.

REQUEST FOR CALL FOR ENTRIES
Please put me on your "Call for Entries" list for the following title(s).
Please check the appropriate box(es).
☐ GRAPHIS PHOTO   ☐ GRAPHIS POSTER   ☐ GRAPHIS DESIGN
☐ GRAPHIS PACKAGING   ☐ GRAPHIS DIAGRAM   ☐ GRAPHIS ANNUAL REPORTS
By submitting material to any of the titles listed above, I will automatically qualify for a
25% discount toward the purchase of the title.   GD 90

BOOK ORDER FORM: FOR EUROPE AND THE WORLD

BOOKS	BRD	WORLD	U.K.
☐ Graphis Design 90	DM 148,-	SFr. 118.-	£ 46.50
☐ Graphis Corporate Identity 1	DM 160,-	SFr. 132.-	£ 48.00
☐ Graphis Photo 89	DM 148,-	SFr. 118.-	£ 46.50
☐ Graphis Poster 89	DM 148,-	SFr. 118.-	£ 46.50
☐ Graphis Packaging 5	DM 160,-	SFr. 132.-	£ 48.00
☐ Graphis Design 89	DM 138,-	SFr. 112.-	£ 45.00
☐ Graphis Diagram 1	DM 138,-	SFr. 112.-	£ 45.00
☐ Graphis Annual Reports 1	DM 138,-	SFr. 112.-	£ 45.00
☐ 42 Years of Graphis Covers (1944-1986)	DM 98,-	SFr. 85.-	£ 35.00

☐ Check enclosed (For Europe, please make SFr. checks payable to a Swiss Bank)
☐ Amount paid into Graphis account at the Union Bank of Switzerland, Acct No 3620063 in Zürich.
☐ Amount paid to Postal Cheque Account Zürich 80-23071-9 (Through your local post office)
☐ Please bill me (Mailing costs in addition to above book price will be charged)

NAME

TITLE

COMPANY

ADDRESS

CITY   POSTAL CODE

COUNTRY

PROFESSION

SIGNATURE   DATE

Please send coupon and make check payable to:
GRAPHIS PRESS CORP., DUFOURSTRASSE 107, CH-8008 ZÜRICH, SWITZERLAND

REQUEST FOR CALL FOR ENTRIES
Please put me on your "Call for Entries" list for the following title(s).
☐ GRAPHIS PHOTO   ☐ GRAPHIS POSTER   ☐ GRAPHIS DESIGN
☐ GRAPHIS PACKAGING   ☐ GRAPHIS DIAGRAM   ☐ GRAPHIS ANNUAL REPORTS
By submitting material to any of the titles listed above, I will automatically qualify for a
25% discount toward the purchase of the title.   GD 90

GRAPHIS PRESS CORP.
DUFOURSTRASSE 107
CH-8008 ZÜRICH
SWITZERLAND

GRAPHIS U.S., INC.
141 LEXINGTON AVENUE
NEW YORK, NEW YORK 10016
U.S.A.

GRAPHIS PRESS CORP.
DUFOURSTRASSE 107
CH-8008 ZÜRICH
SWITZERLAND

GRAPHIS U.S., INC.
141 LEXINGTON AVENUE
NEW YORK, NEW YORK 10016
U.S.A.